The Changing Faces of Journalism

The Changing Faces of Journalism: Tabloidization, Technology and Truthiness brings together an array of top scholars who consider how contemporary journalism has wrestled with its changing parameters and who address how notions of tabloidization, technology and truthiness have altered our understanding of journalism.

Organized into three sections: how tabloidization affects the journalistic landscape; how technology changes what we think we know about journalism; and how truthiness tweaks our understanding of the journalistic tradition, the collection is introduced with an essay by Barbie Zelizer. Section introductions also contextualize the essays and highlight the issues that they raise.

Contributors: S. Elizabeth Bird, Pablo J. Boczkowski, Peter Dahlgren, Mark Deuze, James S. Ettema, Herbert J. Gans, Jeffrey P. Jones, Carolyn Kitch, Julianne H. Newton, Michael Serazio, Michael Schudson, Keren Tenenboim-Weinblatt and Lokman Tsui.

Barbie Zelizer is the Raymond Williams Professor of Communication and Director of the Scholars Program in Culture and Communication at the University of Pennsylvania's Annenberg School for Communication. A former journalist, Zelizer is known for her work in the area of journalism, culture, memory and images, particularly in times of crisis. Previous Routledge publications include *Reporting War: Journalism in Wartime* (2004) and *Journalism After September 11* (2002) – both co-edited with Stuart Allan – and *Explorations in Communication and History* (2008).

Shaping inquiry in culture, communication and media studies
Series Editor: Barbie Zelizer
University of Pennsylvania

Dedicated to bringing to the foreground the central impulses by which we engage in inquiry, the *Shaping Inquiry in Culture, Communication and Media Studies* series attempts to make explicit the ways in which we craft our intellectual grasp of the world.

Explorations in Communication and History
Edited by Barbie Zelizer

The Changing Faces of Journalism
Tabloidization, Technology and Truthiness
Edited by Barbie Zelizer

The Changing Faces of Journalism

Tabloidization, Technology and Truthiness

Edited by Barbie Zelizer

 Routledge
Taylor & Francis Group

LONDON AND NEW YORK

First published 2009
by Routledge
2 Park Square, Milton Park, Abingdon, Oxon OX14 4RN

Simultaneously published in the USA and Canada
by Routledge
270 Madison Ave, New York, NY 10016

Routledge is an imprint of the Taylor & Francis Group, an informa business

Editorial selection and material © 2009 Barbie Zelizer
Individual chapters © 2009 the Contributors

Typeset in Sabon by
Taylor & Francis Books

British Library Cataloguing in Publication Data
A catalogue record for this book is available from the British Library

Library of Congress Cataloging in Publication Data
The changing faces of journalism : tabloidization, technology and truthiness /
edited by Barbie Zelizer.
       p. cm. – (Shaping inquiry in culture, communication and media studies)
    Based on papers presented at a one-day symposium held on November 30,
2007 in Philadelphia, Pennsylvania; sponsored by the University of
Pennsylvania's Annenberg School for Communication.
    1. Journalism–History–21st century–Congresses. 2. Sensationalism in
journalism–Congresses. 3. Journalism–Technological innovations–Congresses.
4. Journalism–Objectivity–Congresses. I. Zelizer, Barbie.
    PN4815.2.C43 2009
    070.9'09051–dc22
                                                                2008047302

ISBN10: 0-415-77824-7 (hbk)
ISBN 10: 0-415-77825-5 (pbk)
ISBN 10: 0-203-87845-0 (ebk)

ISBN13: 978-0-415-77824-4 (hbk)
ISBN 13: 978-0-415-77825-1 (pbk)
ISBN 13: 978-0-203-87845-3 (ebk)

Contents

Contributors

S. Elizabeth Bird is Professor and Chair of Anthropology at the University of South Florida. She is the author of *For Enquiring Minds: A Cultural Study of Supermarket Tabloids*, and *The Audience in Everyday Life: Living in a Media World*, which won the International Communication Association's Outstanding Book Award in 2004. She is also the editor of *Dressing in Feathers: The Construction of the Indian in American Popular Culture*, and has published over 50 articles, book chapters and reviews in the field of media studies, visual anthropology, folklore, and cultural studies.

Pablo J. Boczkowski is Associate Professor in the Department of Communication Studies at Northwestern University. His research program examines the transformation of the social and political institutions of print culture in the digital age. He is the author of *Digitizing the News: Innovation in Online Newspapers* (MIT Press, 2004) and articles in such publications as *Journal of Communication*, *Political Communication*, and *New Media and Society* as well as in edited volumes. He is currently writing a book tentatively entitled "News at Work: Technology and Imitation in the New Media Environment."

Peter Dahlgren is Professor of Media and Communication Studies, Lund University, Sweden. He has written extensively on the role of the media and journalism in the development of a democratic public sphere. Author of the highly acclaimed book, *Television and the Public Sphere* (Sage 1995), along with many other publications, his most recent book is the collection, *Young Citizens and New Media: Learning for Democratic Participation* (Routledge 2007). His current research focuses on the Internet as a civic resource and possible basis for a new political culture.

Mark Deuze holds a joint appointment as Assistant Professor at Indiana University's Department of Telecommunications, and as Professor of Journalism and New Media at Leiden University, the Netherlands. From 2002 to 2003, Deuze was a Fulbright scholar at the University of Southern California's Annenberg School for Communication. His research interests include the social, economic and technological convergence of media culture in general and the creative industries in particular. Publications include most recently *Media Work* (Polity Press, 2007), and the forthcoming *Beyond Journalism* (Polity Press, 2009), as well as articles in journals such as the *International Journal of Cultural Studies*, *New Media & Society*, *Journalism Studies*, and *Media Culture & Society*. He maintains a weblog at www.deuze.blogspot.com

James S. Ettema is Professor of Communication Studies at Northwestern University. He teaches courses focusing on the social organization and cultural impact of the mass media and new communication technologies. Among his books is *Custodians of Conscience: Investigative Journalism and Public Virtue* (Columbia University Press, 1998), written with Theodore L. Glasser of Stanford University. The book won the Frank Luther Mott-Kappa Tau Alpha Award from the National Journalism and Mass Communication Honor Society, the Bart Richards Award for Media Criticism from Penn State University, and the Sigma Delta Chi Award for research on journalism from the Society of Professional Journalists. He served for six years as chair of Communication Studies and for ten years as the faculty coordinator of professional graduate programs in the department. His current research focuses on media coverage of warfare.

Herbert J. Gans is the Robert S. Lynd Professor of Sociology Emeritus at Columbia University. He is the author of 17 books and monographs, including *Popular Culture and High Culture* (1974, 2nd ed. 1999), *Deciding What's News* (1979, 2nd ed. 2004), and *Democracy and the News* (2003). A past president of the American Sociological Association, he received its Career of Distinguished Scholarship Award in 2006. His most recent publication is *Imagining America in 2033* (University of Michigan Press, 2008).

Jeffrey P. Jones is Associate Professor of Communication and Theatre Arts at Old Dominion University in Norfolk, Virginia. He is the author of *Entertaining Politics: New Political Television and Civic Culture* and co-editor of the forthcoming volumes, *Satire TV: Politics and Comedy in the Post-Network Era* and *The Essential HBO Reader*. His research examines the relationship between media and American political culture.

Carolyn Kitch is an associate professor of journalism at Temple University, where she also serves as Director of Graduate Studies for the School of Communications and Theater. She previously taught at the Medill School of Journalism at Northwestern University. She is the author of two books, *The Girl on the Magazine Cover: The Origins of Visual Stereotypes in American Mass Media* (2001) and *Pages from the Past: History and Memory in American Magazines* (2005), both from the University of North Carolina Press. A third book, *Journalism in a Culture of Grief*, co-authored with Janice Hume (University of Georgia), was published by Routledge in fall 2007. Kitch's research areas include media history, magazines, gender issues, and memory studies. Her scholarship has appeared in journals including *Journalism*, *Journalism Studies*, *The Journal of Popular Culture*, *Journalism & Mass Communication Quarterly*, *Journalism History*, *American Journalism*, and *Critical Studies in Media Communication*. She is a former writer and editor for *Reader's Digest*, *Good Housekeeping*, and *McCall's* magazines.

Julianne H. Newton, Professor of Visual Communication and Associate Dean for Undergraduate Affairs, School of Journalism and Communication (University of Oregon), is an award-winning scholar, editor, photographer and teacher. She is author of *The Burden of Visual Truth: The Role of Photojournalism in Mediating Reality* and co-author of *Visual Communication: Integrating Media, Art and Science*. Her visual ethics publications span scholarly, professional and public forums, and her documentary photographs have been shown in more than 50 exhibitions in three countries. Newton's honors include the Marshall Award for Teaching Innovation, NPPA Garland Educator Award, and NCA Visual Communication Research Excellence Award. She was editor of *Visual Communication Quarterly* 2001–6.

Michael Schudson is Professor of Communication and Adjunct Professor of Sociology at the University of California, San Diego where he has taught since 1980. In 2006, Professor Schudson was appointed Professor of Communication at the Graduate School of Journalism, Columbia University, and splits his time between UCSD and Columbia. He is the author of six books and editor of two others concerning the history and sociology of the American news media, advertising, popular culture, and cultural memory. He is the recipient of a number of honors, including a Guggenheim Fellowship, a resident fellowship at the Center for Advanced Study in the Behavioral Sciences, Palo Alto, and a MacArthur Foundation "genius" award. His current research examines growing freedom of expression in the United States from 1960 to the present, and its complicated consequences.

Michael Serazio is a doctoral candidate in Communication at the University of Pennsylvania's Annenberg School for Communication. As a professional journalist, he holds a master's degree from Columbia University's Graduate School for Journalism and was a finalist in the national Livingston Awards. His scholarly agenda focuses on popular and consumer culture, journalism, and religious and political media and his research articles have appeared in *Popular Music & Society*, *The Journal of Popular Culture* and a sports media anthology.

Keren Tenenboim-Weinblatt is a doctoral candidate at the Annenberg School for Communication at the University of Pennsylvania. Her research focuses on the cultural dimensions of journalism and the intersection of journalism, politics, and popular culture. Her work has appeared in *Media, Culture & Society*, *Journalism: Theory, Practice and Criticism*, and *The Communication Review*. She received her Master's degree in Communication from the University of Haifa.

Lokman Tsui is a doctoral candidate at the Annenberg School for Communication at the University of Pennsylvania. His dissertation examines the impact of citizen journalism on global news production. He has co-edited a book *The Hyperlinked Society: Questioning Connections in the Digital Age* (2008) with Joseph Turow. His research has also appeared in *Global Dialogue*, *China Information* and in the newsletter for the *International Institute for Asian Studies*. He was guest editor of a theme issue in *China Information* on the socio-political impact of the internet in China. His research interests center on the areas of new media, global communication and journalism. He divides his time between Philadelphia, Amsterdam, and Hong Kong.

Barbie Zelizer is the Raymond Williams Professor of Communication and Director of the Scholars Program in Culture and Communication at the University of Pennsylvania's Annenberg School for Communication. A former journalist, Zelizer has authored or edited eight books, including the award-winning *Remembering to Forget: Holocaust Memory Through the Camera's Eye* (Chicago, 1998). A recipient of a Guggenheim Fellowship, a Freedom Forum Center Research Fellowship, and a Fellowship from Harvard University's Joan Shorenstein Center on the Press, Politics, and Public Policy, Zelizer is also a media critic, whose work has appeared widely. Coeditor of *Journalism: Theory, Practice and Criticism* and President-Elect of the International Communication Association, she is presently working on a book on about-to-die photographs and journalism.

Introduction: Why Journalism's Changing Faces Matter

Barbie Zelizer

The changing faces of journalism have been part of the journalistic landscape since the inception of news. From early forms of oral delivery to the most recent online exchanges of information, journalism has always been multiple, multi-dimensional, multi-directional and multiply-faceted, and its multiplicity has become more pronounced as journalism has necessarily mutated across region and locale. Despite journalism's variety, however, scholarly inquiry on news has proceeded largely without its recognition. For various reasons associated with the shape of inquiry itself, scholars have tended to favor uniform, unidimensional and unidirectional notions of how journalism works, which over time have moved further out of touch from the forms that the news has taken on the ground. The results of this disconnect have become multiple themselves, generating tensions between journalism's centers and its margins, fights for legitimacy over new tools of information relay, resistance toward new models of newsmaking, and a somewhat stubborn recalcitrance about journalism's necessary attempts to remain relevant in a rapidly changing world.

How would our understanding of journalism look different were we to insist not on a unitary model of journalism – one which assumes that an elevated form of news works in prescribed ways to better the public good across contexts – but on various kinds of journalisms with necessarily multiple facets, definitions, circumstances and functions? This book considers that question. Drawing on the prevailing scholarly understanding of journalism, it queries how the instantiation of predetermined ways for thinking about the news have tweaked and shaped what we believe we know about journalism, the ideas that we hold about what it is supposed to do, and the ways in which we regard and understand what it does in practice. This book thus performs a heuristic exercise which attempts to redefine our pathways to knowledge acquisition, drawing our attention to the linkage between what we know and how we have come to know it.

On change and inquiry

The very presence of change in academic inquiry has long been seen as a necessary but often risky aspect of the landscape of knowledge acquisition. Though academics favor change in principle and argue for its critical role in keeping the academy vital and relevant, accommodating change in practice raises fundamental questions about the establishment and maintenance of academic authority. What happens to longstanding notions of expertise and the individuals associated with them when change forces their topics out of the center of a phenomenon's intellectual consideration? Conversely, how do changing attributes of a phenomenon secure attention, particularly when they challenge or even undermine that which existed before?

How to accommodate change in inquiry without undoing the academic knowledge that exists has long drawn the attention of scholars, particularly in the sociology of knowledge. In recognizing change as a harbinger of the academy's health and relevance, some observers have argued for its critical presence in helping us navigate the problems of the world and our relationship to them.[1] At the same time, change has been associated with instability, risk, threat and potential danger. As Randall Collins remarked, "the paradox is that for an intellectual community to be in a great creative age, it must be both making great discoveries and also overturning them, and not just once but over and again."[2] Navigating competitive demands so as to position topicality and relevance alongside stability and safety has prompted the academy to act in protective ways.

One result has been a slow and gradual incorporation of change into academic thought. Thomas Kuhn argued long ago that our adaptation to the novel and unknown takes place not with leaps of enthusiasm but incrementally, where problems and procedures are named and labeled in ways that can generate consensus while battles over competing insights linger in reduced form long after the new paradigms are established.[3]

Change thus constitutes a double-edged sword in the shaping of academic inquiry. Seen as indispensable for academics trying to remain abreast of evolving developments in the world, it needs to be incorporated gradually into existing notions about what matters so as not to upset or undermine the stability of consensus on which much of academic thought rests. This means that its slow-paced accommodation, strategically useful in maintaining academic authority, may cause academics to miss what is novel and dynamic about a phenomenon at hand. In fitting the concept to the practice, the academy thus runs the risk of lagging in its recognition of the very attributes of its targets of inquiry that make them worthy of academic attention.

How to accommodate change in inquiry

All of this becomes more relevant when change is not only part of the landscape of inquiry but a necessary and critical part of a phenomenon's intellectual understanding. Such is certainly the case with journalism, which has always involved an elaborate set of accommodations surrounding change – the changing practices of newsgathering, the changing tools of news relay, changing economic and political circumstances of news production and its changing audiences. While there is hardly a person among us who has not experienced some form of news, the experience of many has been complicated by degrees of dissonance between what is expected and what is found, between what journalism could be and what journalism is.

This book begins with the presumption that degrees of dissonance exist because journalism scholars have not sufficiently navigated the various pathways between the journalism we imagine and the journalism we have. Many longstanding discussions of journalism have missed the boat in accounting for the various pathways to understanding how the news works and in figuring out how they might be more fruitfully positioned alongside each other, even when doing so complicates the phenomenon at hand.

In a manner typical more generally of knowledge sharing, journalism scholars have tended to privilege an intellectual setting for understanding the news that favors order over messiness, coherence over contradiction, stability over flux, fluidity over unevenness and predictability over contingency. This means that many of the most prevalent scholarly discussions of the news proceed by referencing what is presumed to be the same phenomenon. Laments over errant news practices or the failings of certain reporters or news organizations, kudos and celebration over scoops and newsgathering done well, and ruminations over how journalism might and could look different than it does today all imply at some level that journalism has but one shape in the public imagination. When we discuss its strengths and shortcomings, then, there is an unarticulated presumption that we begin from a shared starting point on our way to addressing what is right about journalism, what is wrong about it, what needs to change and what can stay the same.

This book is an attempt to remind us that what journalism looks like may be far less consensual than what we would like or need it to be. Not only does journalism have myriad forms that are differentiated across regional boundary, technology, workable and unworkable relationships with other institutions, but as we roll it forward across time and space it displays wrinkles and creases that should be causing us to question the originary form from which we thought it evolved. Why is the journalism we imagine not equivalent to the journalism we have? What has gone asunder in the spaces between what we aspire to and what we have in fact settled for?

The changing faces of journalism

The Changing Faces of Journalism addresses these questions by prompting consideration of the consensual landscape that has underlain most scholarly discussions of journalism. It asks us to consider what coaxes us to introduce change into our thinking about journalism. How do we wrestle with tradition and what causes us to reflect upon and change what we think? What makes us reject old paradigms and embrace new ones?

Three focal points are useful in looking more closely at the ways in which discussions of journalism have tended to take shape. They include the points of origin through which we have initially engaged with journalism, the key-words through which we have initiated and maintained its discussion, and the platforms through which we have crystallized what matters and accommodated increases or decreases in its salience.

Points of origin

Where do our notions for thinking about journalism come from? The points of origin for our discussions of journalism are key to understanding the phenom-enon at hand. Existing answers to this question are multiple, for discussions of journalism have many points of origin that rest within different interpretive communities, where tacit knowledge, interpretive strategies and shared ways of determining what counts as evidence for the group rule in certain aspects of a phenomenon and rule out others.[4] When scoped across broad populations, journalism ultimately is defined differently by those who work as journalists, those who educate others to work as journalists and those who study jour-nalism. Not only is each group invested in different answers to the questions of what journalism is and what it could be for, but they often speak at cross-purposes with each other. Each maintains that the others do not understand what is most important about journalism: journalists resent the interference of scholars and educators, scholars decry the pragmatic interests of journalists and educators, and educators say journalists and scholars both lack the wherewithal to navigate concrete detail and conceptual purpose as equal bed-fellows. The heart of everyone's concern – what to do about journalism – gets shunted to the side as everyone fixates on who will be best heard.[5]

Agreement about journalism gets further split by the variant professional and scholarly populations involved in thinking about journalism. We may not find consensus about the craft of journalism if we ask print reporters, photo-journalists and multi-taskers who work across media and news organization; nor will we necessarily find agreement among journalism scholars drawing from different disciplines, where political scientists might concern themselves more with journalism's impact on the polity and historians more with journalism's shape in the past.

The result of all of this is clear: in none of these points of origin do we emerge with a clear and agreed upon notion of what journalism is for across all of the various interpretive communities involved in its definition. And so the very exercise of thinking anew about the points of origin from which we have drawn our assumptions may tell us quite a lot about how – and why – we have come to regard journalism in certain ways and not others.

Keywords

Which keywords do we use to reference what we think we know? Raymond Williams argued that key terms emerge as markers of the "extra edge of consciousness" within which members of a community function, and in that regard they are useful cues to what the community regards as valuable and relevant.[6] The question of which keywords remain relevant and which have outlived their usefulness tells us much about how our thinking is faring in its ability to reflect journalism's state on the ground. If journalism itself is continually changing, have our terms for referencing it kept up with those changes? Equally important, when our keywords for addressing journalism themselves change, what happens to our existing understanding of the phenomenon?

Examples abound. For instance, though the global public sphere has emerged as the central environment in which journalism works, we still regularly invoke the nation-state as a point of reference for journalism. Is there an alternative term – and indeed entity – against which we should be appraising journalism's work instead? Similarly, though we have ample evidence to suggest that newswork has become increasingly diversified, out-sourced and multi-tasked, with individuals working across media and news organizations, often from afar, why do we still insist on "the newsroom" as the metaphoric setting for thinking about journalistic collectivity? And finally, we continue to reference journalistic work primarily through those individuals identified as gainfully employed by a news organization. And yet, a whole world of subterranean tasks – minders, fixers, translators and drivers, among others – are doing the work we formerly expected of bona fide journalists. Why have we not yet developed a way to give them due credit?

Platforms

What are the platforms through which we decide what matters and, equally important, what convinces us to decide that what has long mattered no longer works? Platforms, in Peter Barker's view, are "where we stand when we do our work ... The problem is whether we are ever really entitled to claim knowledge of other platforms."[7] Key here is what is necessary to introduce change in how we think about the journalistic setting. Under which conditions do familiar attributes of journalism fade and new attributes become salient? What induces us to accommodate the novel, the unstable and the dynamic into an intellectual environment which has proven useful and workable over time?

The notion of platforms of inquiry is important in thinking about journalism because they offer recognizable ways to accommodate change in an environment that changes faster than inquiry can track. Platforms facilitate dialogue and generate contestation, negotiation and adaptation in thinking about what matters as evidence in thinking about a phenomenon.

This book identifies three such platforms – tabloidization, technology, and truthiness – because each offsets the traditional core of the journalistic project in its contemporary moment. Though the mainstream of journalism scholarship has long argued for an aspired form of news thought to elevate public reasoning about events in the public sphere, in fact journalism is often, if not always, a blend of tabloid features that further suggests we need to pay more forceful attention to the relationship between the form and content of news. The focus on tabloidization offers an opportunity to address how a default acceptance of non-tabloid journalism has facilitated a certain way of thinking about news more broadly, often to the detriment of our recognizing the value and proliferation of certain tabloid forms, the interweaving of tabloid and non-tabloid aspects of all news, and other similar features that complicate the relationship and suggest it is less of an either-or circumstance than many have argued.

Technology has challenged the core of journalism in similar ways. As journalism has propelled forward across time and space, the emergence of different technological tools for its relay has complicated what we presume is within the parameters of the knowable as news. What would natural disaster look like, for instance, without images to show us its wide-ranging devastation? The repertoire of technological vehicles for news relay is long and varied, and it depends on who is involved in its delineation: do we speak of distinctions between the spoken word, the printed word, the still image and the moving image? Or should we consider the alternative settings of the press, radio, television and the internet? How do we account for news magazines versus talk shows versus reality television? In few cases are all the technological options seen as relevant to the question at hand and yet recent surveys suggest that young people in particular are moved by the alternative settings for news relay more than by its traditional core. While the relevance of technology to knowledge certainly goes beyond journalism,[8] a less forward-looking grasp of technological innovations may have privileged a certain background set of assumptions about how news works technologically that no longer fits the picture.

And finally, the ascent of the notion of "truthiness," coined to address the Bush administration's stance on information relay, has made the journalistic environment newly responsive to irony, parody and satire as part of the journalistic project. Though they have been around for as long as news, they have not been part of its privileged scholarly setting, which has heralded objectivity, distance and impartiality at the expense of perspective. The workability of claims about truthiness and its concomitant neighbors complicates the prism through which to appraise and evaluate the relationship between the polity and the news. In forcing us to think anew about journalism's linkage with politics, it does so in ways that ask us to reconsider the shape of longstanding notions of journalism as the fourth estate.

The Changing Faces of Journalism works from the presumption that journalism is too important to be understood only partially. In fact, journalism's importance is undeniable, for though it has been the target of ongoing discourse both in support and critique of its performance, no existing conversation about journalism suggests its irrelevance. Rather, contemporary conditions insist on journalism's centrality, even if we have not yet figured a way to account for all the ways in which its centrality takes shape. As a mindset, an institution, a set of practices, a profession, a group of people or a business, journalism deserves better from its scholars than it has gotten thus far. A renewed consideration of journalism's points of origin, keywords and platforms may help move us in that direction.

Structure of book

Against these impulses, *The Changing Faces of Journalism* was set in place. The book emerged from a one-day symposium held at the University of Pennsylvania's Annenberg School for Communication in November 2007.[9] The book, like the symposium, was organized around three sessions – each of which addressed tabloidization, technology, and truthiness – and a final session which considered their collective impact on journalism as we move forward. Organized into panels by Annenberg graduate students, three of whom contextualize their offerings in the pages that follow, eight prominent scholars inhabiting the journalistic/scholarly nexus pondered the issues raised here. Taken together, their views comprise this book.

Tabloidization

Herbert J. Gans asks whether new forms of popularization enhance the traditional print and electronic news media. In *Can Popularization Help the Traditional News Media?*, he argues that popularization (aka tabloidization) involves the simplification or other alteration of material and symbolic goods to attract a numerically larger – and thus less educated or lower status – set of buyers and audiences. Consequently, Gans asserts, the original recipients feel that "their" goods are being "dumbed down," creating a situation in which journalism must compete with the internet's already popularized news sites, although the total audience for national and international news has not increased. In sum, he says, as long as the nation has little need of citizens, they have little need of news about it.

In *Tears and Trauma in the News*, Carolyn Kitch embraces the historical definition of tabloidization to mean not just the celebrification but the sensationalism of news. Kitch shows how stories of tragic or violent death, the staple of tabloid newspapers since the 1920s, are more prominent than ever today in mainstream journalism and involve members of even the most elite news media in expressions of grief and outrage as constituents of a community seeking healing and closure. Kitch contends that the emotionalization of mainstream news makes journalists and audiences alike more interested in feeling than fixing the conditions of a violent world, and less able to begin a discussion about their underlying causes.

Tabloidization has long referenced what has been framed as an inexorable decline of "real" journalism, associated with trivialization, celebrity gossip and human interest stories. So argues S. Elizabeth Bird, who, in *Tabloidization: What Is It and Does It Really Matter?*, contends that considering tabloidization in context reveals that it has had many more different meanings and manifestations than we have tended to allow in our discussions of it. Challenging the notion of decline through which scholars have addressed tabloidization, Bird ponders its invocation as a convenient scapegoat for more important challenges to journalism.

Technology

Pablo J. Boczkowski considers how technological transformations have made the journalistic field both more transparent for its members than in the past and have produced an increase in imitation processes in editorial work and homogeneity of news content. In *Materiality and Mimicry in the Journalism Field*, Boczkowski considers how the dynamics and consequences of the links between materiality and mimicry in the journalistic field are altering the role of journalism in emerging democracies.

Julianne H. Newton addresses what happens as the technology of the brain extends through time and space via forms of personal and mass media. In *Guardian of the Real: Journalism in the Time of the New Mind*, Newton argues that understanding the power of journalists and readers to construct social reality is foundational to unraveling contemporary journalism. Building on theory from cognitive neuroscience, media ecology and technologies of the self, she explores the symbiotic nature of information production and consumption in a multimedia, global environment.

Mark Deuze, in *Technology and the Individual Journalist: Agency Beyond Imitation and Change*, challenges the established theories of newswork in the field of journalism studies through the prism of new media. Noting that the creation of content in general and media work in particular have undergone profound changes, Deuze maps new trends, developments and future perspectives emerging out of the fields of new media theory in an attempt to articulate new theories of newswork without necessarily abandoning the existent body of knowledge about journalism.

Truthiness

Michael Schudson queries the need for the term "truthiness" in the contemporary journalistic landscape. In *Factual Knowledge in the Age of Truthiness*, he compares discussions of the Bush administration's rationale for and defense of the war in Iraq with Hannah Arendt's "Lying in Politics," her 1971 essay on the Pentagon Papers, in which she attacked the Johnson and Nixon administrations' "defactualization" of politics. Schudson wonders whether we saw a simple repetition of a perennial lying in politics and disregard of facts or did the Bush administration add a new twist that old concepts do not quite cover?

In *The Moment of Truthiness: The Right Time to Consider the Meaning of Truthfulness,* James S. Ettema situates the notion of truthiness within the contemporary moment of socio-political climate change, characterized by the cooling of a post-9/11 earnestness into the irony-rich atmosphere of the Iraq Period. Arguing that truthiness provides scholars and critics with an opportunity to put the journalistic project in better order, Ettema queries to which notion journalism scholars will subscribe if they do not accept the notion that truth is whatever can be imposed by a regime of power. He contends that though much effort has been spent on deconstructing objectivity, very little has been devoted to developing an understanding of truth that both philosophers and journalists might be willing to accept.

Jeffrey P. Jones argues that truthiness describes much more than the lying of politicians or the polemics of pundits. In *Believable Fictions: Redactional Cultures and the Will to Truthiness,* Jones contends that the term highlights the broader cultural relationships between media, "information" and the widespread creative construction of truth, whether through the echo chambers of opinion talk or virally circulated political myths, Photoshop montages and video mash-ups. Truthiness highlights postmodern tendencies that allow for the construction of believable fictions, where truth *in fact* is less important than truth *in essence*. Jones explores truthiness's place in contemporary political culture as a discursive, media-centered epistemology that operates from a different "regime of truth" than its journalism-centered predecessor.

Afterword

Finally, one additional voice rounds out the conversation, offering summary views of how well the views presented about tabloidization, technology and truthiness have considered an altered journalistic landscape. In a summary piece titled *The Troubling Evolution of Journalism,* Peter Dahlgren reflects on journalism's contemporary dilemmas, considering how the platforms of Tabloidization, Technology and Truthiness engage with the changing nature of news audiences, the notion of positive popularization, and the consequences of new technology not only for journalists but for public participation in the production of journalism. Addressing some of the responses among journalists over the past two decades to the changes that many feel are undermining not only journalism per se but also the democracy to which it is supposed to support, Dahlgren probes the emerging "post-objectivist" situation of journalism and introduces the notion of the news media's "multi-epistemic order" in regard to journalism's role in democracy.

This book, then, is an invitation to begin thinking about journalism. Long ago, Thomas Paine was said to have noted that journalism is there to help us "see with other eyes, hear with other ears, and think with other thoughts than those we formerly used." In thinking about journalism, we might do well to do the same.

Notes

1 See, for instance, Charles E. Lindblom, *Inquiry and Change* (New Haven, CT: Yale University Press, 1992).
2 Randall Collins, *The Sociology of Philosophies: A Global Theory of Intellectual Change* (Cambridge, MA: Harvard University Press, 2000): 32.
3 Thomas Kuhn, *The Structure of Scientific Revolutions* (Chicago: University of Chicago Press, 1964). Also see Barbie Zelizer, *Taking Journalism Seriously: News and the Academy* (Thousand Oaks, CA: Sage, 2004).
4 Stanley Fish, *Is There a Text in This Class?* (Cambridge, MA: Harvard University Press, 1980); Barbie Zelizer, "Journalists as Interpretive Communities," *Critical Studies in Mass Communication* 10 (1993): 219–37.
5 For more on this, see Zelizer, *Taking Journalism Seriously*.
6 Raymond Williams, *Keywords* (New York: Oxford University Press, 1983): 24. See also Benjamin Whorf, *Language, Thought and Reality* (John B. Carroll [Ed.]. New York: John Wiley and MIT, 1956), and George Lakoff and Mark Johnson, *Metaphors We Live By* (Chicago: University of Chicago Press, 1980).
7 Peter Barker, "Kuhn and the Sociological Revolution," in *Configurations* 6.1 (1998): 21–32. Barker offered the so-called "platform problem" as part of a larger critique on Thomas Kuhn's work (also see Paul Hoyningen-Huene, *Reconstructing Scientific Revolutions* [Chicago: University of Chicago Press, 1993]), but for the purposes of this discussion his definition nonetheless bears relevance.
8 Sources are many on this point, but see, for instance, John G. Gunnell, "The Technocratic Image and the Theory of Technocracy," *Technology and Culture* 23 (July 1982).
9 The book began as a symposium run by the Annenberg Scholars Program in Culture and Communication at the University of Pennsylvania's Annenberg School for Communication, under Barbie Zelizer's direction, and with the involvement of the Graduate Working Group in Journalism Studies. Seven ASC graduate students – Caralyn Green, Susan Haas, Angela Lee, Nicole Maurantonio, Michael Serazio, Keren Tenenboim, and Lokman Tsui – developed the launch pad for working through some of the questions raised here, pulling together a wish list of those individuals they wanted to hear address these questions, organizing them into dialogue with each other and following through on the work involved in facilitating their participation. The result was a one-day symposium, entitled *The Changing Faces of Journalism: Tradition, Tabloidization, Technology, and Truthiness*, held on November 30 2007 in Philadelphia, Pennsylvania. Thanks to Emily Plowman and Anjati Gallup-Diaz for helping to organize the symposium, and its transformation into this volume.

On Tabloidization

Chapter 1

Rethinking a Villain, Redeeming a Format: The Crisis and Cure in Tabloidization

Michael Serazio

For journalists and critics alike, tabloidization has long represented something of a shapeshifter bugaboo; it means many things all at once and seems to threaten from equally many angles. It seduces through flashy fashion and vapid content: bold-faced names, red-carpet parties, socialite misadventure and the photogenic news design used to cover these tales. It springs up on street corners in the form of wafer-thin, suspiciously "advertorial" free dailies. We seem to sense it in the splashy infographics of *USA Today* and the vaudevillian bluster of cable news. It feels cheap; and, for practitioners and press observers, that somehow feels wrong.

Above all, in each of its kaleidoscopic instantiations, it seems to give us pause. Something has gone mournfully wrong with the journalistic project – and, in that, it has a built-in nostalgia mechanism. As S. Elizabeth Bird points out, it's like obscenity in that we know it when we see it but can't quite conjure a comfortably clear definition. But, I would add, it shares with obscenity a second, substantive sense: tabloidization as an indecent, unrepressed, wanton form of journalism. We seem to recognize it as much by what it is not. It is not journalism in its lofty form – that journalism with a capital J – a form as often gilded by collective memory as empirically occupying a "pre-tabloidization" Edenic past. Like the industry it plagues, tabloidization is a force with an oursized reputation. The chapters that follow in this section approach this rogue scapegoat undaunted by that reputation. And in different ways they each ask a similar question: what if tabloidization weren't the bugaboo we have long assumed it to be? Indeed, Herbert J. Gans, Carolyn Kitch and S. Elizabeth Bird quickly dispense with that "common sense" blanket damnation to produce more insightful discoveries. While their paths lead in divergent directions, they all produce thoughtful meditations on engagement, emotion and economics in journalism – redeeming, repositioning and rethinking the very concept of tabloidization so that our final judgment of it stays as complex as our shapeshifting encounters with it.

Leading off, Gans issues this provocative notion: could tabloidization actually remedy the ills of journalism today rather than be representative of them? For this, he requires a less pejorative euphemism – "popularization" – to describe shifts in format and content that might, in fact, hold out the possibility of strengthening news and bolstering democracy rather than despoiling both. After all, other cultural products have long been adapted for the simplified palates of a lower class strata – we can think here of the academy lending a public intellect to the op-ed pages or couture fashion trickling down to suburban malls. Though elites initially balk at a less rarefied audience appropriating the popularized form, it nonetheless represents a constructive opportunity for a wider public to engage with accessible content – and this is no small matter in assuring that informed citizens participate in modern democracy. This populist turn – be it through more informal language, inviting humor, audience incentives, or niche tailoring – is not without its limits, however: for Gans rightly notes the *substance* of news must not deviate from the highest of standards, even as its presentation can accommodate less erudite publics. While leavening the didactic tone and stilted language of news should be encouraged, veracity has no more egalitarian incarnate. Its most stringent ideal requires journalists' attention and aspiration, even if the Grey Lady gets a dash more of color. This favoring of pragmatism over perfection and accommodating inclusion over elitist exclusivity may well be the lemonade recipe for a news industry weaned on lemons – after all, the slow-motion death of newspapers and inexorable graying of the nightly news audience could perhaps use a little popularity here and there. Even if it requires a Faustian truce with obscenity.

Carolyn Kitch turns our attention from democratic redemption to emotional catharsis at a time when "feeling" is suspiciously upstaging "knowing" in public culture and journalistic discourse. Just as Gans repositioned tabloidization as popularization, Kitch seeks to locate this often-maligned term in its sensationalized dimension – that which shocks and provokes the audience with touchy-feely coverage of tears and trauma. Increasingly, sensation seems to be quite literally the aim: stories of collective ritual that eulogize the living in their grief so as to find a place of our own as the audience. These shrines, symbols and tributes serve as public ceremony, whereby deaths and mourning are projected as national metaphors and shared sentiments. While there may be nothing new in this communal functionality offering indices of moral identity and markers of group renewal, since September 11, our "Portraits of Grief" seem to have multiplied: we have witnessed a marked increase in feeling over fact, a premature rush to narrative closure, a saturation of performative tears. Here is where caution is warranted in the tabloid turn – where, for Kitch, it *feels* cheap in a different sense – for the living, rather than dead, threaten to become the lead characters and our actions the primary plot. The dependable tropes of tabloidization – shock, heroism, solidarity – may offer us useful proxies for grieving, but they represent a danger in dependency. They seduce with the notion that "feeling fixes everything" while eliding causes and details; they sacrifice context at the altar of emotion; and they perhaps narcissistically foreground catharsis as resolution *in toto*. Sensationalism must not fully eclipse sensibility, even if its uses gratify.

In the concluding chapter of this section, S. Elizabeth Bird poses the necessary challenge: is tabloidization but a red herring – a "convenient demon figure" – for larger industry problems at hand? We have seen three formulaic, if colorful, shifts in style and content that mark the seemingly unavoidable trend: a move away from lengthy, analytical writing; personalized narratives and characters to epitomize complex problems; and the overreliance on visual motifs. And, yet, even having illuminated these typical textures of tabloidization, Bird reiterates that we lack collective consensus on its nature as a phenomenon. Like Gans, she hesitates to classify clarity as the mark of declining standards – particularly at a juncture when journalistic standards are ever in flux. Indeed, the changing faces of journalism today demand effective, efficient communication with the news audience if the news is to survive as economically sustainable and socially relevant. And, yet, the populist turn here too comes with constraints: Bird's vital criticism is that "the cheap, easy, and popular story often wins out over the expensive, difficult, and less popular one" – and that is a bugaboo more real and hazardous than ever. The solution may reside at the very site of so much of journalism's woe and uncertainty: our twenty-first-century new media landscape. Thereby, the Web might not merely be an attendant medium through which to unload content, but a new frontier whereby journalism can explore and renew its vitality, reconstitute its authority and rekindle its bond with audiences.

All three authors in this section perceive pitfalls and potential in tabloidization. Accessibility and emotion need not be the mark of journalistic degradation and can indeed be deployed in effective ways. But if reporters swoon to capture the reader's heart, they cannot fail to attend to his or her mind. If a news outlet shoots to broaden its audience with a friendlier form, it must not allow accuracy or effort to slip. The tabloid story might win out, but the *cheap* story should not. However, in our efforts to redeem a former foe, certain tensions cannot be overlooked: Even if we hope to shy away from an elitist condemnation of tabloidization, doesn't the "rich" nuance of the elite news outlets offer more detail – and therefore accuracy – than populist rags? Even if popularization offers a prism through which we might incentivize the duties of citizenship, doesn't journalism, at some point, still need the audience to make at least some effort of its own to – as they say in the news business about boring stories – "eat your vegetables"? Only so much sugar can coat the often-ineluctably dry prose of policy coverage; only so much effort can be spent trying to "sex up" investigative reporting on the GAO before you realize it'll never look like Paris Hilton. And we remain rightly nervous that the GAO story costs too much for news organizations that increasingly realize they want the cheap and easy Paris Hilton story anyway. For whether tabloidization is marked by popularity or sensationalism, we seem to still fear that its laughter or tears are insufficient unless backed by the fundamentals of good journalism. And if we can't quite come to terms with precisely what tabloidization represents, perhaps it is because we've not yet reached consensus on what it might be defiling. Certainly throughout this section hints are dropped – depth, accuracy, sophistication, reason, indeed, "truth and objectivity" as Bird notes – and we learn tabloidization (in itself) need not be antithetical to these ideals. But we remain suspicious, even if we're trying to give it the benefit of our usual doubt. And, so, sorting out the crisis from the cure requires a careful parsing of trends; Gans, Kitch and Bird lead the way toward making that first cautious peace with a long-time journalistic villain.

Chapter 2

Can Popularization Help the News Media?

Herbert J. Gans

As I understand it, *tabloidization* is a term for the alleged deterioration of the informational and intellectual content of the news media that accompanies their shrinkage to a smaller size and different format. The term is meant to be pejorative and is used to blame all the usual suspects for what is viewed as a decline in the news media. Since moderate and low-income people are the main consumers of tabloid news, tabloidization is a particularly handy verbal weapon used by more educated people to disparage the culture of less educated ones.

I agree with S. Elizabeth Bird that the term is useless and diverts attention from the actual problems of journalism.[1] For this and other reasons, I write instead about *popularization,* which I understand to be a common social process that occurs in many parts of society and is not limited to the media. Although popularization can be as pejorative a term as tabloidization, it has a constructive meaning as well. That will allow me to ask whether some kind of popularization could enlarge and better inform the news media audience and thus perhaps contribute to the strengthening of the news media and democracy.

On stratification

Before considering popularization, I should note my assumption that in a class-stratified society, just about everything cultural is stratified by class to some extent, including the arts, literature and entertainment as well as the news and other kinds of information. When they have a choice, the different classes consume somewhat different kinds of culture, and perhaps with the exception of news, they have a great deal of choice.

The hierarchy of the cultural strata generally resembles that of the class strata, reflecting the differential distribution of income, education and other material and nonmaterial resources. To simplify a complicated structure, in what follows I will mainly distinguish between high culture, upper middle culture and the combination of middle and low or working class culture commonly known as popular culture. I call these taste cultures.[2]

Although the taste culture of the higher classes is generally more expensive than that of the lower ones, the main difference between the cultures reflects the differential cultural schooling of the people who choose them, high culture being the culture of those highly educated in the humanities. Upper middle culture serves the college educated, including those with professional and managerial degrees, and various taste levels of popular culture cater to the rest of the population. However, in the absence of laws and rules determining cultural choice, even people with professional aesthetic training are free to enjoy popular culture – a practice that was once called "slumming."

The news hierarchy resembles the rest of the cultural one, although it is not stratified as sharply. As far as I know no one has ventured to define and describe a high-culture version of the news, at least in the USA. The *New York Times*, commonly thought to be the most "serious" of the news media is a bastion of upper middle taste culture. In fact, culturally, the news has shrunk to two main types: the elite news media and the popular ones – including regular size and tabloid newspapers as well as magazines and electronic and digital news media.[3] Although media critics identify a third type – what is left of the old sensationalist and semi-fictional print tabloids like the *National Enquirer* and their "tabloid TV" equivalents – these are better classified separately as "entertainment news media."[4]

Within the framework of class cultural analysis, popularization is the adaptation of a cultural product initially created in a higher taste culture for consumption and use by a lower one and thus by an audience that is typically of lower status than the original one. Adaptation usually involves simplification as well as stylistic and other alterations, the replacement of technical with popular language, of abstract images with naturalistic and other popular ones, as well as the substitution of inexpensive raw materials for expensive ones.

Popularization takes place in all sectors of society. Academics popularize scientific and technical material to make it intelligible to a student audience; the garment industry takes the newest high fashion from the most prestigious Paris runways and turns it into affordable clothing for the general population; museum shops sell inexpensive reproductions of invaluable original paintings or of very expensive prints.

Marketers call this process "repositioning the product." They adopt this strategy to enlarge the audience and increase sales and profits, just as academics use it to diffuse their knowledge to an audience larger than their peers.

Although popularization itself involves repositioning from a higher to a lower and lower-status culture and audience, cultural products can also be repositioned upward (or upmarket), and can then be said to undergo "depopularization." My favorite example of depopularization can be observed during public television's fundraising periods, when the work of past popular culture musicians such as Lawrence Welk, Xavier Cugat and the Andrews Sisters become entertainment for public TV's predominantly upper middle class culture. Old Hit Parade or Broadway tunes can even move up all the way to high culture, for example, when they show up in the work of composers of contemporary music. Toward the end of the last century, the supporters of the popular magazine illustrator Norman Rockwell sought to elevate his cultural status, but despite a successful exhibition of his paintings in Atlanta's High Museum of Art, the professional critics representing high culture art were cool and the depopularization attempt failed.[5]

However, depopularization can only succeed when the cultural product is no longer used by or associated with an audience of low cultural status. Although today's audience for popular music has never even heard of Xavier Cugat, some of Norman Rockwell's magazine covers became icons of nostalgia and patriotism and are still reprinted in popular media. But imagine the uproar, from the critics and the audience, if public television tried to raise money from its viewers by playing currently popular music, such as the latest gangster rap or the newest Britney Spears album.

Because popularization adapts the products of a higher culture for a lower one, they become downwardly mobile and so does the audience for which the products were first created if it continues to use them. Needless to say, it rarely does so, for once popularized, the products are stigmatized as having been "dumbed down." In the fashion industry, the dumbed down product is called a "knockoff."[6]

In effect, the higher cultural classes are either unhappy about the downward mobility of what they believed to be *their* product, or they are unhappy with the tastes and social standing of the people who will now be able to use it.

Although the term dumbing down is of recent origin, I imagine that popularization is as old as the yet unexcavated hills of Mesopotamia. Someday we will discover that as soon as our ancestors started making pots, better off or more powerful people wound up with longer lasting or more highly decorated ones, and expressed their disdain at the simpler or more breakable pots of the lower orders.

Whatever the era, if popularization is looked at from the top-down perspective of the higher status population, it is as much a pejorative as tabloidization. However, the people who buy the knockoffs that they cannot possibly afford as originals undoubtedly feel pleased, but their perspective is bottoms-up.

Nonetheless, popularization is sometimes viewed as a desirable and even constructive process, even by the people who condemn tabloidization and dumbing down. The best example is the popularization of the natural sciences, especially biology, psychology, physics, astronomy and archaeology. Their newest findings are regularly popularized for the general but scientifically less educated audience. Many of the actual popularizers are science journalists but a sizeable number are themselves professional scientists who have made part or fulltime careers out of popularizing the work of their colleagues who stay in the labs or on their computers.

Although not all scientists whose work is simplified or shorn of its contextual findings and qualifications are happy with their popularizers, generally speaking, scientific popularization is not thought of as dumbing down. Even if scientific writing in high-culture journals differs from that in popular journals and the Sunday supplements, the latter is not disparaged in class-related terms. Instead, scientific popularization seems to be perceived as the transfer of knowledge from one of C.P. Snow's Two Cultures to the other, and both cultures are assumed to be class equals.[7]

Evaluating popularization

So far, I have taken a detached and non-normative view of popularization. However, applying the popularization process to the news in order to help enlarge the news audience is a normative task that raises normative questions.

The creators, suppliers and supporters of, and the audiences for high culture have traditionally argued that culture, whether artistic, informational or entertaining, should be judged from their top-down perspective, claiming that only their high-culture forms are aesthetically acceptable, intellectually valid and socially desirable. To put it another way, the partisans of high culture have long tried to universalize their aesthetic criteria and standards, condemning all other cultures, other than what they view as "folk culture" as unacceptable or harmful.

To be sure, their attempts to universalize their standards have not been successful, and the imposition of their culture even less so. Most Americans, having different aesthetic criteria and standards, do not accept the high culture ones. They make cultural choices on the basis of their own aesthetic criteria and standards. However, these are not written down and taught, for there are few aestheticians and critics, at least outside the academy, who defend the popular taste cultures and legitimate their standards. Although the people who choose popular culture often look pejoratively at upper middle and high culture, they express their views privately and rarely make it into the public prints.

The normative conclusion I draw from these observations is relativist, or, if you will, populist. I argue that everyone is entitled to the arts, entertainment and other cultural products they believe meet their own standards, unless it can be proven that their choices are hurting them, others or the society as a whole. Although the researchers who study the effects of popular culture and the mass media continue to disagree, none have yet demonstrated that the popular failure to follow high-culture standards results in physical or psychological harm to members of society or society as a whole.

I would, however, suggest a different evaluation for news and other kinds of information, and on two grounds. First, news is not judged on the basis of taste and aesthetics but on the basis of empirical accuracy, and inaccurate news can hurt individuals and the larger society. If the news media misreport a known danger to social life, people and society can get hurt.[8]

Second, although a democratic society, or at least this one, does not prescribe what art and entertainment people should choose, it does urge that its citizens are sufficiently informed to properly carry out the responsibilities of citizenship. Consequently, even if many people might prefer human interest stories or fictionalized docudrama over the "hard" domestic and foreign news supplied by the news media, as citizens, they are expected to at least keep up with such news on a reasonably regular basis.

The news audience's "need to know" as citizens should not vary by taste culture or class; after all, facts and explanations are the same in elite as in popular news media. Consequently, the *substance* of the news should not vary by taste or class. However, such variation is acceptable for the *presentation* of news, for example, in the language and the level of detail. If the aim is to reach the parts of the news audience with limited education, the words used to report the news and the complexity of its analysis cannot be the same as that used for graduates of selective colleges. If keeping to a single set of the "highest" presentation standards means losing a significant part of the audience, then the public's need to know cannot be properly satisfied.

Popularization and the news media

In the remainder of this chapter, I consider whether and how popularization should and can be used to enlarge the news audience and increase its interest in and attentiveness to the news, among other things as one step to increasing the American public's role in what is supposed to be a representative democracy.

The popularization of science offers a useful model, for while the substance of the science the popularizers report remains the same for elite and popular media, their presentation methods will vary. Indeed, the methods of the scientific popularizers working for the popular media might be studied by journalists undertaking the further popularization of the news media.

Should further popularization of the news be attempted? After all, the national news media audience, though smaller than a generation ago, remains respectably large. For example, daily newspaper circulation is still over 50 million and daily readership is much higher. The three network evening news programs attract an average daily audience between 20 and 25 million and more when especially newsworthy events are taking place.

If further popularization is considered desirable, it should probably be used to reclaim some of the people who left the news audience and to add new ones, especially but not only young people. An enlarged audience and the new advertising that follows in its wake would presumably help the news media reduce their current economic difficulties, although I am more interested that people obtain the news that they are thought to need as democratic citizens.

Before asking how such popularization might be accomplished, I have to raise two other questions. One question is whether the news audience has in fact decreased, or whether it has just moved from the handful of traditional print and electronic news media to a much larger set of news media now also including the internet. Most people agree the news audience has been fragmented; whether or not there has been an increase or decrease, both in the size of the audience and in the amount of news they attend to is not known, however. Journalism likes to look back to a golden past, but it is possible that today more people obtain more news than ever before, and not just that supplied by Jon Stewart and Stephen Colbert.

Still, for the purpose of this chapter, I accept the pessimistic conventional wisdom and assume the audience has shrunk or not increased, especially among young adults. That assumption leads to my second question: do we know enough about the news audience to know how it could be enlarged and become more involved with the news?

Good answers to this question are currently unavailable. While there are figures and estimates of how many people receive a variety of news media, we know much less about whether and how they consume the news. The Pew Research Center for the People and the Press reports regularly in its "News Interest Index" on what stories their respondents say they follow more or less closely, but we do not have a good sense of what news people choose to pay attention to on a day-to-day basis, why they do so, and how attentive they are.

In addition, we lack good data on how much news various sectors of the news audience decide they need to feel informed or "keep up." However, judging by the amount of daily hard news on the network evening news programs, now and in the past, 10 minutes a day may be sufficient for most, at least as a minimum. Admittedly, not everyone keeps up on a daily basis and there are people who treat the news somewhat like a soap opera, joining the news audience once or twice a week to keep up and to stay informed about the stories of major interest to them and the people with whom they talk.

Even when the news media were awash in money, they did little audience research other than that needed to keep their advertisers happy, while academics, at least in the USA, seem never to have been particularly interested in understanding the audience or learning more about it.[9]

Proper audience research is hard to carry out, and asking audiences to talk about their consumption of the news is methodologically and otherwise extremely difficult. Moreover, researchers who are interested in the news and the news media may not see the audience as part of their field, despite the fact that it plays a significant role in shaping news content.

Even less is known about how much the news audience comprehends the news to which it does pay attention. Although as far back as the mid-twentieth century, the BBC's audience research unit regularly carried out comprehension studies – and found comprehension to be very low – such research never earned a place on the American audience research agenda.

In the 1970s, one of the network TV evening news programs hired a well-known political scientist to carry out a comprehension study and asked him to redesign the program to raise the comprehension rate. The study was never made public, and all I could ever learn was that the results were discouraging. His redesign of the program so that audience comprehension would increase also increased the length of each story to such an extent that the number of the day's stories that could be reported had to be reduced from about 20 to six.

My unsophisticated Googling discovered only one academic comprehension study, carried out in 1986 by John Robinson and Mark Levy.[10] They found that "on average, somewhat less than one-third of the major news stories examined each week were comprehended by the respondents sampled" (p. 166). Moreover, "comprehension was often ... higher for stories with dramatic or 'human interest' content" (p. 167). Perhaps these findings are now out of date, particularly since the number of people who attend and graduate from college has increased, although the typical college curriculum does not teach its students how to comprehend the news.

The Robinson–Levy study also discovered that about two-thirds of the interview sample talked "about things in the news" with friends, workmates and family members, and that those participating in such conversations scored higher on news comprehension. One can assume that some of the sample members first heard their news from these personal sources rather than from journalists, in line with two-step flow communication theory.[11]

Some popularizing changes in the news

A great deal of comprehension and other audience research, as well as learning from experiential data, is necessary before changes in the news can be discussed intelligently. Nonetheless, I suspect that two types of changes would be included in any list – changes in the language of news and changes in audience incentives.

Clearly, the parts of the news audience with comprehension problems need a simpler language, with more description and explanation of the events and issues of greatest universal importance. Perhaps the network half-hour evening news program is not the best platform for simplification since it is so brief and the three such programs already assemble by far the largest news audience in the country. Moreover, since simplification has status connotations – and no one will want – or admit to want – "news for dummies," where and how to present such news will have to be worked out carefully. Someday, when the internet is a standard utility for everyone, websites which simplify the news without stigmatizing its audience can perhaps be created.

Simplification is both art and science; it requires decisions on which facts are of first priority when the total number must be limited; and what detail is necessary and what can be omitted when complexity is an obstacle to reaching the audience. Journalists will have to learn how complicated events can be described and explained in a more easily understandable fashion; and how connections between events and their contexts can be made intelligibly. In addition, they will have to learn what news frames other than personalized ones are most effective in reaching the audience.[12]

The tone of the news has almost always been earnest, acting as a symbolic cod liver oil to insure our steady growth as citizens. But perhaps other possibilities can be tried.

For example, if audience research were available to tell us how people talk about the news with each other and about what kinds of news, and whether such informal news conversation also increases interest in the news, some clues might be gained about how to undertake further popularization of the news. Such clues could come from a variety of sources, including the web news stories and blogs produced by so-called citizen journalists, and especially those by amateurs who are likely to report news stories the way they tell them to each other.[13]

Yet another language clue might come from the newswork that all of us do all day long, as suppliers and receivers of the information needed to function as family members, workers, friends and the other roles we play in everyday life. In fact, social life, and thus life itself, would be impossible if it were not submerged in a constant flow of what might be called everyday news. Understanding the scripts of everyday newswork and the language in which we report those news stories to our various audiences would undoubtedly provide substantive and methodological raw material for further popularization of professional or journalistic news.[14] Understanding how the various word of mouth messages that come to us from all over, orally and now on the web, would enhance journalistic style sheets as well.

Everyday news and word of mouth come to us in informal English, while professional news is both formal and serious. Seriousness is necessary to signify the importance of the news, but a certain amount of informality might enlarge the audience and increase its attention even as it underlines the importance of serious, formally told news. Perhaps even the most serious news is sometimes best told in nonprofessional ways.[15]

For example, the popularity of fake news suggests that it and other kinds of humor could be used from time to time as a kind of news commentary that is more directly connected to the news pages than suggested by today's carefully segregated editorials and other commentaries. Cartoons that accompany news stories and political comic strips that provide a regular commentary on long-running stories are other possibilities. For audiences who like opinion and commentary with their news, the barrier between news and opinion pages or sections could be relaxed in yet other ways.

By audience incentives, I mean format and other changes that give the audience new reasons to consume or pay greater attention to the news. Years ago, network television news added medical, health and service news as such an incentive, and if not to increase perhaps to hold on to its audience. True, such news is of interest largely to the older parts of the audience; what incentives, if any would attract younger people to the daily news – which is predominantly about newsmakers who are no longer young – remain to be discovered. Cable television news has used a generous dollop of human interest, crime and suspense news – enough to suggest the accuracy of Carolyn Kitch's analysis of "tears and trauma" in the news.[16] BBC radio and television has always included major sports stories in its news budgets; perhaps equivalent US news media could do the same.

Another possible incentive is greater custom tailoring of the news to specific audiences. Although standardized production for the so-called mass buyer has declined in the "post Fordist" consumer economy, too much news remains standardized, as if it were pursuing a homogeneous mass audience. The print and electronic news media have, with a few mostly ideological exceptions, been reluctant to risk a niche approach but appealing to parts of the total audience should be easier on the internet.

If one stipulates that only a portion of the day's important news will or should be of universal interest and that certain news stories will inevitably be of interest only to some parts of the total news audience, it becomes possible to speculate about and experiment with news programs, or sections of them, for different audiences. If there are stories relevant to old people but not to young ones and vice versa, then why not try formats that appeal to each. Parents and single people, well-educated and poorly educated ones might be attracted to news programs and websites as well as the already existing magazine and newspaper sections designed for each.

In a society which sells watches that cost from between $20 to tens of thousands of dollars, it is even possible to imagine news programming for different income groups. For example, poor people live with very different micro-economies, including labor markets, local polities and bureaucracies than the more affluent. They do not need daily business news written for investors but they do need to be informed about government support programs for the low-income population and the availability of new jobs. Since they cannot afford much of what advertisers advertise, however, news media for the poor would have to be nonprofit.

Needing the news

Journalists and others who make their living in and from the news media need them in many different ways. The news audience does not, however; indeed, most people do not need most of the news available to them, including that with which they keep up regularly. News media analysts and critics should probably remind themselves every so often that for their everyday lives, people need daily news only about the weather and transportation or other problems that might affect work and other scheduled trips they must take and institutions they must use.

People also need to know about threats that could disrupt the day or the days to come – and they might want to know, or not know, certainties or likelihoods about the more distant future. But how much do most people need information about an overseas disaster, a foreign election or the House Appropriations Committee vote on next year's federal budget? In addition, it is not even clear how many depend on the news media for the information they need, and how many obtain what they actually need from family, friends and work mates who have the same needs. Word of mouth remains the most widely and intensively used news medium in human society.

Admittedly, citizens are supposed to need the news as citizens. Although they are expected to inform themselves about government and politics and much of the daily news fare concerns both, the polity also suggests in various direct and indirect ways that government, and even their own elected representatives, do not require – or even want – them to be politically active other than in elections.[17] Perhaps that helps to explain why the news media places such emphasis on elections, and says very little about other citizen political activity.

Furthermore, the news about government and politics as it is now reported, even in the *New York Times*, would not enable people to be politically active other than as voters. For example, the news media could supply only a little of the information that citizens would need to mobilize, or to lobby their elected representatives. Once upon a time, such information was transmitted in political meetings, by special messengers, newsletters and of course word of mouth; today, special and often temporary websites are slowly but surely replacing almost all of these.

Consequently, I find it surprising that, despite the concern about the alleged decline in the news audience and its allegedly declining attention span, people actually follow news stories which play no direct parts in their lives or are not designed to evoke an emotional response. Perhaps they keep up with the news because most people they know do so, or because they could otherwise not participate in the political conversations that do take place. Or maybe the news helps to let people feel they remain connected to the larger society, particularly older ones who have actually been disconnected from it.

In any case, the polls suggest that at least the people who make themselves available to pollsters and can respond to the questions they are asked with more than a "I don't know" response have a general sense of and opinions about the most important domestic and foreign news stories of the day. True, most respondents are under-informed about specifics and technical details, which is why organized interests and politicians are so often able to pass legislation that the majority of poll respondents oppose. But organized interests and politicians all have access to special and even personal news media designed to inform them about the political activities in which they participate.

These observations suggest that further popularization of the news media might not go very far, at least with respect to strengthening representative democracy in the USA. A very differently organized society in which citizens are offered the incentives and resources to be politically active would be required to change news habits – and the country's news media.[18]

Conclusion

The news and news media that would result from these efforts at popularization might not satisfy current professional criteria for excellence. However, in a highly polarized society embedded in a globalizing domestic economy and a combative international polity, every little bit of extra understanding of the national and international news is important. Consider a September 2007 *New York Times*-CBS News poll which found that six years after 9/11, 33 per cent of the sample still believed Saddam Hussein to have been personally involved in the 9/11 bombings. And then imagine how their knowing and accepting the correct information might affect their opinions about the Iraq War, other wars and civil wars as well as related foreign and domestic policy issues.

To be sure, such poll findings cannot be blamed solely or even primarily on the news media or on the country's news consumption. They reflect the Bush administration's continued attempt to connect Saddam Hussein to its war on terrorism, as well as the still widespread resort to foreign villains to justify our Mideast wars, other features of our foreign policy and the evocation of fear built into the homeland security apparatus.

Of course, the people who hold such opinions may feel no need for additional news and might actually be upset by and reject accurate facts. They may even need the foreign villains to cope with threats and perceived threats coming at them from somewhere in US society. Although the news media cannot chase away real and imagined demons, and there are other limits to what they can do and whom they can reach, they can try harder to get the news out to the people who may unknowingly need it most.

Notes

1 S. Elizabeth Bird, "Tabloidization: What is it and Does it Really Matter?" in this volume.
2 My analysis here follows the one I presented in my *Popular Culture and High Culture: An Analysis of Taste* (New York: Basic Books, 1974, 1999); and in Pierre Bourdieu, *Distinction: A Social Critique of the Judgment of Taste* (Cambridge: Harvard University Press, 1984). However, we disagree in the evaluation of the cultural hierarchy.
3 Again it is possible to identify several levels of taste, although all these news media are alike insofar as they are produced by professional and thus fairly similarly trained journalists.
4 These tabloids serve mostly the lower income and lower educational strata, but the concept of entertainment news media also makes it possible to compare them to news media that supply entertainment to the patrons of upper middle and high culture, for example book, art and other review journals.
5 For details, see my "Can Rockwell Survive Cultural Elevation," *Chronicle of Higher Education*, 21 April 2000, B8–9.
6 When the knockoff is sold at the same high price and claims the same high status as the original, it is criminalized as counterfeit or forged.
7 C.P. Snow, *The Two Cultures and the Scientific Revolution* (New York: Cambridge University Press, 1959).
8 I purposely underline known dangers, thereby excluding unknown ones, which cannot be reported, or guesses about such dangers, which can only be reported as guesses, not as news. Another paper would be required to discuss the role of values in the news, since these cannot be judged by accuracy criteria.

9 British scholars have been more interested and active, through ethnography and other methods. For a comprehensive discussion of their activity, see S. Elizabeth Bird, *The Audience in Everyday Life; Living in a Media World* (New York: Routledge, 2003), Chapter 1.

10 John P. Robinson and Mark Levy, "Interpersonal Communication and News Comprehension," *Public Opinion Quarterly*, 50, no. 2, Summer (1986): 160–75.

11 Elihu Katz and Paul F. Lazarsfeld, *Personal Influence: The Part Played by People in the Flow of Mass Communications* (New Brunswick, NJ: Transaction, 2nd ed. 2006).

12 We also need to know what news frames are misunderstood or rejected by audiences, for ideological and other reasons.

13 Even academic researchers can contribute. See, for example, William A. Gamson, *Talking Politics* (New York: Cambridge University Press, 1992), which provides an analysis of focus group members talking about politics and political news.

14 See my "Everyday News, Newsworkers and Professional Journalism," *Political Communication*, 24. no. 2, April (2007): 161–66.

15 A good example often replayed in documentaries about the 1960s is Walter Cronkite, overcome with emotions not normally permitted an anchorman, telling his audience about the death of President Kennedy.

16 See her chapter, "Tears and Trauma in the News," in this volume.

17 If truth be told, citizens can vote without being informed. Moreover, campaigning politicians would prefer the voters to ignore the news and become informed only by their campaign advertising.

18 I have tried to think about such a society in my *Democracy and the News* (New York: Basic Books, 2003) and more recently, in my *Imagining America in 2033* (Ann Arbor: University of Michigan Press, 2008), particularly Chapter 7.

Chapter 3

Tears and Trauma in the News[1]

Carolyn Kitch

A decade ago, in August of 1997, cultural critics claimed to be appalled by the collective weeping of news media around the world, or rather by the conveyance through news media of the collective weeping of millions of people, simply because a popular and beautiful person had died tragically. Two years later, *Time* columnist Roger Rosenblatt, a gifted cultural observer himself, took issue with such criticism when he considered why people (including journalists) were so upset at another tragic death of yet another beautiful, popular public figure, John F. Kennedy Jr.; Rosenblatt argued that it was time for us, including those in elite news organizations, to acknowledge that "there is a news of feeling as well as fact."[2] Only eight years have passed since then, and yet it seems quite a long time ago. Today, feeling is all around us, in public culture and in journalistic coverage of that culture.

One dimension of the presumed tabloidization of journalism is sensationalism, the inclusion in news of elements meant to shock and provoke strong emotional responses among readers. Conventional wisdom tells us that displays of raw emotion, from sorrow to outrage, are to be avoided by journalists and, if expressed by news subjects, not to be exploited by journalists. And yet current journalism is saturated with tears and trauma. Whether the news is about a natural disaster with mass casualties, a local police officer killed in the line of duty, a young woman murdered on a college campus, or a child struck and killed by a drunk driver, it will be reported and produced in news media as a story of the living who grieve, a story about public ritual. The focus will be on mourners who erect spontaneous shrines, who stand outdoors holding candles or American flags, and who very publicly pay tribute to the dead.

Increasingly these stories are told in journalistic prose and pictures that, themselves, express grief and pay tribute to the dead, a ceremonial representation of public ceremony. Such news content has escalated along with casualties of the war in Iraq. In May of 2007, *The New York Times* visually marked Memorial Day with a front-page photograph of a young woman, her shoulders bare in a sundress, weeping, prostrate on the Arlington National Cemetery grave of her fiancée, who had been killed in Iraq three months earlier.[3]

How have we arrived at this point? What are the consequences of such an emotional shift in even the most elite news media? This essay seeks some possible answers to those questions. Specifically, it examines the expression of emotion in news about deaths that are seen as nationally meaningful, in which local and personal feelings are understood as national feelings. War deaths are among these, as are disasters, dreadful accidents, and shocking murders. All of these kinds of stories are newsworthy, not only because they are unexpected events, but also because they inspire sympathy and outrage, sorrow and moralizing. In journalism, these kinds of stories exist at the intersection of hard news and heart-tugging feature, making headlines in elite as well as tabloid publications, in small-town newspapers as well as on international television news networks.

Stories of shocking death, especially murder, have been a staple of journalism since at least the turn of the twentieth century, first in the "sob sister" reporting of lurid murder trials in "yellow journalism" newspapers competing for a mass audience, and then when a new kind of crime-filled newspaper, produced in a new size, introduced the word tabloid into American journalism in the 1920s. But news stories about crime and crisis always have cultural value, not just shock value; they tell us something about the times in which they happen and are reported.[4] Reaching back farther into history, to the Penny Press, journalism historian Andie Tucher argues that *The New York Herald*'s sensational coverage of the 1836 murder of prostitute Helen Jewett was in fact a moral tale about religion and class identity at the dawn of the industrial revolution. She writes that:

> [James Gordon] Bennett and the other editors were fulfilling their public duty as journalists. ... They were confirming their audience's general assumptions of how the world worked ... and upholding the beliefs and ethics they already cherished. They were allowing readers to cement their own sense of self and communal identity. ... They were making sense of a society growing ever more confusing by assuring their readers that things happened in understandable, even predictable ways.[5]

These social purposes of news – affirming collective identity, making sense of the senseless, upholding beliefs – are ways in which journalism functions as a ritual process, to use James Carey's well-known term.[6] They are especially evident in news coverage of disaster and other upsetting, prominent deaths, and it is not surprising that, in such cases, journalists search for themes that provide explanation and offer consolation. It also is not surprising that coverage should focus on mourners who are ordinary people; many scholars, including Herbert J. Gans and John Hartley,[7] have noted the powerful symbolic appeal, and therefore the routine inclusion, of "the common man" in news as a way of personalizing complex events and promoting audience identification with news topics. In this symbolic system, Gaye Tuchman explains:

Tears and other displays of emotion. ... do not function as an attribute of the individual. They are social indicators of the plight of a group, whether the group is parents with incurably ill children, wives of soldiers missing in action, or families made homeless by a natural disaster.[8]

Through such news characters – who lose their regional specificity when they become symbols, typical people who could be "any of us" – private emotions are transformed into public ones.[9] Journalists explain shocking news events by placing such characters into familiar narratives through which audiences recognize the meaning of those events.[10]

This construction process is not new, nor is it uniquely suited to recent events. Over the past several years, however, there has been a marked shift in the sheer amount of emotion in news narratives about death, the repeated use of certain kinds of symbols, and, most of all, a rush to narrative closure. This growing urge to make truly horrific events understandable favors certain explanatory narratives at the expense of others, masking or eliminating other lessons we might have learned from these stories.

The most spectacular murder and disaster story of recent years was one of the most deadly serious news topics in modern journalism history. I would argue that it was out of *that* story – not the death of Princess Diana, but the deaths of September 11 – that journalism has become a regular blend of fact and feeling whenever death is seen as publicly meaningful.

So many events have been covered in recent years in ways strikingly reminiscent of the coverage of September 11 and its aftermath. That coverage highlighted public emotions through many photographs of weeping and stunned witnesses and survivors, especially young women, and declared the country's "Lost Innocence," the title of an article in *U.S. News & World Report*.[11] That coverage represented so much public ritual, some local to the sites of disaster, such as firefighters' funerals, and some nationwide, such as candlelight vigils and prayer services. That coverage searched for and celebrated heroes, from the firefighters to the passengers of Flight 93 to workers who had helped each other in the World Trade Center and Pentagon buildings. *The New York Times*'s "Portraits of Grief" series and other newspaper and magazine eulogies described the victims as typical people with hopes and dreams just like any of us.[12] Indeed, the story of September 11 quickly became, in news, a tale of a disaster that *had* happened to all Americans; it was, according to the sole headline on a front page of the Cleveland *Plain Dealer*, "America's Tragedy."[13] In that final narrative shift, healing and closure were pronounced through very public statements of solidarity, statements that were made by real people in particular places but that ultimately were communicated through news media. "We" were, as a country, "Back on Our Feet" just two weeks after the attacks, proclaimed *Newsweek* in a headline under a double-page photograph of baseball players surrounding a giant American flag.[14]

Since then, other prominent news stories have been covered in ways they probably wouldn't have been covered a decade ago.

The journalistic frenzy that ensued when nine miners were trapped in the Quecreek coal mine near Sipesville, Pennsylvania, in the summer of 2002 at first seemed surprising, since mine accidents have occurred with regularity for more than a century. Yet here was a potential disaster story that was linked overtly to September 11, happening in a place 10 miles away from where Flight 93 had crashed only 10 months earlier. And its happy, if atypical, outcome was explained in news as a redemption tale, one that seemed to compensate for the story of September 11 while also repeating it, a parable of brave working-class men and the "first responders" who saved them. *The New York Times* repeated President George Bush's claim that the miners represented the "spirit of America," while one of the rescued men told *Dateline NBC*, "I couldn't even imagine how many people was out there behind us. ... that just tells us what kind of country we live in. I mean, we always pull together."[15]

Miners' inherent bravery was declared again four and a half years later, when 12 miners were killed in an explosion at the Sago mine near Tallmansville, West Virginia. Grief was represented on newspaper front pages by photographs of girls and young women, some of them daughters or granddaughters of the dead miners. These news characters were foremost in declaring outrage that the mine company, and the news media, had conveyed an erroneous report of the miners' survival. On the front page of *The Washington Post* was a picture of a shocked and furious Daniele Bennett, who cried out to an *NBC Nightly News* reporter, "my granddaddy is dead because people has lied on the TV ... We had a miracle, and it was taken away from us."[16]

In order to create closure in this story, reporters turned to a much broader narrative about working-class heroes, evidenced by a long eulogy from ABC reporter Chris Cuomo, which concluded: "It is much more than a job for them. ... They say that every time they leave their families they know they might not come back. ... these men [are] part of something that is bigger than just themselves. It is a tradition of sacrifice that truly helped build this country."[17] News photographs showed black bows attached to a chain-link fence, blowing in the wind, and a row of crosses, each marked with a dead miner's name, capped by a helmet, and next to an American flag.[18] These gestures, made locally by the West Virginia community but then made nationally through news media, blended memory of September 11 and military ritual.

Given that military framing, it seems as if it would be hard to compare the story of the Sago mine explosion with what happened in Nickel Mines, Pennsylvania in October 2006. Initial news reports called the shooting of 10 Amish schoolgirls, resulting in the death of five girls plus the gunman, "inexplicable" and described the shooter as "a killer out of nowhere."[19] Very quickly, however, familiar visual symbols appeared in news coverage. Newspapers were full of pictures of teenage Amish and Mennonite girls walking through fields. Buggies were the visual symbol in which, literally, grief traveled across public

view. The older victims, who reportedly had said "Shoot me first," were pronounced brave and heroic, as were the state troopers who were first on the
scene. With no access to the grieving families and no apparent motive for the
killings, journalists still faced the question of how to provide narrative closure.
The answer was the theme of "grace," a journalistic focus on, and celebration
of, the kindness of the victims' families toward the gunman's family, and their
statement that they forgave him for his sins.

This was in fact a strange form of closure after a heinous murder in a
broader American culture that tends to expect justice rather than forgiveness.
The refusal of the Amish to seek retribution or show anger was, as Diane
Zimmerman Umble and David Weaver-Zercher have written, a radical statement quite atypical of American norms.[20] Yet it was embraced in journalism
as the theme through which this story became about "us," a story in which the
Amish came to stand for the best part of *our* nature. In news, forgiveness
turned into "solidarity" among people in a "small town," words used in news
media ranging from the *Lancaster New Era* to *People* magazine.[21] Such a
construction of both the Sago mining community and the Amish are evidence
of the survival of the news value, identified by Herbert J. Gans three decades
ago, of "small-town pastoralism," the portrayal of a good, simple life that,
according to Katherine Fry, "exists as a repository of fundamental values" and
symbolically stands for "the cultural strength of the nation as a whole."[22]

The same portrait was painted of the university community at Virginia Tech
after the deadly shooting of 33 students and faculty there six months later, in
April 2007. "Tragedy Defies Comprehension" was one newspaper headline the
next day.[23] Yet from the start of the coverage, the many photographs depicting
mourning and sorrow described those emotions as national ones. The front
page of *The Dallas Morning News* featured a close-up photograph of a young
woman looking upward, with tears running down her face, and this caption:
"A Virginia Tech student expressed the sentiment of the nation Tuesday
during a memorial service."[24] The entire front page of the Denver *Rocky
Mountain News* was a photograph of a nighttime candlelight ceremony,
focusing on three young women with sorrowful expressions, with the headline
"America's Anguish."[25]

This was one of hundreds of news-media images of this candlelight vigil and
of other rituals through which the campus community expressed its solidarity,
even while reporters were still trying to find a motive for the killings. The
victims were eulogized as "the fallen," as though they had died fighting for a
cause, and brief profiles of these "lives cut short" painted a collective portrait
of typicality.[26] News coverage emphasized heroes, including a professor who
had been a Holocaust survivor, who had died in an effort to save others. News
media used words including "strength," "prevail," and "pride," suggesting an
act of uniting against an opponent. The rush toward closure was especially
pronounced in the Virginia Tech case; in some newspapers, "healing" was
reported to have begun the same night as the killings.[27]

In all of these nationally prominent death stories, even though they were really very different kinds of news events, journalists told the tale of each tragedy as one of shocking loss, pride in heroism, and strength through solidarity. In this kind of story, it is not the dead but the typical people of the community, and by extension the grieving nation, who become the main characters; their behaviour – assembling memorial shrines, holding prayer services, and then quickly healing – becomes the main plot.

The central role of journalism in publicly conveying this communal process is among the most convincing evidence that journalism is, indeed, a ritual process, even a form of civil religion, a process of "upholding and reaffirming at regular intervals the collective sentiments" of a society.[28] If this is true, then journalism exists in a symbiotic relationship with vernacular culture, taking cues from citizen ritual even as it provides cues for Americans' behavior during grief events. Journalists' uses of patriotic rhetoric are part of a much broader public acknowledgment of the affirming power of, to use Carolyn Marvin and David Ingle's term, "violent blood sacrifice [that] makes enduring groups cohere. ... a sacrificial system that ... has a sacred flag at its center."[29] Reporters' and editors' willing and consistent participation in such ritual situates them within culture, rather than outside it, and confirms that they too are citizens who react to terrible events with feeling and sometimes outrage. These aspects of journalism, like the reportorial use of recognizable news characters and narratives, are probably inevitable in the coverage of crisis, and are not necessarily undesirable at a time when journalists are criticized for being out of touch with their audiences' needs, beliefs, and feelings.

And yet the cases discussed in this essay – and there are, and will be, others – have troubling implications. Their common narrative trajectory transforms a news story about other people who have died in atypical, horrific, and often outrageous circumstances to a story *about us*, typical people whose ordinary lives affirm the patriotic way these deaths are made sense of in news. What is lost when this happens? What lessons *don't* we learn from these news stories?

Certainly we don't learn much about violent crimes that happen in depressed urban areas, crimes that are not regarded as inexplicable and whose victims and their families are not portrayed in news as symbolic of the nation. In late September 2006, more than 1000 residents of Philadelphia, where more than 400 homicides had occurred the previous year, marched outside the state capitol building in Harrisburg to urge passage of gun-control legislation. This protest received some coverage but disappeared from the news less than a week later, when the Nickel Mines murders became the central focus of not just Pennsylvania news, but international news. In Philadelphia and other cities, homicide is a routine event, although news coverage of urban crime does at least tend to acknowledge its causes.

On the other hand, when we understand the victims and community of a crime primarily as symbols – of grief, of "pride," of "the American spirit" –

then we don't learn about them as actual people living in specific circumstances. A more accurate picture of both the Quecreek and Sago mining communities would have been one of rural poverty, or at any rate, limited
economic opportunities for many Americans. Moreover, there were reasons
the Quecreek mine flooded and the Sago mine exploded, reasons having to do
with the erosion of mine-safety standards over the past 20 years in this country,
especially in bituminous coal mines in western Pennsylvania, West Virginia,
and Kentucky (where two miners were killed in an explosion one month after
the Sago incident). That contextual backdrop was lost when the emotions of
the local people involved in those events were generalized to the trauma of (as
television news anchor Brian Williams put it, covering the Sago story) "millions of Americans from the East Coast to the West" waiting for "word from
deep underground."[30]

When tragic deaths are understood in news as having happened to "America," this storyline almost always requires the erasure of the details and causes
of the specific news event. While they were inarguably shocking, neither of the
massacres at Virginia Tech and Nickel Mines was really inexplicable. Only a
few media raised the question posed on the front page of the Fargo, North
Dakota *Forum*: "Are Guns the Problem?"[31] That headline referred to Virginia
Tech, while a headline in a Lancaster newspaper asked "What's Wrong Here?"
after the Amish murders.[32] The latter feature made the provocative claim that
murder is now not uncommon in rural Lancaster County, and that the
McMansionization of the area has led to "isolation and a sense of entitlement."[33] The front page contained a picture of Carl Roberts, the killer of the
Amish girls, alongside the faces of two other young men who had committed
multiple murders in Lancaster County within the 11 months preceding the
Amish murder: 18-year-old David Ludwig of Lititz, who shot and killed his
14-year-old girlfriend's parents before running off with her; and 21-year-old
Jesse Dee Wise, who murdered six members of his own family in Leola. Lititz
was described in news as a "pastoral ... village dotted with quilt shops and
Amish handicrafts,"[34] yet it turned out that David Ludwig had grown up in a
house containing a basement bunker and 54 guns. Except for the killer, there
were no survivors in the Wise family murder case, so newspapers used photographs of girls leaving teddy bears outside the home and interviewed neighbors,
who said, "How could this happen here?"

In early October 2007, when a 20-year-old deputy sheriff in rural Wisconsin
shot and killed six people at a homecoming party, the same question formed
headlines. But one area resident also told a *New York Times* reporter: "He
didn't have a lot of friends because he was arrogant. ... After he became an
officer, it was a power trip to him."[35] Less than a week later, a 14-year-boy
was arrested in Norristown, Pennsylvania when he admitted to planning a
Columbine-style attack at Plymouth Whitemarsh High School. He was found
to have dozens of knives, several swords, homemade explosives, and three
guns, which his mother had helped him obtain; he told police he was "tired of

being bullied" in school.[36] Reviewed together, these cases suggest some consistent themes: isolation, entitlement, bullying, and very angry young men with guns and knives.

A related issue is the use of girls and young women as symbols of loss. Such a gesture is hardly new; it is rhetorically linked to the labeling of murder coverage as "sob sister" journalism a century ago and rooted in the imagery of art, sculpture, and literature of even earlier historic periods. And yet it is particularly ironic that these figures are repeatedly offered in journalism as a visual "explanation" of the meaning of violent crime, especially crimes committed by angry young men. The majority of victims who are targeted and killed in workplace and school shootings in America are female, as are the overwhelming majority of victims of domestic violence, and in nearly all cases the criminals are angry men. Because we are used to seeing female figures used symbolically, it may be that we are distracted from noticing the misogyny present in such crimes.

There are, in fact, causes and motives for most murders and disasters. But in the news coverage of the crises discussed here, causes and motives were lost in proclamations of disbelief and grief. When awful things happen, the now-routine journalistic turn to tears and tribute creates a narrative bridge from dreadful events, proof of the worst of America, to patriotic affirmation, proof of the best of America. This reframing of the disaster event is accomplished by much visual display of girls, candles, and the American flag, and by frequent comparisons, in news text, between heroic civilians and soldiers.

There may be no greater hero in US journalism today than a soldier. This is especially true in local journalism, in which each casualty of the Iraq War is eulogized as the ultimate hero as well as the ultimate common man. Like the murder and disaster victims, the soldier's grieving-but-united family and community could be ours. Generalized feeling, anchored by national pride, wins out over fact or context. Private emotions become presumably public ones, as the audience is encouraged to feel part of the heroism and solidarity.

The commonness of this narrative in journalism today is cause for concern, for many reasons. It constructs an imaginary America in which feeling fixes everything. It promotes unearned self-satisfaction among people wholly unconnected with the tragedy, while prematurely declaring the healing of wounds that remain, for the actual victims, quite raw. It presents violent crimes and deadly accidents as unanticipated exceptions rather than foreseeable consequences of chronic social and political problems. And it employs patriotism in order to foreclose serious public discussion of those problems.

And yet this news narrative of national grief has the potential to be critical as well as conservative, and we are beginning to see evidence of this. We first saw it two years ago in coverage of Hurricane Katrina, in which the American flag, waved by people stranded on rooftops and wrapped around the shoulders of an elderly woman, became a symbol of protest, conveyed widely through journalism. Not only was there no immediate closure to this story, but since then it has become clear that the nation has badly failed to stand in solidarity with these victims. The fact that the news media emphasized the faces of women and girls (as well as the flag) in coverage of the hurricane's aftermath rhetorically situated this story within the gallery of other disasters in which victims received more sympathy and help. Journalists have gone out of their way to emphasize this contrast.

Coverage of Katrina revealed that patriotic rhetoric can take on new meaning when the events of the news stubbornly resist closure and remain in public view. In such situations, conventional symbols gain critical strength. Over time, the sheer number of weeping mothers and fiancés of the Iraq War dead may signify not patriotic closure, but unending emotion and loss. With more incidents of school shootings and terrorism, spontaneous shrines and candle-holding may no longer be enough, in public culture as well as media, to provide closure. Journalists will inevitably continue to provide consolation and emotional leadership in coverage of tragedies, and they will continue to try to make those events understandable. But even as they search for inspirational heroes, journalists may soon need a new kind of grief narrative, one that asks the usual question – Why? – but that then seeks different kinds of answers. In such a story, a "news of feeling" could be a powerful form of communication as well as sensation.

Notes

1 This essay is based in part on the author's studies included in Carolyn Kitch and Janice Hume, *Journalism in a Culture of Grief* (New York: Routledge, 2008).
2 Roger Rosenblatt, "The Measure of a Life," *Time*, August 2 1999, 56.
3 "In Memoriam [photo caption]," *The New York Times*, May 28 2007, A1.
4 See, for instance: David L. Altheide, *Creating Fear: News and the Construction of Crisis* (New York; Aline de Gruyter, 2002); Doris Graber, *Crime News and the Public* (New York: Praeger, 1980); and Dan Nimmo and James E. Combs, *Nightly Horrors: Crisis Coverage by Television Network News* (Knoxville: University of Tennessee Press, 1985).
5 Andie Tucher, *Froth and Scum: Truth, Beauty, Goodness, and the Ax Murder in America's First Mass Medium* (Chapel Hill: University of North Carolina Press, 1994), 75.
6 James Carey, *Communication as Culture* (Boston: Unwin Hyman, 1989).
7 Herbert J. Gans, *Deciding What's News: A Study of CBS Evening News, NBC Nightly News, Newsweek and Time* (New York: Pantheon, 1979); John Hartley, *Understanding News* (London and New York: Routledge, 1982).
8 Gaye Tuchman, *Making News: A Study in the Construction of Reality* (New York: Free Press, 1978), 123.
9 Dana L. Cloud, *Control and Consolation in American Culture and Politics: Rhetorics of Therapy* (Thousand Oaks, CA: Sage, 1998).
10 See, for instance: S. Elizabeth Bird and Robert W. Dardenne, "Myth, Chronicle, and Story: Exploring the Narrative Qualities of News," in *Social Meanings of News*, ed. Dan Berkowitz (Thousand Oaks, CA: Sage, 1997): 333–50; David Eason, "Telling Stories and Making Sense," *Journal of Popular Culture* 15 (1981): 125–29; Walter R. Fisher, "The Narrative Paradigm," *Journal of Communication* 35 (1985): 74–89;

Carolyn Kitch, *Pages from the Past: History and Memory in American Magazines* (Chapel Hill: University of North Carolina Press, 2005); Jack Lule, *Daily News, Eternal Stories: The Mythological Role of Journalism* (New York: Guilford Press, 2001); Robert K. Manoff, "Writing the News (by Telling the 'Story')," in *Reading the News*, ed. Robert K. Manoff and Michael Schudson (New York: Pantheon Books, 1986), 197–229; Paul Rock, "News as Eternal Recurrence," in *The Manufacture of News*, ed. Stanley Cohen and Jock Young (London: Sage, 1973), pp. 226–43; and Barbie Zelizer, "Achieving Journalistic Authority through Narrative," *Critical Studies in Mass Communication* 7 (1990): 366–76.

11 Linda Kulman, "Lost Innocence," *U.S. News & World Report*, October 8 2001, 44.

12 Janice Hume, "'Portraits of Grief,' Reflectors of Values: *The New York Times* Remembers Victims of September 11," *Journalism & Mass Communication Quarterly* 80, no. 1, Spring (2003): 166–82.

13 "America's Tragedy," *The Plain Dealer* (Cleveland, OH), September 16 2001, A1.

14 Kenneth Auchincloss, "Back on Our Feet," *Newsweek: Commemorative Issue* (Fall 2001): 14–15.

15 Elizabeth Bumiller, "Bush Meets Rescued Miners, Saying They Represent Spirit of America," *The New York Times*, August 6 2002, A10; *Dateline NBC*, National Broadcasting Company (NBC), July 28 2002.

16 Emily Bazar, "Despite Tragedy, Miners' Way of Life Will Live On," *USA Today*, January 6–8 2006, 1A; *NBC Nightly News*, National Broadcasting Company (NBC), January 4 2006.

17 *Good Morning America*, American Broadcasting Company (ABC), January 5 2006.

18 Gardiner Harris, "Endemic Problem of Safety in Coal Mining," *The New York Times*, January 10 2006, A13; Ian Urbina, "Senators Have Strong Words for Mine Safety Officials," *The New York Times*, January 24 2006, A17.

19 "Inexplicable," *The Patriot-News* (Harrisburg PA), October 3 2006, A12; Larry King, Wendy Ruderman, and Christine Schiavo, "A Killer, It Seems, Out of Nowhere," *The Philadelphia Inquirer*, October 8 2006, A1, A22.

20 Diane Zimmerman Umble and David L. Weaver-Zercher, eds., *The Amish and the Media* (Baltimore: Johns Hopkins University Press, 2008), 256.

21 Cindy Stauffer, "The Sound of Solidarity," *Lancaster New Era*, October 9 2006, A1; Bill Hewitt, *et al.*, "Heartbreak in a Small Town," *People*, October 16 2006, 62–63.

22 Herbert J. Gans, *Deciding What's News: A Study of CBS Evening News, NBC Nightly News, Newsweek and Time* (New York: Pantheon, 1979), p. 48; Katherine Fry, *Constructing the Heartland: Television News and Natural Disaster* (Cresskill, NJ: Hampton Press, 2003), 42, 37.

23 "Tragedy Defies Comprehension," *The State* (Columbia SC), April 18 2007, A1, A12, A13, available online at: www.newseum.org

24 "Heartbroken," *The Dallas Morning News*, April 18 2007, A1.

25 "America's Anguish," April 18, 2007, *Rocky Mountain News*, 1, available online at: www.newseum.org

26 "The Fallen: A Gallery of Lives Cut Short," *Time*, April 30 2007, 62–63.

27 For example, Gordon Trowbridge, "After Day of Terror, the Healing Begins," *The Detroit News*, April 18 2007, 1A, 6A, available online at: www.newseum.org

28 Emile Durkheim, *The Elementary Forms of Religious Life*, trans. Karen E. Fields (New York: Free Press, 1973; originally published in 1915).

29 Carolyn Marvin and David W. Ingle, *Blood Sacrifice and the Nation: Totem Rituals and the American Flag* (Cambridge, UK: Cambridge University Press, 1999), 2.

30 *NBC Nightly News*, NBC, January 4 2006.

31 "Are Guns the Problem?" *The Forum* (Fargo-Moorhead, ND), April 18 2007, A1, available online at: www.newseum.org

32 Gil Smart, "What's Wrong Here?" *The Sunday News* (Lancaster PA), October 8 2006, A1.
33 Smart, "What's Wrong Here?," A1.
34 Ashley M. Heher, "Pa. Man Accused of Killing his Girlfriend's Parents Captured," Associated Press, November 14 2005, n.p.
35 Monica Davey, "A Tiny Town, Suddenly Smaller by Seven, Mourns and Wonders, Why?" *The New York Times*, October 9 2007, A16.
36 Maryclaire Dale, "Teen Accused in School Plot was Target of Bullies," Associated Press report in *The Patriot-News* (Harrisburg PA), October 13 2007, A5.

Chapter 4

Tabloidization: What is it, and Does it Really Matter?

S. Elizabeth Bird

The word "tabloidization" is relatively new, achieving wide currency since the 1980s. The process itself – which has come to be understood as stylistic and content changes that represent a decline in traditional journalistic standards – has been "lamented"[1] for a century or more. The problem with the word is that, perhaps like "obscenity," everyone seems to recognize it when they see it, but no one really agrees what it is. Tabloids and their earlier precursors have long functioned as a convenient demon figure for "real" journalism, which has used them to draw boundaries between good and bad journalistic practices.[2] Those boundaries, however, have constantly shifted with changing tastes and media environments. And today, when the environment for journalism has been so radically transformed, my concern is that the still-continuing lament about "tabloidization" may be a distraction from forces that are much more real, a point to which I will return.

Tabloidization: desperately seeking a definition

First, a word about tabloids and tabloidization. Strictly speaking, the term "tabloid" simply refers to certain newspapers' size, which is half that of a standard broadsheet. However, over the years it has taken on a much broader definition that has less to do with size and more to do with the presentation and style of news. Tabloid style has come to be understood as a particular kind of formulaic, colorful narrative related to, but usually perceived as distinct from standard, "objective" styles of journalism. The tabloid style is consistently seen by critics as inferior, appealing to base instincts and public demand for sensationalism. True "tabloids" emerged in Britain during the first decade of the twentieth century, and in the USA in the 1920s. Entertainingly sensational, they were written in the idioms of the people, as William Randolph Hearst proudly declared when launching the American *Daily Mirror* in 1924.[3] The tension between a perception of tabloid style as representing the legitimate desires and voice of the people, or as representing a vulgarization of public discourse, has been at the heart of the debate about tabloidization ever since, as Gans suggests in this volume.

The tabloid is not necessarily defined by content; tabloids may cover the same topics as mainstream journalism, although typically more briefly and flamboyantly.[4] British daily tabloids, such as the *Sun*, cover politics and "hard" news, although much more briefly and superficially than "quality" newspapers, while much of their space is devoted to celebrity news, sensational human interest stories, advice, and so on.[5] Their US daily counterparts, such as the *New York Daily News*, have a similar mix of news and entertainment, while US weekly supermarket tabloids, such as the *National Enquirer* or *Star*, rarely touch hard news at all. Publications recognizable as tabloids across the world contain variable mixes of news, entertainment, sports, and other features, usually with heavy use of illustration.[6]

If "tabloid" has come to mean a specific style, "tabloidization" is a more recent term developed to describe an inexorable move toward that style by "real" journalism. Long before the term was actually coined, tabloidization was a focus of criticism and concern that began with the emergence of more popular journalistic formats, such as the "penny press" of the 1830s, whose writers drew on the formulaic conventions of broadsheets and ballads to produce dramatic, human interest news of crime and mayhem, frequently with an implied or overt moral. In the nineteenth and early twentieth centuries, critics bemoaned the cheapening of public discourse represented by such popularization of news, and this lament has gathered speed over the last 100 years. In the late twentieth century, the term "tabloidization" appeared, and came to connote a serious decline in journalistic discourse, whether in television or print. As Colin Sparks wrote, tabloidization implied that "the high standards of yesterday are being undermined by sensationalism, prurience, triviality, malice, and plain, simple credulity."[7]

The problem, as I have mentioned, is that tabloidization is not a clearly defined term; neither journalists nor critics agree precisely what it is, or even whether it is invariably a negative force. Indeed, as Sparks showed, empirical attempts to demonstrate the process have been inconclusive. However, there appear to be some key areas in which most critics (as well as the general public) recognize the phenomenon. Generally, these can be seen as issues of either style or content, although these are clearly closely related. Under style, we can look at writing techniques, observed in a movement away from longer, complex, analytical writing into shorter, punchier sentences, primarily in a narrative, rather than analytical mode. Second, we see an increasing emphasis on the personal; for instance, journalists handle major economic themes through personal stories about individual people and the way they cope. A third symptom of tabloidization is a greater use of visual images, including photos, artists' sketches and so on, as well as increased reliance on such techniques as re-enactments and dramatizations, primarily in electronic news.

Tabloidization of content is usually framed in terms of increasing trivialization. Celebrity news and gossip are seen to be crowding out serious news, and human interest stories receive more coverage than important international events. Critics also point to changes such as the move toward covering political debate as horse races (in election coverage) or as shouting matches on talk shows and other venues, both of which detract from serious and nuanced debate and analysis.[8] For Tannen, tabloidization is one feature of what she dubs the contemporary "argument culture."[9]

The specific term tabloidization arose in the context of changes in traditional news that created great anxiety. It was first used widely in the USA to describe and often decry the emergence of the national newspaper USA Today, launched in 1982 by Al Neuharth, then heading the Gannett chain. Many critics and journalists despised the paper, but of course it went on to become a great success, and by the early 2000s Neuharth enjoyed the status of a press elder statesman. Without a doubt, USA Today's stylistic innovations led to significant changes in print journalism, and by now such changes are generally regarded as positive and revitalizing. This progression points to the way in which the very meaning of "tabloidization" continually shifts, as changes once seen as evidence of decline become mainstreamed, if they prove successful.

The contexts of tabloidization

So it is important to consider tabloidization in context. A movement to clearer, more accessible news that speaks more directly to readers does not necessarily equate with a decline in standards. For instance, Hallin[10] reports that in Mexico, these kinds of stylistic changes have signaled positive forces for social reform and democratic participation, as elite controls on news have loosened. Similar changes are noted in former Eastern bloc nations, where the emergence of more personal, snappier, and tabloid-like styles go hand-in-hand with a more open and accessible press – just as they did in Europe and the USA as journalistic style changed in the nineteenth century. Several commentators have pointed out that if done well, "tabloid" features, such as emphasis on the personal over the institutional, can make news more direct and effective.[12] The downside of this is of course that a focus on the personal can obscure larger social, political, and cultural factors, a point made by many writers, such as Campbell.[11]

Thus it is important to understand cultural specificities when discussing tabloidization, or any other journalistic quality. For instance, even in two societies as apparently similar as Britain and the USA, there are significant differences in tabloid media, and thus the implications of tabloidization can also differ. US supermarket tabloids and UK daily tabloids feature similar layouts, writing styles, and a celebrity focus, and journalists have moved comfortably between the two genres for years. However, they are in many ways different, reflecting quite distinct cultural milieus. British tabloids are explicit, visually and verbally, about sex, while US weeklies avoid direct references. And while some US weeklies are far more interested in paranormal and religious topics, such as biblical prophecies and faith healing, British tabloids reflect a much greater sense of working-class consciousness than those in the USA, where "everyone is middle-class." Tabloid-style media in other countries also reflect a range of social, political, and cultural characteristics; when we discuss "tabloidization," we may mean very different things depending on context.

So there simply is no single, clear definition of tabloidization. When broken down to its constituent elements, such as changes in style, a move toward accessibility and personalization, it becomes a difficult target to see clearly. In part this is because, although tabloidization is usually seen as antithetical to traditional journalistic standards of truth and objectivity, exactly what those standards are has never been entirely clear. For instance, there has always been some degree of discomfort both within journalism and among news audiences about whether news can be genuinely informative when using a narrative or storytelling format. "Mere storytelling" is often cited pejoratively as a significant marker of tabloidization, while at the same time, journalists know (and research is confirming) that telling compelling stories can reach audiences in ways that "objective" accounts cannot.[13] Journalists have long been encouraged to see large issues in personal terms, knowing that members of the public are not well informed if they simply reject the news out of boredom. Is writing that speaks to the heart necessarily symptomatic of tabloidization and is thus bad? Consensus simply doesn't exist.

As an example, I have noted elsewhere consider the regular balancing act newspapers must perform when they try ambitious, basically ethnographic stories. My local newspaper, the *St. Petersburg Times*, fairly regularly offers extended, often multi-part stories that explore various kinds of human experience, such as a 2003 series that used a total of almost 40,000 words and several reporters to look in depth at the lives of a few adolescents.[14] The reaction from readers, as expressed in letters to the editor, was bi-polar; some found it "well written, truthful," or praised its "justice, explanation, sympathy, and beauty." Others were "astounded, disgusted, and outraged," calling it a "silly series." Inevitably, comments included comparisons with tabloids – "I expect this kind of thing in the *National Enquirer*, not a respectable newspaper." Indeed, this is a constant refrain from readers whenever something offends them, showing how entrenched the demonization of the tabloid actually is, even though one person's outrage is another one's admiration.

The lack of consensus about what tabloidization means is one of the reasons to argue that tabloidization does not matter – how can we fix it if we don't know what it is? Furthermore, there is ample evidence to suggest that a certain tabloidization of style, such as the emphasis on storytelling that engages senses and emotions, actually enhances good journalism. Nevertheless, some of the issues that surface in the tabloidization discussion are still important. Journalism is changing because the tradition of newspaper reading is clearly on the decline, with younger readers apparently not taking up the habit as they grow older. The competition for news has become increasingly fierce, with proliferating broadcast outlets, as well as the enormous impact of the internet, which has led traditional media to rethink many of their familiar practices. The internet's promise of democratization raised hopes that this would offer a much greater variety of serious, international news. To some extent it has, but at the same time it seems clear that what has often happened is that more time than ever is being devoted to the kind of stories that are typically seen as tabloid.

I have long argued that storytelling is an essential component in effective journalism,[15] and I still believe that. Indeed, the ability to tell complex stories effectively and authoritatively may be the key to the survival of newspapers. Nevertheless, the proliferation of some kinds of stories and the marginalization of others does, I believe, constitute a threat to journalism as a cultural force. Arguably frivolous, tabloid-style narratives are important; as I have argued elsewhere,[16] they allow audiences to interrogate morality, explore values, and connect with others – they are not about passing on essential information. They have always been part of news, in spite of critics who see them as anathema to real journalism. Stories about Anna Nicole Smith, the "runaway bride" and the tribulations of Brittney Spears or Paris Hilton produce massive amounts of attractively open-ended speculation that makes such tales gripping. Audiences apparently want them; the most googled news topic for 2006 was Paris Hilton, followed by Orlando Bloom, although the top 10 also included Hurricane Katrina and "bankruptcy."

However, the domination of the celebrity and human interest "celebrity for a day" story is not just about giving audiences what they want; it is also about the bottom line. That is why it is essential to add economics to the other terms we are addressing in this volume – tabloidization, technology, and truthiness – even if it doesn't start with "t." Editors find these stories easy, cheap, *and* popular. In a competitive, digital environment in which news organizations struggle to maintain independence and profit levels, the cheap, easy, and popular story often wins out over expensive, difficult, and less popular ones. Pages of news space and hours of airtime can be filled without ever having to assign a reporter, as news outlets simply feed off each other.

And this *is* a major threat to journalism. The irony is that as more and more outlets for news open up, the range of alternative stories actually seems to be shrinking. And along with that, those in power seem to be becoming even more effective than ever at controlling the stories that then flood the mediascape.[17] High-profile narratives of terrorism and war provide dramatic examples. The first Bush administration succeeded brilliantly in the first Gulf War in framing the story of a just, heroic, clinically scientific and very clean war, in an era when the internet was less fully developed. Surely, one would think, the second Bush administration would find this harder in the new news world? Yet, the government actually succeeded in framing the second Iraq War similarly, at least in the early stages.[18] Indeed, its success in providing terms and frames that journalists found compelling helped form the backbone of the "story" of the war. The press used them so consistently that they become "natural" and therefore "true," from the highly successful "weapons of mass destruction," to "shock and awe," which formed the central frame of countless news articles and television broadcasts. This, along with government-supplied notions of "smart bombs" from the first war and the reluctance to provide images of "collateral damage" resulted in a particular and narrow "story" of a clean and successful war, established early in 2003 and built carefully since.[19] Certainly that story started to fall apart, but arguably too late.

In addition to the larger story of the war, the administration was extremely effective in building and spreading particular narratives that both served its purpose and offered audiences emotional, resonant experiences. For instance, it took some years for the truth to emerge about the "heroic" death in Afghanistan of former National Football League star Pat Tillman in 2004. Most stories relied on a military spokesman, who said that Tillman was killed "in a firefight." Reports of his last, heroic battle were steeped in the American cultural resonance of football and war, and received eagerly. Later, the "story" unraveled into a tale of military bungling and bureaucratic cover-up of a sorry "friendly fire" incident. A similar unraveling occurred in the Jessica Lynch story, originally presented as a tale of the teenage "girl soldier," captured while fighting "like a man," only to be rescued by brave troops. Later, Lynch herself repudiated the heroic nature of the tale. Deepa Kumar argues that "constructed as hero, Lynch became a symbol of the West's 'enlightened' attitude toward women, justifying the argument that the United States was 'liberating' the people of Iraq."[20] At the same time, the story evoked the cultural lexicon of "captivity narratives," involving fair, lovely young women actually or potentially brutalized by dark, menacing savages. The story, in other words, was especially powerful (and dangerous) because it perfectly meshed existing, culturally resonant images with the needs of the US administration to create specific heroic tales, and, no doubt, the needs of the people to have such tales.

Of course, alternative accounts of such events are physically more available than ever – the new media environment has in some ways opened up the world, suggesting a kind of utopia in which we might see a true, Miltonian struggle from which truth emerges. Indeed, for the news consumer with significant tenacity and time, alternative stories abound. For instance, one might turn to the reporting of American independent journalist Dahr Jamail, which resulted in a book, *Beyond the Green Zone: Dispatches from an Unembedded Journalist in Occupied Iraq*[21], which paints a much more comprehensive picture of life in Iraq than that provided by mainstream media. In his book, blogs, and public presentations, Jamail expresses his frustration that so few mainstream journalists in Iraq made any attempt at all to report news unfiltered through official sources. At one level, we might argue that Jamail's success shows that the new media environment *has* allowed unprecedented freedom of knowledge – his dispatches have been used by significant media outlets around the world. At the same time, the domination of mainstream US media still renders such alternatives largely invisible to most of the public, partly because most people simply do not have the time to pursue different versions, and partly because the economic cost of aggressive, investigative journalism is too high. As the sheer volume of information continues to increase, it seems that fewer and fewer competent journalists are actually out there gathering and creating new information. As Amy Goodman and Dennis Moynihan write in the forward to Jamail's book: "If only the corporate networks would devote a small per centage of their resources to the type of reporting that Dahr Jamail accomplishes with next to nothing. The prospect of such a media system depends on the demands and activism of the public, a public that holds the networks, the reporters, and elected officials accountable, and a public that supports independent media."

I think in some ways we are at a critical point for journalism, as it relates to the public sphere. Multiple narratives now appear to compete with mainstream journalism to define the day's stories. News audiences pick and choose stories they want to believe, from a seemingly endless supply of information from which to assemble their own versions of reality. Yet many choose to receive only news that is tailored to their existing opinions, even if drawn from multiple forms – Sean Hannity's story is the same whether one receives it via his TV show, radio show, web site, or books. Others may be much more creative, disseminating their own stories on blogs, wikis, and personal websites. The internet does have the potential to provide genuine forums for alternative participation and even real action.

The production of content and tabloidization

However, how is all the root content actually being produced? Part of the earlier critique of tabloid journalism was that reporters gathered information through paid informants, gossip-mongers, and simple rumor; this outrage seems almost outdated now that anyone can post anything, without regard for verification, ethics or "truth" – resulting in the "truthiness" that others address more fully in this volume. In many ways, the conception of a huge world of information is an illusion, since so much of it is either unreliable or simply a variation of official accounts. And the growth of niche markets means that no news consumers ever need to leave their comfort zones.

As the latest report from the Pew Excellence in Journalism project suggests, news organizations seem very uncertain about how to participate in the new web environment.[22] Mainstream journalism often seems to be simply replicating its content in various different contexts – for instance, a regular newspaper, a smaller, tabloid version designed for young people, a website, a partnership with a TV news station, and so on. As Pew reports, "Sites have done more, for instance, to exploit immediacy, but they have done less to exploit the potential for depth." I believe this potential for depth is where the mainstream media could go to reclaim their relevance. Part of that is, I think, a need to re-establish some kind of journalistic authority – not as an omniscient arbiter of truth, but as a profession whose practitioners have knowledge and reporting skills that can offer audiences something more than mere "truthiness" and special interest information.

Of course the problem for news organizations is that their ability to undertake serious, in-depth, independent reporting, whether at home or abroad, is compromised by economics. As Pew also points out, the advertising base of newspapers has seriously eroded, and advertising on their internet branches has not replaced lost revenue. Attempts to charge for internet content have largely been abandoned; audiences will not pay for material they can get elsewhere. So what can newspapers do that makes them distinctive, and offers something different from everything else on the web?

One possibility is a renewed focus on significant reporting of local and regional news in a mixed print/online environment. For instance, Robinson reports on the vibrant and award-winning on-line presence of the Spokane, Wash., *Spokesman Review*. In a case study, she looks at coverage of a pedophilia scandal involving the mayor of Spokane, in which a coherent, conventional story emerged in print over the course of a month-long investigation. However, simultaneous with the printed story, a "cyber newsroom" on the paper's own website made available interviews, documents, and multiple forms of information, and people dissected and analyzed the information, often offering their own sometimes radically different versions of the "official" stories. Readers, interacting with journalists, the news content, and other readers, helped form an online news narrative:

> If readers took issue with the coverage, they had the newspaper's own space to criticize the journalism ... Like reporters, readers utilized quotation marks and hyperlinks to source the material ... This sharing of information production changed the dynamics of the journalism resulting in a re-negotiation of the news paradigm within cyberspace.[23]

Nolan notes that this kind of connectivity means that journalists become "less of an authority and more of a guide," which some might see as a threat to journalism.[24] However, in today's highly relativistic, skeptical and cynical news environment, audiences may be very appreciative of an impartial voice to provide information and facilitate discussion – perhaps recreating some kind of political "center." Newspapers can still tell stories of consequence that otherwise go untold and that resist government- and corporate-provided terms and themes, and they can invite readers into those stories in a form of participatory democracy. These stories require time, resources, and skills, but they help meet journalism's obligations to do more than narrate the increasingly inconsequential tide of amusement, diversion and official spin that pervades the news media.

A recent experiment by the *St. Petersburg Times* offers another way for established news organizations to contribute in authoritative ways. In September,

2007, the *Times* launched PolitiFact.com, a website that attempts to sort out the truth of politician's campaigning, and run-in partnership with *Congressional Quarterly*. Managing Editor Neil Brown described the effort:

> We believe our journalists can play a greater role as an honest broker for voters bewildered by the barrage of campaign talk. So in a move rare for a news organization, we're dedicating a team of reporters and researchers to meticulously examine the rhetoric of candidates and their partisans, and then make a call: Is the claim true or not?[25]

Acknowledging the reality of the new media environment, Brown continues:

> many news organizations can spend less money and get less grief if their political reporting sticks to stenography and puffery. It's easier to record the words and claims of competing candidates than to vet their accuracy. It's easier to write about the strategy of using negative advertising than to do the painstaking research to sort out whether the claim is actually true or false.

In the same introduction, Brown writes:

> You might think such work would be standard journalistic fare. In fact, of course, the long-standing, if rather tattered, journalistic ideology of objectivity has meant exactly the opposite – journalists are supposed to report, not make judgments about whether something claimed is real. It is the very ideology of objectivity that supermarket tabloid writers evoke in justifying stories with patently outlandish claims; they are simply reporting objectively what someone told them.[26]

Such initiatives as PolitiFact point to the potential for a new kind of authority for journalism, which actually takes on "truthiness" head on. This role has not traditionally been tried by news organizations, being left largely to such outfits as Factcheck.org, run by the Annenberg Public Policy Center, University of Pennsylvania.

Significantly, both the *St. Pete Times* and the *Spokesman Review* constitute increasingly rare independent voices in journalism. The *Times* is owned by the Poynter Institute, the *Review* by the Cowles family – the present publisher William Stacey Cowles representing the fourth generation of his family to oversee the paper. In this environment, there is clearly more freedom to minimize the bottom line in favor of a fourth estate role that seems to have become increasingly irrelevant. As *Times* editor Brown writes, "we are true believers in journalism as an instrument of democracy. Even as we seek to reach customers in new ways, we see our primary obligation as helping citizens participate fully in the democratic process ... PolitiFact fits with that mission."

Tabloidization and the future of journalism

So, where is journalism going? Journalism is losing the confident sense of authority that still allows the *New York Times* to claim "all the news that's fit to print," and increasingly the profession seems to be panicking in an era when anyone can set up a virtual shop and claim to be a journalist. It seems journalism may have two choices. It can accept that its claim to truth is no better or worse than anyone else's, cling onto traditional notions of objectivity, and continue a struggle to survive in a relativistic, cynical world in which whatever sells leads. Or it can try to develop new ways of doing business, that involve a renewed commitment to actually doing journalism, and perhaps a rethinking of objectivity. One strategy might be a positive embrace of significant, ethnographic stories that invite readers into an experience that is simply not replicable in the point-and-click world of the internet. Another would be to reduce dependence on official sources of information, and do more independent reporting. And another would be to embrace the participatory potential of the internet, drawing readers into dialog by providing good information and facilitating reasoned, democratic participation and discussion, where truth can be conceptualized without irony.

To return to my original question: I don't believe tabloidization is a particularly useful term any more (if it ever was). And I don't worry that journalism includes supposedly trivial or emotion-laden stories of celebrities, everyday heroes, and so on. These have always been part of news, and they perform an important cultural role. The problem is when that role swamps the other important dimensions of what journalism can and should be. And so some of the themes that are often included in the imprecise term, tabloidization, are still vital to the future of journalism. But as long as we still fuss about the tabloids as representative of everything bad, we will be distracted from seriously addressing the more real challenges of maintaining journalistic authority in the age of truthiness.

Notes

1 John Langer, *Tabloid Television* (New York: Routledge, 1997).
2 See for example, Howard Kurtz, *Media Circus: The Trouble with America's Newspapers* (New York: Three Rivers Press, 1994).
3 S. Elizabeth Bird, *For Enquiring Minds: A Cultural Study of Supermarket Tabloids* (Knoxville: University of Tennessee Press, 1992).
4 S. Elizabeth Bird, "Taking it Personally: Supermarket Tabloids after September 11," in *Journalism after September 11*, ed. Barbie Zelizer and Stuart Allen (London: Routledge, 2002), 141–59.
5 For a good history of the British tabloid press, see Martin Conboy, *Tabloid Britain: Constructing a Community Through Language* (London: Routledge, 2006).
6 Colin Sparks and John Tulloch, eds. *Tabloid Tales* (New York: Rowman and Littlefield, 2000).
7 Colin Sparks, "The Panic Over Tabloid News," in Colin Sparks and John Tulloch, eds. *Tabloid Tales* (New York: Rowman and Littlefield), 1–40.

8 See, for example, David J. Krajicek, *Scooped!* (New York: Columbia University Press, 1999) and Kurtz, *Media Circus*.

9 Deborah Tannen, *The Argument Culture: Stopping America's War of Words* (New York: Ballantine, 1999).

10 Daniel Hallin, "*La Nota Roja*: Popular Journalism and the Transition to Democracy in Mexico," in Sparks and Tulloch (eds.), *Tabloid Tales*, 267–84.

11 Myra MacDonald, "Rethinking Personalization in Current Affairs Journalism," in ed. Sparks and Tulloch, *Tabloid Tales*, 251–66.

12 Richard Campbell, *60 Minutes and the News – A Mythology for Middle America* (Urbana: University of Illinois Press, 1991).

13 Marcel Machill, Sebastian Köhler and Markus Waldhauser, "The Use of Narrative Structures in Television News: An Experiment in Innovative Forms of Journalistic Presentation," *European Journal of Communication* 22, no. 2 (2007): 185–205.

14 S. Elizabeth Bird, "The Journalist as Ethnographer: How Anthropology Can Enrich Journalistic Practice," in Eric Rothenbuhler and Mihai Coman, eds. *Media Anthropology* (Thousand Oaks, CA: Sage, 2005), 220–28.

15 See, for example, S. Elizabeth Bird and Robert W. Dardenne, "Myth, Chronicle, and Story: Exploring the Narrative Qualities of News," in ed. James W. Carey, Media, Myths, and Narratives (Beverly Hills: Sage, 1988), 67–87; and S. Elizabeth Bird, *For Enquiring Minds*.

16 S. Elizabeth Bird, *The Audience in Everyday Life: Living in a Media World* (New York: Routledge, 2003).

17 S. Elizabeth Bird and Robert W. Dardenne, "Rethinking News as Myth and Storytelling," in ed. Karin Wahl-Jorgenson and Thomas Hanisch, Handbook of Journalism (London: Blackwell, 2008) 205–16.

18 See, for example, James R. Compton, *The Integrated News Spectacle: A Political Economy of Cultural Performance* (New York: Peter Lang, 2004); Douglas Kellner, *Media Spectacle and the Crisis of Democracy: Terrorism, War, and Election Battles* (New York: Paradigm, 2005).

19 Compton, *The Integrated News Spectacle*; Kellner, *Media Spectacle*.

20 Deepa Kumar, "War propaganda and the (Ab)uses of Women: Media Construction of the Jessica Lynch Story," *Feminist Media Studies*, 4, no. 3 (2004): 297–313.

21 Dahr Jamail, *Beyond the Green Zone: Dispatches from an Unembedded Journalist in Occupied Iraq* (New York: Haymarket Books, 2007).

22 Project for Excellence in Journalism, "The State of the Media Report," available online at: www.stateofthenewsmedia.org

23 Susan Robinson, "The Cyber Newsroom: A Case Study of the Journalistic Paradigm in a News Narrative's Journey from a Newspaper to Cyberspace." Paper presented at the International Symposium on Online Journalism. March. Available online at: www.online.journalism.utexas.edu

24 Sybil Nolan, "Journalism Online: The Search for Narrative Form in a Multilinear World." Proceedings of Melbourne DAC, the 5th International Digital Arts and Culture Conference, available online at: www.hypertext.rmit.edu.au

25 Neil Brown, "The Truth is PolitiFact.com," *St Petersburg Times*, September 2, available online at: www.sptimes.com

26 S. Elizabeth Bird, *For Enquiring Minds*.

On Technology

Chapter 5

Rethinking Journalism Through Technology

Lokman Tsui

Has technology changed journalism to positive or negative effect? The praise for technological advances and their enrichment of journalism have been accompanied by lamentations over the role of technology in impoverishing the news. While journalism seems to benefit from technological developments in news gathering (digital and smaller cameras, digital voice recorders, convergent technology), distribution (the internet, satellite), and exhibition (the world wide web, colour print, mobile phones), there is also a sense that technology is responsible, partially or wholly, for a devaluation of journalistic standards – amateur bloggers who do not adhere to practices of fact-checking, deadlines that become shorter or even continuous because the internet is "always on", sloppier writing, and more inaccuracies.

The essays in this section, while hopeful, seem mostly to converge on the idea that technology does more to impoverish journalism than enrich it. Julianne H. Newton suggests that "technology appears to be changing journalism more for negative effect than positive" (p. 78, of this book). Mark Deuze, though cautious, is perhaps more optimistic as he makes the case that trends caused by new technologies open up "creative affordances for individual journalists"; at the same time, however, they potentially restrict journalists' editorial autonomy (p. 93, of this book). How justified is the pessimism being voiced here? It is worth stepping back momentarily to consider the landscape against which technology's ascent in journalism has been implemented.

Looking at the relationship between journalism and technology from a historical perspective nearly a decade ago, John Hartley helped us understand that the two domains have always been inextricably intertwined with each other.[1] Modern journalism was born of the necessity to streamline journalistic processes – news gathering, news interpretation, and news distribution – we ended up outsourcing them to specialists, the journalists, who could devote time and energy specifically to gather information deemed relevant for the community. Over time the public increasingly became reliant on what Hartley called "representative journalism." It is representative because the public granted the journalistic community permission to represent the public and its right to communicate. However its development produced a gap between the ability to read and the ability to write, with journalists taking over the ability to write, particularly in public, and maintaining that right over time as journalism evolved into new forms. Now is the time to ask how this situation has changed with current advances in technology. Has new technology made old constraints obsolete? Is it true, as Ian Hargreaves has argued, that now "everybody is a journalist"? If it is, then what is left of the meaning of journalism?

In that the three essays in this section invite us to rethink the meaning of journalism in the face of technological changes, we need to consider what we mean by journalism – its process, its people, or the news itself? Two ways to address this question are fruitful in light of the essays – journalism as an institution and journalism as a set of principles and values.

Looking at journalism as an institution suggests addressing the enduring rules and constraints that shape journalism and how technology affects them. What changes occur when new technology and its social practices are layered on top of already proven, legitimized and institutionalized practices? When refracted through the lens of the institution, journalism is most often seen as an institution in decline. It tries to catch up with technology but is forced to do so within the organizational constraints of the newsroom and the institutional ecology it operates in. The first essay by Pablo J. Boczkowski illustrates the problem of incorporating technology within the institutional tensions of the existing journalistic organizational field. Boczkowski helps us understand how the longstanding practice of monitoring competitors, accelerated by technology, has changed qualitatively. Coining the term, he argues how technology and the market have produced a trend that nobody actually chooses to practice but that nobody can afford not to practice. Information transparency and the increased mimicry it produces have powerful implications for the normative role of the media in providing a healthy and diverse public sphere.

A second way to think about journalism is as a set of principles and values. Here the exercise reconceptualizes what journalism can and should be, given the new technological constraints and affordances. How would journalism look if we could reinvent it from the bottom up in present time, current technology in hand? In the second essay, Julianne H. Newton engages us in exactly this kind of thought experiment by regarding the brain – and by extension, journalism – as a technology. Arguing that journalism has not benefited enough from advances in cognitive neuroscience and media ecology, Newton calls for a "journalism in the time of the new mind," which would actively twin the "practices of reporting and conveying information of significance to human perception, survival and decision making" together with "unprecedented opportunities to understand how the brain makes use of information it perceives" (p. 74, of this book). Noting that the space in which journalism operates is being taken over by competitors in persuasion, advertising and entertainment, who exploit an understanding of the new mind to reach audiences, Newton contends that journalism needs to do the same, leaving aside its moral high ground enough to reconceptualize journalism as a technological system run and processed by new minds.

Lastly, Mark Deuze balances a vision of journalism as an existing institution and as a set of principles and values when he explores the implications of new technologies on the agency of individual journalists and their work. Noting how technology both supercharges and accelerates existing practices, Deuze considers how it also opens windows for new kinds of "journalistic acts" – acts that are in themselves journalistic but are not necessarily performed by those whom we traditionally regard as "journalists". Focusing on the individual, Deuze sensitizes us to a broadened and changing definition of who is a journalist and identifies factors that contribute to this trend.

Does technology impoverish or facilitate journalism? If seen through the lens of journalism as an institution, Boczkowski demonstrates that journalism is struggling to come to terms with the new media environment. Seen as a set of values and principles, Newton points to a vast field of opportunities that technological advances present on which journalism has yet to capitalize. Deuze suggests that technology has raised critical questions about the changing role of the individual in today's field of journalism. What all three essays in this section show is that technology is at the heart of a reorientation of power and knowledge, where incumbents and new players are seeking to redefine and reinterpret the meaning of journalism. Using technology as a frame for understanding journalism allows us to reflect on what journalism can be and raises normative questions about what journalism should be. The three essays are important contributions in starting to address these questions that have become once again urgent to ask in the new media environment.

Notes

1 Hartley, J. "Communicative Democracy in a Redactional Society: The Future of Journalism Studies," *Journalism* 1,1 (2000): 39–48.

Chapter 6

Materiality and Mimicry in the Journalism Field[1]

Pablo J. Boczkowski

Analysts increasingly suggest that much has changed in journalism in the past couple of decades, partly in relation to technological developments that have taken place during this period.[2] This article focuses on one phenomenon – journalists' tendency to mimic their competitors and other media – to examine the difference that technology makes and to think about the more general role of materiality in journalistic practice. Mimicry in news production can shed light on how materiality matters in contemporary journalistic practice because it has long been recognized as a staple of editorial routines and because technology has been largely overlooked as a relevant factor in scholarly analyses of imitation in the news.[3]

Crouse's *The Boys on the Bus*[4] is commonly seen as the canonical text on what he called "pack journalism." The book examines a situation that is extraordinary – news production by journalists who travel together on the campaign trail – and therefore exposes with great intensity certain dynamics related to mimicry that are less visible in more ordinary situations. Two such dynamics are particularly relevant for this article: the primacy of journalists' unmediated monitoring of the work of colleagues[5] and the prevalence of risk aversion in decision-making among reporters and editors.[6]

One telling episode about how legendary *New York Times* reporter Johnny Apple was observed and imitated by many of his colleagues as he was writing up the results of the Iowa caucuses, during the 1972 presidential campaign, illustrates the dynamics of unmediated monitoring:

> Johnny Apple ... sat in a corner and everyone peered over his shoulder to find out what he was writing. The AP guy was looking over one shoulder, the UPI guy over the other and CBS, NBC, ABC and the *Baltimore Sun* were all crowding in behind ... He would sit down and write a lead, and they would go write leads. Then he'd change his lead when more results came in, and they'd all change theirs accordingly ... At midnight, the guy announced that Muskie had 32 per cent and McGovern had 26 per cent, and Apple sat down to write his final story. He called it something like "a surprisingly strong showing for George McGovern." Everyone peered over

his shoulder again and picked it up. It was on the front page of every major newspaper the next day.[7]

Risk aversion in the selection of what stories to cover and in how to cover them has long been paramount in the decision-making processes of reporters and editors. Although exclusives and scoops have "good press," a reporter knows that her editor is likely to punish her for not having a story that other media outlets have – while running with the pack is normally a safer option. Similar dynamics are in place between section editors and the top editors to whom they report. One typical manifestation of this pattern of risk aversion is the propensity of a journalist to be influenced by wire service content, in part due to the assumption that the content will appear in other media. According to Crouse:

> [Reporters] wanted to avoid "call-backs" – phone calls from their editors asking them why they had deviated from the AP or UPI. If the editors were going to run with a story that differed from the story in the nation's 1,700 other newspapers, they wanted a good reason for it. Most reporters dreaded call-backs. Thus the pack followed the wire-service men whenever possible. Nobody made a secret of running with the wires; it was an accepted practice. At an event later in the campaign, a *New York Daily News* reporter looked over the shoulder of Norm Kempster, a UPI man, and read his copy. "Stick with that lead, Norm," said the man from the *News*. "You'll save us a lot of trouble." "Don't worry," said Norm. "I don't think you'll have any trouble from mine."[8]

Have new technologies, their appropriation by journalists and their incorporation in daily journalistic routine been tied to changes in monitoring and decision-making? If so, have any of these changes affected mimicry in news production? Drawing from an ethnographic study of content production in the leading Argentine online and print newspapers and a content analysis of their resulting news products from the mid 1990s to the mid 2000s, this chapter addresses these questions so as to make sense of novel connections between materiality and mimicry in contemporary journalism.

Contextual matters

The largest print newspapers in Argentina are national in scope. The industry exhibits clear signs of ownership concentration: the top two players account for half of the national newspaper market and the top five for almost two-thirds of it.[9] Print newspapers' share of the advertising pie was in the 40 per cent range during the period analyzed here.[10] The two leading newspapers, Clarín and *La Nación*, are both headquartered in Buenos Aires, the nation's capital. Their online editions, produced largely autonomously from their respective print newsrooms throughout the period examined here, are also top players in the national market for online news.

Clarín is the country's largest daily – with a 36% share of the national newspaper market – and is the flagship news enterprise of Grupo Clarín, a large and mostly privately owned multimedia conglomerate. Clarín has a centrist political orientation and appeals to a broad audience. In the first quarter of 2006 it had an average daily circulation greater than 420,000 and an average Sunday circulation greater than 807,000.[11] The paper's online site, *Clarin.com*, was launched in March 2006 and had 6.2 million unique users in August 2006.[12]

La Nación is Argentina's second largest daily, with a 14 per cent share of the national newspaper market, and is part of a family-owned media conglomerate that is smaller and less diversified than Grupo Clarín. La *Nación* features a conservative political outlook and targets a public with a relatively high socioeconomic status. In the first quarter of 2006, it had an average daily circulation of more than 165,000 and an average Sunday circulation that was greater than 251,000.[13] *Lanacion.com* debuted in December 1995 and had 2.3 million unique users in August 2006.[14]

Like sites of traditional media in other regions of the world during the early years of news on the internet, *Clarin.com* and *Lanacion.com* initially mostly reproduced the news stories of their respective print counterparts. Site usage peaked in the morning and was comparatively much lower the rest of the day. The dominance of print material began to gradually recede around 2001, when editors of both online papers started to increase the volume and frequency of news published during the day – these news sites relied on content first featured in wire services, broadcast media and overseas news sites. This increase was tied to a rise in number of visitors to these sites and to more usage in the afternoon and early evening hours. The realization that there seemed to be a strong link between more news during the day and more site traffic led, in the case of *Clarin.com*, to a major site redesign and organizational restructuring in May 2004. The new site devoted two-thirds of the homepage to breaking and developing news coverage. The new organizational structure determined that most full-time staff were devoted to the production of this news. Making this news unfolded in a relatively similar direction at *Lanacion.com* during the first few years of the 2000s. Moreover, constant and ongoing publication of news throughout the day – slowing down between late evening and early morning hours – became the norm among online news sites in Argentina by the mid 2000s.

For journalists in print and online newsrooms, the growth in volume and frequency of publication of online news led to unintended and major transformations in monitoring practices, which are critical to understand the role of materiality in contemporary news production.

Materiality

Between April and December 2005, the author directed a research team that undertook an ethnographic study of content production at *Clarin.com*. It included three months of observations of work practices and 40 semi-structured interviews with full-time newsroom staffers.[15] One of the most repeated and intensive work practices among staff in charge of producing breaking and developing news content was monitoring competitors and a wide spectrum of other news outlets, from cable television to wire services to news sites from around the world. Reflecting on his own routine, an editor of the site said that "I [look at the other online news sites] all the time ... I don't want to miss anything of what they have."[16] In addition to regularly monitoring the news space, this practice often intensified before and after story publication. In the case of developing news, monitoring helped to calibrate one's coverage vis-à-vis that of competitors. As he recalled coverage of one such developing story, a staffer said that "looking at the competition is inescapable. When we defined the headline and the lead we were going to use, the first thing we did was to look at the sites [of the two main competitors] to see their [headlines and leads]".[17] He added that "this is something that happens almost naturally: 'this is how we frame the story, in principle, let's see how the others do it'." Journalists monitored the news field often also immediately after publishing a story, partly to contrast coverage and partly to see if they had been the first to post the story. For instance:

[At 18:13 a local cable news channel announces the verdict of the Michael Jackson trial, which triggers a rush to publish the story]. 18:20: The updated story is published. The editor [in charge of the story] immediately looks at the sites of [the main competitors] and says "we published it first." The homepage editor congratulates him, shakes his hand and says something along the lines of "it's a great to work with you."[18]

A comparison between these monitoring patterns at *Clarin.com* and the Johnny Apple vignette from *Boys on the Bus* yields an obvious difference: a shift from face-to-face to mediated monitoring. This shift does not mean that there was no mediated monitoring then or that there is no face-to-face monitoring now, but that the balance between the two seems to have been altered in the contemporary environment. This is also consistent with research that shows a rise of "sedentary journalism,"[19] marking a general growing reliance on technological mediation for information acquisition and a parallel decline of opportunities to interact with fellow journalists as part of the daily news-making routines. Moreover, the constant publication of news by online sites has greatly increased the volume of content available and the frequency of new content. In turn, this seems to have intensified the pace of mediated monitoring.

Interviews conducted with journalists at Clarín, *La Nación*, and *Lanacion. com* in 2006 and 2007[20] confirmed the growing prominence of mediated monitoring among reporters and editors, and the quickening of the pace of this practice. For instance, Ariel Tifferes, sports editor at *Lanacion.com*, said he looked at the sites of Spain's sports dailies *Marca* and *As*, "all the time."[21] If a relevant story were found on these dailies – for instance, about an Argentine soccer player who plays for a team in Spain – *Lanacion.com* typically posted an article referring to it. Thus, it is not surprising that Julio Chiappetta, a reporter in the sports desk of *Clarín*, remarked on this practice by Argentina's leading online newspapers: they "look a lot at overseas [sites] now, before they did not do it so often. So, [a story] that is published on *Marca* or *As* is also featured on *Clarin.com* or on *Lanacion.com* since the morning."[22] According to Chiappetta, the presence of these stories on local online news sites has become an added factor in putting together the news budget for his section.

In print newsrooms, the intensification of mediated monitoring and the rising importance of online news sites – in addition to the long utilized alternatives of wire services, television, radio and print – has been particularly salient among editors. Inés Capdevila, deputy foreign editor at *La Nación*, said she spends a couple hours of each working day monitoring the sites of leading news operations around the world. "I probably look at *The New York Times* [*on the Web*] twenty times a day."[23] Julio Blanck, who as one of three editors-in-chief at Clarín is partly in charge of the daily operation of its 500-journalist newsroom, said he looks at *Clarin.com* "all the time."[24] Blanck added that in his own experience one of the main effects of the time spent on his paper's site primarily, and on other news sites secondarily, is that he rarely reads the wire service copy anymore.

This last issue ties to an important development in the organization of content production at *Clarin.com* that underscores the centrality of unmediated monitoring in particular and helps to make sense of the role of materiality in contemporary journalistic work more generally: the reinvention of the *cablera*. In traditional newsrooms, this Spanish neologism, which means the "cable box," has been used to refer to the device that receives wire-service copy. But after the May 2004 redesign at *Clarin.com*, the *cablera* was reinvented into a new position and given a new space in the newsroom. One of the employees who occupies this position describes the job as follows:

> When I started I was told [by my bosses] 'we want you to be a news hunter' ... a person who not only receives content, which is also part of the function, but who also looks for it. This does not mean that I go on the street ... [because] it is possible to generate content from here [referring to the newsroom] ... hunting everything that circulates around many places [referring to different outlets in different media].[25]

In order to undertake this task of actively 'hunting' news from the world of mediated information, the *cablera* morphed technologically from a single device to a space, centrally located in the breaking and developing news area of the newsroom, populated by a wide array of hardware, software, and connectivity devices. The hardware includes two television sets with their respective remote controls, two computer workstations with their respective sets of keyboards, mice and speakers, a telephone, a number of printed materials such as notebooks, calendar books, and press clippings, and writing instruments. These artifacts are arrayed in a semi-circular fashion, with the two television sets at the two ends and the computer monitors in the middle, thus providing a semi-enclosed space for the *cablera* staffers. Surrounded by these multiple windows to the world of news and information, these staffers utilize an assortment of computer programs to scan the content digitally – including wire service copy, online news sites, and radio, television and cable newscasts – to capture potentially relevant news items, and unrelentingly distribute a synopsis of them via instant messenger to the editors.

How are we to think about these contemporary practices of monitoring in the newsroom? Put simply, they would not be possible without technology. More importantly, technology is not efficacious through one decisive piece of hardware or software but through a vast and multifaceted ensemble of old and new hardware, software, and connectivity devices that amount to an "infrastructure of mediation." The notion of infrastructure emphasizes that technologies are often socially consequential in complex bundles of artifacts, protocols, and standards together with the predisposition and skills to use them in particular ways that are always layered on top of an installed base.[26] The idea of an "infrastructure of mediation" makes visible the shifting balance from face-to-face to mediated monitoring and helps to make sense of one difference that technology makes not in terms of a single decisive artifact but as an infrastructure that ties materiality, skills, and specific modes of appropriation by the actors.

Mimicry

The growing intensification and mediation of monitoring has meant, among other things, that reporters and editors have far more knowledge about the output of their competitors and other media than ever before. When this greater knowledge is combined with the prevailing risk-averse editorial decision-making culture of journalists, what results is, at least partly, an expansion of mimicry. According to an editor at *Clarin.com*, "there is a criterion that says that we have to provide [consumers] with everything that the others [referring to competitors] have and more. And the news are part of that ... so we have to offer them the same news that the others have, although framed differently."[27] The following vignette illustrates a typical scene in the production of breaking news at *Clarin.com*:

> Reporter does 'copy-paste' of a piece of news that the cablera staffer sent her. Then she does 'copy-paste' of what she found on a Web page that has news from the wire services. With the text in Word, she changes phrases, adds words, modifies [things] a bit, but the basis of the news story is what she gets from the wire services.[28]

A growth in mimicry has also seemed to mark print newsrooms. *La Nacion*'s Capdevilla said that she regularly monitored *Clarin.com* several times a day and that one thing she discovered was that "there was a period at around 6:00 or 7:00 p.m., in which it [prominently displayed] on its homepage what were going to be the main stories of [its print counterpart] the following morning. ... And if we saw a headline that we did not have, we added [the story to the next day's edition]."[29] The issue of similarity in editorial products was also addressed during an interview with Alberto Amato, a journalist in the national desk of Clarín. Amato was asked whether he had noticed an increase in similarity in the stories supplied by the different news media in Argentina in recent years. With a gesture of frustration on his face, he said: "well, today the three newspapers [referring to Clarín, *La Nación*, and the small leftist daily *Pagina/12*] published the same picture on [their respective] front pages. The three newspapers!".[30] That was a picture of Argentina's President Néstor Kirchner and Venezuela's President Hugo Chavez, taken on occasion of the launch of a joint endeavor between the two countries. What Amato did not mention was that the front pages of Clarín and *La Nación* also featured two other headlines about similar events – a political incident in a Buenos Aires slum and a transportation accident – and Clarín and *Pagina/12* had headlines about a government crisis in Italy.

To better ascertain whether the views noted above reflect a more systematic field-level expansion of mimicry – and, if so, to estimate its magnitude – a content analysis of front page and top home page news stories was conducted for samples of coverage in Clarín and *La Nación* in 1995, 2000, 2004, and 2005, and on *Clarin.com* and *Lanacion.com* for 2005, respectively.[31] The study operationalized mimicry in story selection as to whether a story published on a front page – or a home page – was about an event that was also featured in a story on the front page of the other print paper in the same day – or the home page of the other online newspaper at the same time in the day. The analysis centered on news stories – as opposed to features, commentary, and other types of editorial content – as the dominant content type of both samples. On average, news stories constituted 86 per cent of the print sample and 69 per cent of the online sample.

Regarding the news stories on the front pages of Clarín and *La Nación* between 1995 and 2005, there is a major growth in the number of items about the same event featured in both papers on the same day that coincides with the increase in the frequency and volume of publication by their online counterparts. That is, 37 per cent and 33 per cent of the stories were about the same event in 1995 and 2000, respectively. But the per centages of stories with overlap rose to 42 per cent and 47 per cent in 2004 and 2005, respectively. Because the stories from 1995 and 2000 were from years before *Clarin.com* and *Lanacion.com* intensified the publication of breaking and developing news during the day, and because the differences in content overlap between them were not significant, they were combined into a "before" period for additional analysis.

For similar reasons, the 2004 and 2005 stories were blended into an "after" period. The comparison of these two periods shows a significant ($p < 0.01$) increase of 10 per centage points, from 35 per cent to 45 per cent (see Table 6.1). In relative terms, this is a growth in content overlap of 29 per centage points from the baseline level of 35 per cent in the before period.

Conversely, the analysis shows remarkable similarity in levels of content overlap between the print and online samples for 2005: 47 per cent for both samples (see Table 6.2). Thus, the main differences are not across media but between the before and after periods. Furthermore, consistent with print journalists' concern about the increasing anticipation of their content by other media, the analysis reveals that the news stories on the top portion of the home-page of *Clarin.com* and *Lanacion.com* at 10:00 pm anticipate 58 per cent and 51 per cent of the subjects of the stories on the front pages of Clarín and *La Nación* the following morning. Finally, there is also substantive cross-newspaper anticipation of content: news stories on the 10:00 pm homepage of *Lanacion. com* anticipate 48% of those in the front page of Clarín the next day, and those on *Clarin.com* anticipate 36% of the *La Nación* front page news stories.

The increase in overlap of news stories in the front pages of Clarín and *La Nación* between 1995–2000 and 2004–2005, and the similarly high level of overlap across the print and online media in 2005, are evidence of increased mimicry across the journalistic field. The convergence of the mediated mon-itoring processes described in the previous section with the imitation practices

Table 6.1 Evolution of content overlap in front page news stories of Clarín and *La Nación*, 1995–2005.

	Before samples (1995 and 2000)		After samples (2004 and 2005)		Difference
	%	No.	%	No.	%
Stories with overlap	35	140	45	178	10*
Stories without overlap	65	258	55	221	10*
Total	100	398	100	399	

* $p < 0.01$.

Table 6.2. Content overlap of news stories in front pages of Clarín and *La Nación*, and in top portion of home pages of Clarin.com and LaNacion.com in 2005.

	Print sample		Online sample		Difference
	%	No.	%	No.	%
Stories with overlap	47	98	47	350	0
Stories without overlap	53	109	53	394	0
Total	100	207	100	744	

and products outlined in the current section suggest a critical connection between materiality and mimicry in contemporary journalism.

Conclusion

This chapter asked whether new technologies and their appropriation by journalists have been tied to changes in monitoring and decision-making processes and, if so, whether any of these changes have affected mimicry in the construction of news. The account presented here shows discontinuity regarding monitoring and continuity concerning decision-making. That is, journalists have appropriated novel technologies – in combination with the already existing ones – in ways that have shifted the balance from unmediated to mediated monitoring while maintaining the patterns of risk aversion in editorial judgment. In turn, this has led to an increase in mimetic practices during the production of news and in the resulting news products. Beyond the specifics of the cases examined here, the analysis has implications for understanding technology and its relationships to the current media environment more broadly.

How does materiality matter in current practices of news production? This analysis suggests a three-part answer. First, material changes do not determine editorial transformations. The emergence of online publishing, with its associated technological innovations, did not mean any major modifications in monitoring and mimicry during the initial years of *Clarin.com* and *Lanacion.com*. It was only after online journalists appropriated the capabilities of the internet for constant publishing during the day that other editorial changes took place. Second, these changes were not planned but emerged spontaneously as an unintended consequence of this particular appropriation of new technological capabilities. In other words, online staffers did not start publishing constantly to affect the pace and intensity of mediated monitoring or to increase the rate of mimicry, but these were unforeseen developments that happened when the growth in the volume and frequency of content interacted with a pre-existing risk-averse editorial decision-making culture. Third, in the current context, materiality matters mostly in an infrastructural way that blends together old and new, hardware and software, tool and skill.

How does the elucidated link between materiality and mimicry help in making sense of contemporary journalism? Simply put, it illuminates the dynamics whereby more might actually mean less. The proliferation of outlets and the growth of content associated with the internet and other digital environments have often been positively received because they might mean more diversity of voices among producers and more choices for consumers. While this is an adequate characterization of certain kinds of news and certain contexts, it is also the case that, as a report from the Project for Excellence in Journalism has stated, "the new paradox of journalism is more outlets covering fewer stories."[32] The analysis presented in this paper is one step towards understanding the technological and cultural processes that account for this paradox in which more means less. Therefore, it might also help to think about ways to decrease their potentially negative consequences for journalism and society at large.

Notes

1 Portions of this article are published in Pablo J. Boczkowski, "Technology, Monitoring and Imitation in Contemporary News Work," *Communication, Culture & Critique* (2009): 39–58. Reprinted with permission from the publisher. The research reported in this paper would not have been possible without the cooperation of *Clarín.com*, Clarín, *La Nación*, and *Lanacion.com*. I would like to thank all the people who participated in the field studies, and especially acknowledge the support received from Guillermo Culell and Marcelo Franco at *Clarín.com*, Ricardo Kirschbaum and Miguel Wiñazki at Clarín, Fernán Saguier at *La Nación*, and Gastón Roitberg at *Lanacion.com*. I would also like to acknowledge the outstanding assistance of my Buenos Aires-based team – Diego López, Martin Walter and, in particular, Romina Frazzetta and Victoria Mansur. Simply put, this project would not have been feasible without their creativity and responsibility. Special thanks to Barbie Zelizer, for her always insightful comments and for inviting me to take part in the Symposium on "The Changing Faces of Journalism," held at the University of Pennsylvania's Annenberg School for Communication, where an earlier version of the ideas contained in this paper was presented. For helpful conversations on issues discussed in this paper, I also thank Amahl Bishara, Dominic Boyer, Guillermo Culell, Daniel Fernandez Canedo, Jean-François Fogel, Marcos Foglia, Marcelo Franco, Tom Gieryn, Shane Greenstein, Elihu Katz, Karin Knorr Cetina, Omar Lavieri, Eugenia Mitchelstein, Dan O'Keefe, Michael Schudson, Jim Webster, and seminar participants at Chicago, Indiana, MIT, Northwestern, and Penn. The research reported in this paper was in part supported by Northwestern University's Research Grants Committee and the School of Communication's Innovation Fund.
2 Pablo J. Boczkowski, *Digitizing the News: Innovation in Online Newspapers* (Cambridge: MIT Press, 2004); and Dominic Boyer and Ulf Hannerz, "Introduction: Worlds of Journalism," *Ethnography* 7 (2006): 5–17; Mark Deuze, "Participation, Remediation, Bricolage: Considering Principal Components of a Digital Culture," *Information Society* 22 (2006): 63–75; Eric Klinenberg, "Convergence: News Production in a Digital Age," *Annals of the American Academy of Political and Social Science* 597 (2005): 48–64; Tom Rosenstiel, "Political Polling and the New Media Culture: A Case of More Being Less," *Public Opinion Quarterly* 69 (2005): 698–715; Barbie Zelizer, "On Finding New Ways of Thinking About Journalism," *Political Communication* 24 (2007): 111–14.
3 Warren Breed, "Newspaper 'Opinion Leaders' and the Processes of Standardization," *Journalism Quarterly* 32 (1955): 277–84; James Halloran, Philip Elliot and Graham Murdock, *Demonstrations and Communication: A Case Study* (Harmondsworth: Penguin Books, 1970); Doris Graber, "The Press as Public Opinion Resource During the 1968 Presidential Campaign," *Public Opinion Quarterly* 35, (1971): 162–82; Elisabeth Noelle-Neuman and Rainer Mathes, "The 'Event as Event' and the 'Event as News': The Significance of Consonance for Media Effects Research," *European Journal of Communication* 2 (1987): 392–414; Michael Schudson, *The Sociology of News* (New York: W. W. Norton, 2003).
4 Timothy Crouse, *The Boys on the Bus* (New York: Random House, 2003 [1972]).
5 Pierre Bourdieu, *On Television* (New York: The New Press, 1996); Sharon Dunwoody, "The Science Writing Inner Club: A Communication Link Between

Science and Lay People," *Science, Technology & Human Values* 5 (1980): 14–22; Pamela Shoemaker and Stephen Reese, *Mediating the Message: Theories of Influences on Mass Media Content* (New York: Longman, 1996); Olav Velthuis, "Inside a World of Spin: Four Days at the World Trade Organization," *Ethnography* 7 (2006): 125–50.

6 Crouse, *The Boys on the Bus*. Dunwoody, "The Science Writing Inner Club"; James Hamilton, *All the News that's Fit to Sell* (Princeton, NJ: Princeton University Press, 2004); Vincent Kiernan, "Embargoes and Science News," *Journalism & Mass Communication Quarterly* 80 (2003): 903–20.

7 Crouse, *The Boys on the Bus*, 79.

8 Crouse, *The Boys on the Bus*, 22.

9 Standard & Poor's, *Arte Grafico Editorial Argentino S. A.: Rating report* (Buenos Aires, Argentina: Autor, 2005).

10 Asociación Argentina de Agentes de Publicidad, *Informe oficial de inversión publicitaria* (Retrieved April 15, 2005, from www.aaap.org.ar).

11 Instituto Verificador de Circulaciones, *IVC online datos gratuitos* (Retrieved June 8, 2006, from www.ivc.com.ar).

12 Internet Advertising Bureau – Argentina, *El IAB publica ranking de audience de sitios de Internet de Agosto 2006* (Retrieved March 22, 2008, from www.iabargentina. com.ar).

13 Instituto Verificador de Circulaciones, ibid.

14 Internet Advertising Bureau – Argentina, ibid.

15 For details on the methodology, see Pablo J. Boczkowski, "Rethinking Hard and Soft News Production: From Common Ground to Divergent Paths," *Journal of Communication* 59 (2009): 98–116.

16 Personal communication, December 15 2005.

17 Personal communication, July 28 2005.

18 Field note, June 13 2005.

19 Olivier Baisnee and Dominique Marchetti, "The Economy of Just-In-Time Television Newscasting: Journalistic Production and Professional Excellence at Euro-News," *Ethnography* 7 (2006): 99–123.

20 For details on the methodology, see Pablo J. Boczkowski, *News At Work: Imitation in an Age of Information Abundance* (unpublished book manuscript).

21 Personal communication, December 14 2006.

22 Personal communication, March 20 2007.

23 Personal communication, February 21 2007.

24 Personal communication, December 14 2006.

25 Personal communication, November 28 2005.

26 Pablo J. Boczkowski and Leah Lievrouw, "Bridging STS and Communication Studies: Scholarship on Media and Information Technologies," in *The Handbook of Science and Technology Studies*, third edition, ed. Olga Amsterdamska, Edward Hackett, Michel Lynch and Judy Wajcman (Cambridge, MA: MIT Press, 2007): 949–77; Geoffrey Bowker and Susan Leigh Star, *Sorting Things Out: Classification and its Consequences* (Cambridge, MA: MIT Press, 1999); Paul Edwards, "Infrastructure and Modernity: Force, Time, and Social Organization in the History of Sociotechnical Systems," in *Modernity and technology*, ed. Thomas Misa, Paul Brey and Andrew Feenberg (Cambridge, MA: MIT Press, 2003): 185–225; Steven Jackson, Paul Edwards, Geoffrey Bowker and Cary Knobel, "Understanding Infrastructure: History, Heuristics, and Cyberinfrastructure Policy," *First Monday* 12, no. 6 (2007). Retrieved October 24 2007 from www.firstmonday.org; and Susan Leigh Star and Karen Ruhleder, "Steps Toward an Ecology of Infrastructure: Design

and Access for Large Information Spaces," *Information Systems Research* 7 (1996): 111–34.

27 Personal communication, July 28 2005.

28 Field note, April 11 2005.

29 Personal communication, February 21 2007.

30 Personal communication, February 22 2007.

31 For details on the methodology, see Pablo J. Boczkowski and Martin de Santos, "When More Media Equals Less News: Patterns of Content Homogenization in Argentina's Leading Print and Online Newspapers," *Political Communication* 24 (2007): 167–90.

32 Project for Excellence in Journalism, *State of the News Media*. Retrieved June 9 2006 from www.stateofthemedia.org.

Chapter 7

The Guardian of the Real: Journalism in the Time of the New Mind

Julianne H. Newton

Within the dream, the dreamer is usually unaware that he is dreaming. ...
Gregory Bateson[1]

Society has ... become alarmed as never before without possessing ... the cognitive means for predicting and directing action because it not only changes its environment but also undermines the conditions for its own continued existence.
Niklas Luhmann[2]

Most of our mental life is unconscious; it becomes conscious only as words and images.
Erik Kandel[3]

It's learning to live at ... the speed of mind that counts.
Marshall McLuhan[4]

This essay issues a call to arms for journalism: to combine unprecedented knowledge about the workings of the mind with new forms of professional practice to disseminate vital, accurate information throughout the world. In a time when multiple truths, untruths, half-truths and make-believe truths dominate media content, journalism has an opportunity – indeed the obligation – to step up as guardian of the real. By making effective use of new technologies and social practices, good journalism can demonstrate not only that it is worth public attention but also that it is worthy of public trust.

We can trace reporting practices back to human survival instincts and to ancient images and symbols painted or carved onto rock walls to communicate with those who came after us. Traditionally, the practice of journalism has involved talking face to face with people, directly observing and recording events, gleaning documents and preparing accounts for dissemination in printed words and images. The relationship between reporting and the real world – the world of material things – was reinforced by the physical properties of the processes involved. Today, journalism technologies range across hand-made symbols, hand-cast type and engravings, machine-cast type and images, electromagnetic transmission of sound and images and computer-generated type, images and sounds. Journalism practices have evolved, too, developing writing styles and formulae, editing standards, longer and larger story packages, wider audiences, and new formats such as the internet and the infotainment, profit oriented genres that increasingly blur boundaries among reportage, persuasion and entertainment. Although the new processes and practices still are physical – in that electromagnetic energy is physical – to users they may seem less tangible and thus less credible.

The human brain as command center

The one constant driving these shifts is the human brain, the command center of an information system reaching throughout the body. The brain also creates the means for reaching beyond the body through the perception of external stimuli and creation of tools of extension such as journalism and other media forms. This makes it possible to gather information, create word and image packages, and send them around and even beyond the earth. The brain and all that it creates are bound in this co-evolutionary dynamic through time and space.

One way to gain perspective on the profound shifts occurring in contemporary media culture is to consider the discovery by archeologist Denise Schmandt-Besserat[5] that written language itself evolved from a Sumerian system of tokens developed between the ninth and seventh centuries BCE. Early tokens, which kept account of livestock and other trading goods, consisted of individual clay forms engraved with symbols indicating sheep, jars of oil and so forth. Then the Sumerians devised larger clay envelopes for carrying multiple, related tokens. On the outside of the envelopes they drew symbols indicating the nature of the tokens held inside. Eventually, the system of envelopes and tokens evolved into small tablets bearing symbols that represented such goods as sheep and jars. This shift from one-to-one physical correspondence with the real to increasingly symbolic representation offers insight for twenty-first-century evolutions in media technologies.

We can think of today's expansive communication systems as mega-envelopes, carrying 0s and 1s representing letterforms, other numerical notations, our thoughts and creations, images and sounds to every location on the earth that can receive them. With motivations not so dissimilar from those of early humans who physically scoured their environments for information left by other creatures and humans, we scour the internet for bits of information to help us understand the world and shape our lives. We also enjoy playing in virtual worlds – the escape of interacting through the variety of media available to us today, and the multiple ways in which we can express our thoughts and feelings.

Although such savvy journalism businesses as the Associated Press led the field with its Electronic Darkroom in 1979, journalism as a whole has yet to fully exploit these new ways of gathering, conveying, using and interacting with information. Many in journalism hold onto the 150-year tradition of newspapers in printed broadsheet and tabloid forms. One reason for resistance to new electronic formats may be the idealized association of the physical, printed page with the role of a free press announcing news of significant consequence to people's lives in a democratic society. Another reason may be the lingering perception that legitimate journalism requires the relative permanence of the printed page, especially in this time of great flux and the "age of the instant."[6] It is no wonder that many journalists feel threatened by the angst of antiquation. Persuasion, art and entertainment media long ago surpassed news and information media by engaging audiences through highly sophisticated media forms that tap multiple modalities of mind.

The issue for journalism, however, is guarding the real, by which I refer to journalism's social responsibility to seek and disseminate accurate, fair and significant information affecting people and their lives. This guardianship requires creative diligence, the ability to adjust to the unpredictable in ways that continue to foster the ideals of democratic citizenship. There is much that was right about the "old journalism" ideals of free expression, social responsibility, fairness and accuracy. Nevertheless, if we are serious about our commitment to journalism as the guardian of the real, we might reconceptualize the process of "doing journalism" in light of our contemporary knowledge of mind and media. Developments in cognitive neuroscience, for example, have enhanced our understanding of how the brain creates the mind, thereby generating a sense of self, other and environment, and shaping behavior. In addition, theoretical work in media ecology has strengthened our understanding of how humans and technologies external to the body co-evolve as mutually dependent systems through which each entity extends itself in a perpetual dynamic. These two theoretical fields intersect to help us comprehend the constantly shifting, highly mediated minds that perceive and act in a globalized twenty-first-century arena. By confirming the urgency of journalism as a fundamental force in the development of personal, cultural, political, economic and environmental survival systems, these approaches light a path for revolutionizing the practice of journalism. They suggest thinking about journalism systemically as a primal and primary source of personal and global knowledge production and dissemination, and as the key to opinion formation, perception and decision-making in a free society. They position journalism as a knowledge frame, a system for gathering, producing and conveying verifiable information through the media. In this way, journalism can be seen as akin to a technology through which we extend and form personal and public mind.

Defining terms

A number of terms are central to reconceptualizing journalism and technology in this way. In everyday use, "technology" refers to equipment or tools that help us do things and to the ability to use those tools. Moss offers a broader definition that is especially useful to our discussion: "the means by which human societies interact directly with and adapt to the environment. Technology can also refer to the steps taken, or manufacturing process used, to produce an artifact."[7] Applying this definition, the brain becomes a form of technology, serving as the means by which we interact, adapt to our environments and create artifacts of living. We also can view technology as both "tool" and "content." As a communication tool, technology encompasses hardware, software and the human capacity for innovation in communication strategies across journalism, advertising/public relations and long-form narrative, across platforms and across sub-genres. As content, technology encompasses the human extension of body and mind through material and virtual worlds. From a journalism perspective, this means developing ways in which to enhance freedom of expression with journalistic integrity in a globally diverse society. Beyond journalism, this means understanding not only the positive and negative ways in which technologies impact the environments in which we live but also what it means to be one kind of organism living in a larger system with countless other organisms – all seeking to survive.

The word "brain" has multiple meanings, too. Neuroscientist and Nobel Laureate Eric Kandel defines the brain as "the organ that mediates all mental functions and all behavior."[8] Beyond the standard definition as the key organ of the central nervous system, the word "brain" sometimes refers to a computer operating system or communication network. Contrary to popular application, however, some neuroscientists do not conceive of the human brain as working like a computer. They point to fuzzy or mosaic logic, to nondefinable, less linear and more intuitive ways the brain interprets self and world to work for the survival of the individual. Also important for our discussion is the concept of the "mind," which Kandel asserts is inseparable from the brain. It is worth reminding ourselves that the:

> brain is a complex biological organ of great computational capability that constructs our sensory experiences, regulates our thoughts and emotions, and controls our actions. The brain is responsible not only for relatively simple motor behaviors, such as running and eating, but also for the complex acts that we consider quintessentially human, such as thinking, speaking, and creating works of art. ... mind is a set of operations carried out by the brain, much as walking is a set of operations carried out by the legs, except dramatically more complex.[9]

This means that for journalism, "the brain" refers to 1) an individual's means for mediating feelings, thoughts, and behaviors, including the production and consumption of news, and 2) a communication system's means for mediating thoughts and actions, including collective memory and awareness. For journalism, "the mind" refers to the set of informational operations made possible by worldwide communication systems.

By "new mind," then, I refer to recent understandings of brain and mind that are made possible by the discoveries of cognitive neuroscience in the last part of the twentieth century and early twenty-first century, which many call the "century of the brain." This research reminds us of the evolving, organic nature of human ways of knowing and can help us reconceptualize journalism. In addition to the inseparability of the brain and the mind, the new science of mind is based on the idea that mental functions are executed by "specialized neural circuits in different regions of the brain."[10] Neural circuits in turn are composed of nerve cells and "use specific molecules to generate signals within and between nerve cells."[11] Some of these molecules, retained:

> ... through millions of years of evolution. ... were present in the cells of our most ancient ancestors and can be found today in our most distant and primitive evolutionary relatives: single-celled organisms such as bacteria and yeast and simple multicellular organisms such as worms, flies, and snails. These creatures use the same molecules to organize their maneuvering through their environment that we use to govern our daily lives and adjust to our environment.[12]

Most of this signaling activity occurs as nonconscious processing in the brain.

How does something as practical as journalism relate to the brain and the mind, much less to the abstract concept of "global mind"? For journalism, an understanding of the mind connects the single unit of one brain with the seemingly limitless expanse of brains participating in worldwide communication systems. The term "global mind" refers to the idea that the internet and other forms of media have connected people across the earth (and beyond via space exploration) to the extent that the media operate as a kind of brain, mediating our understandings of reality and our behaviors and creating a kind of worldwide consciousness, or global mind. Entrepreneur Nova Spivak, who calls himself a "technological visionary" and ontologist, believes:

> ... that the Internet (the hardware) is already evolving into a distributed global brain, and its ongoing activity (the software, humans and data) represents the cognitive process of an increasingly intelligent global mind. This global mind is not centrally organized or controlled, rather it is a bottom-up, emergent, self-organizing phenomenon formed from flows of trillions of information-processing events comprised of billions of independent information processors.[13]

We can define traditional journalism as the profession or practice of gathering information, compiling the information into a story, and disseminating the story as part of a package or alone via radio, print media, television or the internet. Traditional journalism at its best is associated with the social responsibility of serving as the "fourth estate," or a watchdog, check/balance on the judicial, legislative and executive branches of a democratic government. At its worst, traditional journalism is associated with careless and sensational exploitation of people and events for profit. As a guardian of the real, journalism has the responsibility to ferret out and disseminate a "reasonable truth," the most accurate information "a person can perceive and convey at any given moment."[14]

An important related term to clarify is "media." In everyday use, people use the word to refer to the mass media, that amorphous collective of print and electronic platforms that disseminate informative, entertaining and persuasive messages to large audiences. However, a medium is simply an environment, which can be the body, a room, a book or magazine, a computer screen or virtual reality. Media ecologists draw on multiple disciplines to study the evolution, effects, forms and environments of communication. The human body is the original multimedium – thinking, feeling, sensing, seeing, hearing, smelling, tasting, touching, creating and extending its own organic technologies through various media platforms around the globe. Addressing the "effects" of such media, we can define them as results, consequences or influences. Positive effects are those that enhance, benefit or improve. Negative effects are those that damage, harm or discredit. To change is to make or become different, or to transform from one state to another. Media today engage in a process Bolter and Grusin call "remediation," through which one medium, such as the internet, adapts forms of other media, such as newspapers and television.[15]

By "time,", I mean a period or duration in which definable events occur. The "time of the new mind," then, is our present era, a period of years in which science, art and media are converging to understand and exercise an extended form of consciousness. Kandel might describe this time as one in which we are trying to determine "how each person's brain creates the consciousness of a unique self and the sense of free will."[16] It is also a time in which we are critically exploring how we integrate that sense of self and free will in a global culture of instantaneously mediated communication. Note the concept of integration, a process through which the mind balances nonconscious processing with conscious processing. This involves both rational intelligence, knowing through a process of reason, and intuitive intelligence, knowing without direct evidence of reason.[17] Many educational systems emphasize, or bias, rational intelligence. Williams theorizes that this rational bias has, in turn, created an "intuitive void," which advertising and entertainment media have become expert at filling.[18] The brain uses this information on both conscious and nonconscious levels of cognition to shape perceptions of reality and guide behavior. In fact, most advantageous decision-making is generated on primarily nonconscious levels of communication.[19] What this means for journalism is that readers and viewers make decisions and form opinions based on media content that is not necessarily intended to be read as true. Journalism content is part of the mix of words and pictures people perceive in everyday media consumption. Increasingly, people also are contributing to that mix through blogs, citizen journalism, social networks and other forms of interactive media. Journalism, therefore, would do well to look beyond its traditional formats – even newly formed internet canons – to communicate its messages. Journalism also can benefit from sharing its standards of excellence with users and citizen producers through education and journalistic media.[20]

Thus, "journalism in the time of the new mind" refers to the idea that current practices of reporting and conveying information of significance to human perception, survival and decision-making are operating in a period of history in which we have unprecedented opportunities: 1) to understand how the brain is drawn to and makes use of information it perceives, and 2) to determine how best to get significant, life-enhancing information to all people of the earth in ways that maintain the integrity and value of the communication.

Application

Were we to move beyond thinking of technologies as only external, inorganic entities, we might recognize that technologies can refer to almost everything. Communication technologies, such as journalism, are frames that reflect or facilitate knowledge flow. In the practice of journalism, technology as a frame limits, expands and creates meaning through the imposition of structure on story forms, codes of ethics, and social responsibility to a free society. The structure is both hard and soft, material and ideological, a kind of design that shapes, reduces, distorts, clarifies and makes possible ways of knowing on conscious and nonconscious levels of cognition. Technology employed in the name of journalism carries a particular burden for facilitating straightforward, accurate, truthful communication of information that is vital to people's lives. Yet any frame imposes figure/ground relationships upon the elements that lie within the frame. In this way, elements of communication are foregrounded or backgrounded, seen as significant or less significant, positive or negative. Other elements are excluded from the frame, thus excluded from attention.

Those who practice journalism often view their work as a voice of reason expressed through a carefully investigated, crafted news story – the epitome of experience and professionalism. Yet we also talk about going into the profession of journalism as a kind of calling, driven by a passion for showing the world to itself in hopes of improving that world. The demands of daily work on the mind, body and heart of a journalist who has dedicated her life to seeking truth in the interest of the public exact a heavy price, one paid through sustained passionate commitment or through succumbing to the numbness and automaticity – the "almost nonconsciousness" – of routines. On the other side of the professional spectrum are those who rely on sensationalism and persuasion to garner interest in the spectacles of society and sell publications or user time.

On the whole, journalism tends to be practiced as a process of learned behavior and codes, a process that facilitates rapid information gathering, production and dissemination – and profit making. Many scholars have investigated this process through multiple approaches, searching to understand how news media communicate, how people perceive the news, how organizational and governmental policies are set, and how news media affect individual perceptions and behavior and thus create society.

Meanwhile, persuasion and entertainment media have for decades drawn on carefully conducted experimental and qualitative psychological and brain research with another variable in mind: emotion. Often devalued as the source of irrational behavior, emotion has captured the attention of cognitive neuroscientists such as Antonio Damasio[21] and Joseph LeDoux.[22] Their research asserts the foundational role of emotion in human decision-making and problem-solving. In fact, research strongly suggests that without consideration of the nonconscious role of emotion and other intuitive ways of knowing, conscious decision-making often is based on a kind of "rationalization," the conscious mind's effort to make sense of behavior the nonconscious mind has already determined.[23] Gazzaniga, who calls the part of the brain that creates the story of the self the "Interpreter," writes, "It appears that the inventive and interpreting left hemisphere has a conscious experience very different from that of the truthful, literal right brain."[24] The left hemisphere, Gazzaniga says, even makes things up (or rationalizes) to make behaviors the nonconscious mind already has initiated seem like logical, consciously derived decisions.

Williams and Newton suggest the term "intuitive intelligence" as an inclusive concept referring to the human "ability to learn or understand and apply knowledge directly and nonconsciously without the intervention of conscious rational processing."[25] Understanding how people use nonconscious cognitive processing and intuitive intelligence to make meaning – as both perceivers and creators – and learning to integrate intuitive and rational mental processing can help journalists "find new solutions to old problems,"[26] such as declining interest in significant news of the day. Ironically, journalistic venues often are the dissemination platforms for both persuasion and entertainment messages. Advertising, public relations and entertainment industries have successfully exploited intuitive cognitive modalities on highly sophisticated levels for professional and corporate profit for at least the last 60 years.

It is time for journalists to better understand how their media platforms are used by the competition (persuasion and entertainment) and by consumers. Professional journalists are competing for the same limited, but crowded, visual, aural and verbal space as their advertising and public relations colleagues – and as bloggers and other internet content producers. This is a call to arms for journalism and education. If we want people to pay attention, and if we want the integrity of our messages to get through to people, we might have more success if we learned to produce and disseminate messages in ways that communicate effectively from a perspective of the whole mind. That means employing a deep understanding of the interplay of conscious and nonconscious, rational and intuitive cognitive modalities – modalities the persuaders use with unparalleled expertise and finesse.

For 150 years, journalism has depended on news itself to take the "center ring" in the big tent of the media circus. In a world overwhelmed with media communication and competition, everything else, particularly messages designed to entertain and persuade, seems more interesting in comparison with the reportage of the daily news. One significant reason this is true is the form of the messages presented. This in turn is linked directly to the concept of appealing to the whole mind or the new mind. Research in education strongly suggests that the more cognitive modalities or intelligences that a communicator engages in an integrative, congruent manner, the more readers/viewers are engaged and the more they learn and remember. Persuasive media have long understood and exploited the tactic of engaging both the rational and intuitive minds in their message designs. This does not suggest that we sensationalize stories in order to get and hold readers' attention. It does suggest, however, that we more fully engage attention by engaging the whole mind. At the most basic levels, we would benefit from more research (and from the use of research in advertising and persuasion, cognitive neuroscience, and media ecology) into how we can better integrate graphic design, psychology, visual and aural perception, and metaphor to communicate reportage. Being realistic about our competitive role in the mass media environment can foster the development of new strategies for using visual, verbal and aural media to communicate via the new mind. We need *not* leave Second Life, Facebook and other virtual environments to themselves to fill the "intuitive void" felt by many media users today. Journalists can employ intuitively driven techniques to draw users to explore significant issues from multi-modal perspectives.

The new mind is both an extended collection of individual user brains and an unlimited extension of an individual's brain through space and time. This has implications for journalism practice: the beat is the universe, audiences are as diverse as those who populate the earth, access is more uneven than ever, dissemination timeframes are instant/real time, and participatory journalism is changing content, standards and effects. Just as the human mind mediates stimuli to create meaning for living, the collective mind of external media "remediate" information in a perpetual dynamic of meaning making. New Mind Journalism is not a practice of either/or "factness" but a continuum of conscious and nonconscious, rational and intuitive ways of knowing and communicating. New Mind Journalism embraces the continuum of the one and the many, the local and the global.

A number of theoretical approaches from a variety of fields echo aspects of this approach. I refer to only a few here. Certainly Marshall McLuhan, drawing on the ideas of anthropologist Edward T. Hall,[27] developed his concepts of the "extensions of man" in *Understanding Media* and the "global village" in *The Gutenberg Galaxy*.[28] In *Laws of Media: The New Science*,[29] Erik McLuhan expanded his father's notion of the tetrad, a metaphorical means of predicting and perhaps altering potential effects of media evolutions. Especially interesting is McLuhan and Powers' *The Global Village: Transformations in World Life and Media in the 21st Century*.[30] Published after McLuhan's death through the efforts of his colleague Bruce Powers, *The Global Village* draws on brain science to suggest ways in which the world could avoid a monumental cultural clash in the twenty-first century. In his classic *An Ecology of Communication*, symbolic interactionist David Altheide maintains that "social order is increasingly an electronically communicated and mediated order, and this has tremendous consequences for social life and especially for freedom and justice."[31] Arguing that "modern society creates too little as well as too much resonance because of its structural differentiation into different function systems,"[32] sociologist Niklas Luhmann calls for new values and an environmental ethics that expands our understanding of ecology to include human communication and behavior. Neuroscientist Michael Gazzaniga believes that becoming conscious of "a universal set of biological responses to moral dilemmas, a sort of ethics, built into our brains" could help eliminate "a lot of suffering, war, and conflict."[33] No one scholar proposes to have "the" answer to solving the world's problems. Yet collectively, they point to concurring ideas that might offer insight for helping journalism find a strong, compelling voice above the din of media noise.

Conclusion

In sum, communication engages mental processes that operate from both rational and intuitive, conscious and nonconscious cognitive arenas to convey knowledge that shapes reality and behavior. The nonconscious mind is the primary facilitator of perception, memory, decision-making and behavior. Journalism needs to employ the new knowledge we hold about the workings of the mind:

> Ultimately, the mediation of knowledge through visual, aural and other means of perception is best examined through both empirical and theoretical approaches that consider how individuals, as living organisms, survive and create as small parts of large systems. The individual and collective memories of human consciousness comprise countless neural data points—the combination of centuries of genetic encoding; months of light, darkness, sounds and chemical and electrical signaling acquired in utero; the dream worlds of millions of nights and quiet afternoons; and the mental and physical galleries constructed as each person and group experience the multiple stimuli of time, space and media.[34]

Technology is a fluid construct that frames information and is framed by information at the same time that it forms systems and is formed by systems. The nonconscious mind biases and generates our responses to environment; the conscious mind tries to make rational sense out of the intuitive bias and behavior and often introduces distortion as it reframes the primary response. This reframing process can result in both positive and destructive biases. Our conscious minds believe we have rationally arrived at something we call truth. Often, it is not truth but truthiness.[35] We are aware of many previously unacknowledged biases of which we used to be unaware: race, gender, age, disability, sexual orientation, ethnicity, and national origin. But we have much to learn about the biases hidden deep within us – those biases formed through years of experiencing and negotiating our environments. And some of those biases – toward words, toward print, toward traditional story formats, for example – are holding journalists back.

Thus far, technology appears to be changing journalism more for negative effect than positive effect. Journalism as a whole would benefit from moving forward with a critical understanding of the new mind. By developing practices that disseminate both highly intuitive and rational messages, journalism can acknowledge its fundamental role in the construction of social reality, as well as its ability to influence thinking and behavior across space and time on multiple cognitive platforms. If Journalism – with a capital "J" – can embrace the new mind of global media, new understandings of how people interpret and use information, and new applications of the basic concepts of reporting and conveying significant information, the potential for positive change is unlimited.

I want to suggest three guidelines for twenty-first-century journalism. First, we might figure out different ways of telling "the story." That means drawing on brain research to get the attention of reader/viewer/user and to present information in forms that facilitate comprehension and recall. Second, we might expand the frame of journalism beyond the goal of objectivity to more often offer context for the "whole story" and the "meta-story," the stories that professional journalists are best at discerning and communicating. This means cultivating alternative narrative forms that make sophisticated use of multiple modalities for telling, showing, and teaching. Third, we need to "attend to the attender." By that I mean we might draw on the best of perceptual researchers to ascertain how to get and hold the attention of readers/viewers/users. This process might mean embracing the move toward "participatory journalism," a term coined by communication scholar Wayne Danielson (personal communication) during the early rise of amateur involvement in news production in the 1990s. Rather than feel threatened by citizen participation, journalism can benefit from inviting further participation, setting standards for amateur contributions, and fulfilling journalism's destiny of a free press for a free people protected by – and responsible to – the First Amendment. I believe that applying these guidelines will move journalism a long way toward competing more successfully with highly sophisticated persuasive and entertainment media – on our own terms, rather than theirs.

One example of a journalist who not only balances rational and intuitive mental processing but also is applying her wisdom to solving problems in professional practice is international photojournalist Maggie Steber. Steber is trained in both word and visual journalism, has won the World Press Award for Spot News for her coverage of Haiti, and has developed multiple stories for *National Geographic*. At the *Miami Herald*, where Steber was director of photography and features editor, Steber once stood in the newsroom and yelled, "Photojournalism is the Rosa Parks of the news room!"[36] Determined to forge a path for journalism in the time of the new mind, Steber proposed a plan for the "New American Newspaper" to the Knight Foundation, which awarded her a grant through the Knight Center for International Media at the University of Miami School of Communication. Through an innovative seminar, Steber and her students "are working hard at designing a new visually driven paper and website."[37] The goal is to create a paper that will "reach backward to entice a generation of print readers toward the Internet. ... and to reach forward and entice younger generations toward deeper investigation into major issues through dynamic visual presentation and articles that cannot be found anywhere else."[38] Instead of lamenting the loss of verbal literacy, Steber's group is working to bridge the gap between generations of different brains and minds. Research in cognitive neuroscience supports this move toward increased integration of the visual with the verbal. It is estimated that at least 75 per cent of all information the brain processes is visual. Furthermore, brain researchers estimate that at least 90 per cent of mental processing itself is visual. Neuroscientist Antonio Damasio[39] asserts that all mental processing involves imaging patterns. Visual communication is the primary intuitive intelligence that helps shape behavior and make decisions that guide behavior.[40]

Enhancing the role of visual messages in journalism is an important but singular form of enhancing the practice of journalism. Embracing, rather than fighting, the new mind can facilitate better journalism – a journalism that reaches, engages and influences more people with its urgent messages. Reconceptualizing journalism as a technological system created and consumed by new minds connected with multiple cognitive modalities through local and global systems will help our most significant form of communication reach diverse audiences with diverse media – and increase the likelihood that people will see, listen and attend to issues at hand as they make critical decisions for their lives and society at large.

This intense level of transformation requires redesigning education throughout journalism schools, as well as developing strategies for educating current professionals and the citizens of the world. Research already is advancing this integrative approach to engaging the new mind. Interdisciplinary efforts toward integrative mind technologies are being developed in scholarship that merges communication, education, art, media, cognitive neuroscience, biology, and psychology, among others. It is time, in this century of the new mind, for journalists to lead the way to a communication system that engages the whole mind with the integrity of the whole truth.

Notes

1 Gregory Bateson, *Steps to an Ecology of Mind* (New York: Ballantine, 1972).
2 Niklas Luhmann, *Ecological Communication*, trans. John Benarz, Jr. (Chicago: University of Chicago Press, 1989), 1.
3 Eric R. Kandel, *In Search of Memory: The Emergence of the New Science of Mind* (London: Norton, 2006).
4 Matie Molinaro, personal communication, June 7 2004.
5 D. Schmandt-Besserat, *How Writing Came About*. [Abridged edition of *Before Writing, Volume I: From Counting to Cuneiform*, Austin: University of Texas Press, 1992] (Austin: University of Texas Press, 1996).
6 Dennis Dunleavy, *In the Age of the Instant: The Influence of the Digital Camera on the Photojournalistic Routines of Productivity, Empowerment and Social Interaction Between Subject and Photographer* (Unpublished Ph.D. dissertation, University of Oregon School of Journalism and Communication, Eugene, 2004).
7 Madonna L. Moss "Anthropology 150 – Glossary" (2001). Available: www.darkwing.uoregon.edu (February 11, 2007).
8 Kandel, *In Search of Memory*, 432.
9 Kandel, *In Search of Memory*, xxi.
10 Kandel, *In Search of Memory*, xii.
11 Ibid.
12 Kandel, *In Search of Memory*, xiii.
13 Nova Spivak, Minding the Planet: From Semantic Web to Global Mind. Available: www.novaspivack.typepad.com (Spivak, 2004, para. 10) (November 8, 2007).
14 Julianne H. Newton, *The Burden of Visual Truth: The Role of Photojournalism in Mediating Reality* (Mahwah, NJ: Lawrence Erlbaum Associates, 2001), 86.
15 J. David Bolter and Richard Grusin, *Remediation: Understanding New Media* (Cambridge, MA: MIT, 1999).
16 Kandel, *In Search of Memory*, 11.
17 Rick Williams and Julianne H. Newton, *Visual Communication: Integrating Media, Art and Science* (New York: Lawrence Erlbaum/Taylor Francis, 2007).
18 Rick Williams, "Transforming Intuitive Illiteracy: Understanding the Effects of the Unconscious Mind on Image Meaning, Image Consumption, and Behavior," *EME* 2 (2003): 119–34.
19 Antoine Bechara, Hanna Damasio, Daniel Tranel and Antonio Damasio, "Deciding Advantageously Before Knowing the Advantageous Strategy," *Science*, 275 (1997): 1293–95. See also Chun Siong Soon, Marcel Brass, Hans-Jochen Heinze and John-Dylan Haynes, "Unconscious Determinants of Free Decisions in the Human Brain," *Nature Neuroscience* 11 (2008): 543–45.
20 Williams and Newton, *Visual Communication*.
21 Antonio Damasio, *The Feeling of What Happens: Body and Emotion in the Making of Consciousness* (New York: Harcourt Brace, 1999).
22 Joseph LeDoux, "Sensory Systems and Emotion," *Integrative Psychiatry* 4 (1986): 237–43, and Joseph LeDoux, *The Emotional Brain* (New York: Simon & Schuster, 1996).
23 Michael S. Gazzaniga, "Cerebral Specialization and Interhemispheric Communication: Does the Corpus Callosum Enable the Human Condition?" *Brain* 123 (2000): 1293–1326; Michael Gazzaniga, "The Split Brain Revisited," *Scientific American* 279 (1998): 1, 50–56; and Michael Gazzaniga, *The Ethical Brain* (New York: Dana Press, 2005).
24 Gazzaniga, "The Split Brain Revisited," npn.
25 Williams and Newton, *Visual Communication*, 18.
26 Williams and Newton, *Visual Communication*, 10.

27 Edward T. Hall, *The Silent Language* (Garden City, NY: Doubleday, 1959).
28 Marshall McLuhan, *The Gutenberg Galaxy: The Making of Typographic Man* (Toronto: University of Toronto Press, 1962), and Marshall McLuhan, *Understanding Media: The Extensions of Man* (New York: McGraw-Hill, 1964).
29 Marshall McLuhan and Frik McLuhan, *Laws of Media: The New Science* (Toronto: University of Toronto Press, 1988).
30 Marshall McLuhan and Bruce Powers, *The Global Village: Transformations in World Life and Media in the 21st Century* (New York: Oxford University Press, 1989).
31 David Altheide, *An Ecology of Communication: Cultural Formats of Control* (New York: Aldine de Gruyter, 1995), xi.
32 Luhmann, *Ecological Communication*, xvii.
33 Gazzaniga, *The Ethical Brain*, xix.
34 Julianne H. Newton, "Memory and Visual Communication: The Meaning Connection," ed. Elena Agazzi and Vita Fortunati, *Memoria/Memorie* (Percorsi transdisciplinari, Roma: Meltemi, 2007).
35 Please see other chapters in this volume for expositions on truth and truthiness.
36 Maggie Steber, personal communication, 2007.
37 Maggie Steber, personal communication, 2007.
38 Knight Center for International Media, "Knight Foundation Sponsors America's Newspaper of the Future," press release, University of Miami School of Communication, September 18, 2007.
39 Damasio, *The Feeling of What Happens*.
40 Williams and Newton, *Visual Communication*.

Chapter 8

Technology and the Individual Journalist: Agency Beyond Imitation and Change

Mark Deuze

Journalism as a profession is important to democratic society not just because of what it produces but also how news is produced: under what conditions, for what purposes, within which institutional mindset and professional identity. Consequently, the field of journalism studies has many canonic texts investigating and documenting who journalists are, how they do what they do, and how news cultures and occupational ideology give meaning and provide structure to their work.[1] Yet considering the significant transformations in the creation of content in the journalistic field that have emerged during the past couple of decades, which have been supercharged by rapidly changing disruptive technologies, it is crucial to reconsider sedimented ways of understanding and the work that journalists do under contemporary conditions.[2]

The fundamental perspectives with which scholars study and interpret the work of journalists are generally framed in terms of the economic, social, and cultural organization of newswork.[3] In this contribution I will focus on such economic, social and cultural explanations as a structure for my argument. This structure is set against the contemporary rapidly changing realities of newswork and employment in the field of journalism. The perspective used to make sense of these changes is that of the individual newsworker. In order to do so, journalism is first conceptualized as the ensemble of attitudes and behaviors of individuals (rather than as a set of institutions, social system, professional group or news industry). Theories of newswork are then reconsidered in terms of recent changes and challenges in the ways in which journalism as a field of work is managed and organized in society.

Running through these considerations is a specific focus on the amplification effect of technology. Considering the role of technology as an amplifier and accelerator of change in journalism means focusing on how journalists appropriate technologies in the service of established goals, strategies, and relationships in ways that accelerate current constituent trends, developments and activities of journalism. Technology in this sense is neither a necessary change agent nor a vehicle for seamless reproduction. It is seen as a "supercharger" of emerging trends and developments affecting the work of journalists.

The emphasis here refers to the explanatory potential of re-theorizing dominant perspectives in the social sciences on newswork so as to understand the individual news producer. The essay concludes with a brief discussion of the opportunities for reinvigorating journalism studies and education with a specific focus on the evolving "workstyles" of journalists: their ways of working and being at work.[4] In making this argument, I regrettably sidestep a number of definitional issues (what is journalism and who is a journalist), and cross-cultural complexities (specifying differences in markets and news cultures in various countries and regions). However, as this paper intends to make a point rather than prove one, I hope to argue that the study of journalism needs to engage with the changing nature of employment and the creative process.

Contingency and individualization in newswork

Contingency defines the lived experience of many if not most media professionals today. Of all professions in the media production industries (such as advertising, film and TV, and digital game development), the labor market for journalism has arguably been among the most stable.[5] This is rapidly changing, however. In April 2006, the International Federation of Journalists (IFJ) released a report on the labor conditions of journalists around the world, concluding that "[j]ournalists and media workers are increasingly being employed in atypical and contingent employment relationships – casual employment, use of contract work and the rise of the use of triangular, ambiguous and disguised employment."[6] Atypical newswork makes up around one-third of the membership of IFJ affiliates. This figure is much higher among newcomers in the industry, and among those working in television, for print magazines, and online. In the Netherlands the number of freelance or otherwise contingently employed journalists has grown from 13 per cent in 1993 via 23 per cent in 2000 to roughly one-third today.[7] In South Africa the number of freelancers is relatively low (estimates are less than 10 per cent), but an ongoing conglomeration of big media companies such as Naspers has resulted in a practice of directing journalists across their increasingly diversified title range. A growing number of journalists are thus doing freelance work, but they are still employed more or less full time somewhere else.[8] The situation is similar in Europe and Australia, where freelancing has grown exponentially during the 1990s and the early parts of the twenty-first century.[9] Some reporters are still permanently employed, most others only parachute in for a couple of weeks to work on a certain aspect of a project (a special issue or supplement, a specific program or reportage, a part of a news website); several people move in and out of projects and temporary labor arrangements all the time, and many if not most media workers swim in a pool of underutilized talent.[10] Contemporary trends in new media technologies, changes in the ownership structures and production networks of cultural industries, an ongoing hyper-fragmentation of media audiences, as well as a gradual convergence of production and consumption through an increasingly participatory media culture contribute to this precariousness.[11]

The increased contingency in work and employment does not mean media professionals are without power or resources to counteract.[12] The creative process of work in the media industries in general and in journalism in particular is a fascinating object of study, because newswork is itself a cultural process.[13] This means that neither the individual, the owner nor the corporation completely controls the production of news. Elements of social structure (the organization of work, the parameters set by time, budget and space, media ownership, and so on) and the norms, values, and ways of doing things of the practitioners involved mutually influence each other. The dialectic of cultural and structural concerns in the context of present-day media work can be seen as constituent material practice: the combination of specific technical and organizational arrangements as these influence and are shaped by the generally idiosyncratic habits of individual media practitioners.[14] One particular example has been the formation of specific online journalism units within news organizations exclusively dedicated to putting ("shoveling" or "windowing") the news online. As online newsrooms traditionally have been organized separately from their parent institutions and tend to be populated mostly by newcomers and contingent employees, these departments grew into their own "mini-cultures."[15] Such online journalism units have developed since the mid-1990s and are quite distinct; in some cases they constitute countercultural departments within the profession, where their values, practices and ideals are gradually changing the cultural mosaic of established news organizations.[16]

At the outset of this essay, I want to emphasize the necessity of considering journalists as individual meaning-makers in the context of today's media ecosystem. This approach may be counterintuitive, as the profession of journalism and the larger media industry within which it operates are known as rather bureaucratically structured and market-driven enterprises where individual voices tend to be forced out under pressures of workplace socialization, routinization of newswork, and a rather homogeneous professional population.[17] However, an argument can be made that this system is giving way to new practices and ways of working under the influence of current social and technological trends. There are four reasons for explaining contemporary journalism as the ensemble of attitudes and activities of individuals. First, what Richard Sennett calls the "culture of the new capitalism" draws our attention to the current reorganization of the workplace and the field of work towards an almost exclusive emphasis on individualized responsibilities.[18] Several scholars have noted how in the field of cultural production, managers and employers increasingly stress the importance of "enterprise" as an individual rather than organizational or firm-based attribute.[19] Shifting the notion of enterprise – with its connotations of efficiency, productivity, empowerment and autonomy – from the company to the individual employee makes it part of the professional identity of each and every worker, however contingently employed or not. This subtle shift can be seen as a deliberate managerial attempt to regulate professional identity as a form of organizational control, with the intent "to reconstitute workers as more adaptable, flexible, and willing to move between activities and assignments and to take responsibility for their own actions and their successes and failures."[20]

Journalism is no exception to the trend of labor individualization in a context of managerial efforts to expand workforce control.[21] No doubt, the individualization of labor allows for workforce flexibility and adaptive production, but it also makes media management dependent on the availability of appropriate talent, and allows competent workers greater individual autonomy, the acquisition of a wide variety of skills and experiences, and a reduced dependence on a single employer.[22]

Second, the production of news increasingly takes place both within and outside of professional news organizations, as well as within and across multiple media forms and formats – where fragmentation of newswork is furthermore facilitated by practices of outsourcing, subcontracting, and off-shoring, as documented by the World Association of Newspapers in a 2006 report.[23] Outsourcing has become a staple of newswork, as documented, for example, by the shift of part of the workforce of the news agency *Reuters* and several local US and UK newspapers to India, or the attempt of German national newspaper *Süddeutsche Zeitung* to offshore its online newsroom to the Czech Republic (as reported in the *International Herald Tribune* of November 20, 2006 and the *OnlineJournalismus.de* weblog on October 29, 2006).[24] Although these are extreme examples, the practice of functional flexibility in the workforce is common throughout the news industry. Functional flexibility relates to the division of the workforce in a multi-skilled core, consisting of privileged professionals enjoying greater job security and career development performing many different tasks throughout the organization, and a periphery of semi-affiliated professionals.[25] The peripheral group tends to be temporarily employed in subcontracted or outsourcing arrangements and consists mainly of freelancers (in broadcast news called "stringers," in print journalism "correspondents"). Especially in broadcast production (of news and entertainment television shows) and magazine journalism, such a peripheral group can be quite substantial, where professionals compete with each other for assignments, budget and space. This in turn partly shifts the control over labor to the company, as workers compete for employment rather than employers compete for talented, skilled workers. Of course, the same practice enables individual newsworkers to shop around their work and talent, which in a continuing fragmentation of media platforms and niche marketing of titles is perhaps less problematic than it used to be.

Third, on a more abstract level, in today's advanced communicational democracies, society can be conceptualized as "redactional."[26] A redactional society is one where editorial practices are required for survival and are therefore not exclusive to a particular professional group such as journalists. A redactional society is one where everyone tells stories, where many if not most of these stories get distributed via the one billion or so users of internet, and thus where the storytelling of journalists is to a large extent limited to editing, annotating and packaging, rather than original writing. Under these circumstances everyone is (or can be) a journalist, in that journalism is an editorial act, one that can be equally found among the millions of amateur bloggers as among the tens of thousands of professional journalists. It would be a mistake to see the "work" of people online as part of the journalistic profession, yet one has to acknowledge the fact that the user-turned-producer significantly influences the relationship between a journalist and his or her audience.

It would also be a mistake to see the emergence of consumer-generated content alongside professional media production solely as a consequence of a widespread diffusion of ubiquitous and easy-to-use new technologies. Reporting on studies in 43 countries, Ronald Inglehart has observed a global shift of people in their roles as citizens away from nation-based politics and institutional elites, towards a distinctly skeptical, globally interconnected yet deeply personal type of self-determined civic engagement.[27] This shift occurs in the context of a trend, particularly found among the populations of Western democratic countries, towards post-materialist values and ideals. This development – which started in the early 1970s – is indicated by a shift in emphasis on economic and physical security towards goals that emphasize self-expression and quality of life. The countries where people rank self-expression values highest are nations in Scandinavia, North America, and Western Europe, as well as Australia and New Zealand, which are also among the top countries represented in the "blogosphere" according to *The Blog Herald* (reporting on February 2 2006).[28] One could add to this the high numbers of bloggers in South Korea, Iran and China, perhaps suggesting a similar spillover effect of digital culture into the wider social context as observed on a much smaller scale between an online newsroom and a journalism organization as a whole. The work of a journalist today is thus difficult to conceptualize as that of a distinct group of professionals serving a mass audience. Especially online, every journalist is on his or her own – not only because of the millions of bloggers and hundreds of millions "other" websites but also because of widespread practices such as deeplinking to specific articles or clips (e.g. *Google News/Google Video*) and subscribing to particular RSS feeds (e.g. *Google Reader*).

A fourth and final argument in favor of framing perspectives on newswork in terms of the individual is the pervasive and ubiquitous role (new) technologies play in the gathering, editing, and distribution of news. Today's printing press is the desktop or laptop personal computer equipped with broadband internet access and standard outfitted with easy-to-use publishing tools, open source software applications, and converged hardware (camera, microphone, and keyboard). If anything, this means that potentially anyone with access to such technologies and the literacies required to wield them successfully can produce (and remix) news – regardless of who or where they are. The combination of mergers and vertical integration of media conglomerates and the fast-paced diffusion of digital and networked technologies throughout the profession creates a strong impetus for individualized storytelling in journalism. Studies in the Netherlands, Canada, the USA, Britain and Spain, for example, note that technological convergence and corporate concentration must be understood as part of a strategy by media owners to acquire new sources for profit, extending their control over the relations of production and distribution of news (e.g. through forced deskilling and multiskilling practices), and aiming to undermine the collective bargaining position of journalists through their unions and trade associations by shifting towards an earlier mentioned model of individualized and contingent contracts.[29] Although one must be skeptical about a wholesale emergence of a "free agent nation"[30] among journalists, a trend towards workforce flexibility in journalism among different properties within the same mass media company is common, particularly among newcomers in the profession.

In what follows, I discuss the economic, social, and cultural organization of newswork – a framework originally suggested and developed by Michael Schudson[31] – in the context of new technologies, as seen from the perspective of the individual media professional.

The economy of newswork

The economic foundation of the news organization is a strong predictor of the appropriation and implementation of technologies in newswork. A recurring concern among journalists and scholars about the structure of ownership and control in the news industry is the issue of media concentration. Journalists particularly fear what some see as the inevitable consequences of being subsumed by a bigger company: downsizing, loss of editorial control over the creative process, and homogenization across the older and newly acquired titles. Research does not suggest that either locally independent or corporate ownership is a significant predictor of quality in news reporting.[32] Case studies on the influence of ownership on newswork in multinational organizations such as CNN and the BBC,[33] or News Corporation[34] suggests that while owners or directors can be powerful influencers of decision-making processes throughout the company, the daily management of specific divisions or departments allows for some degree of autonomy. Researchers tend to find multiple and proliferating styles of control and decision-making being tolerated in different parts of such globally networked news companies.[35]

The process of accumulation of media properties has accelerated in the 1990s, resulting in a market where there are more news outlets owned by a smaller number of media companies. This institutional trend has been supercharged by increased worldwide government deregulation on the one hand and the rapid diffusion of digital media technologies on the other. By opening up the media market to transnational ownership, foreign investments and cross-media mergers in local markets, once relatively stable news companies started to shift towards what became an industry-wide buzzword in the 1990s: convergence. The institutional characteristics of convergence are companies developing partnerships with other (journalistic and non-journalistic) media organizations to provide, promote, repurpose, or exchange news, and the introduction of cross-media (integrated) marketing and management projects.[36]

A structure of convergent multimedia news organizations has been emerging since the mid-1990s, with companies all over the world opting for at least some form of cross-media cooperation or synergy between formerly separated staffers, newsrooms, and departments. Perhaps the pioneering example is US-based Tampa Bay Online (TBO), a convergent news operation combining WFLA-TV (an NBC affiliate station), The *Tampa Tribune*, and a news website that provides original content plus material from print and television. The three media are housed in a special building called The News Center, where the different departments work together though a central multimedia news-desk. Several scholarly studies[37] and trade journal articles have reported on the TBO.com case, suggesting the gathering of breaking and daily news across the three platforms "did not happen without a lot of angst, complaints, missteps and aggravation. Some employees quit rather than change their way of doing journalism. Many more grumbled and went along. And a few rode the bull into the ring with equal parts fear and exhilaration."[38] Although the journalists involved were not universally enthusiastic, most perceived convergence ultimately as having a number of advantages relative to the long-standing system in which each news organization was independent and, in the case of the newspaper and television station, competitive. On a personal level, the journalists seemed to agree that the ability to work in more than one medium could be seen as a career booster or at least a useful addition to their resumé. Among the crucial issues involved were the lack of a common language in which to discuss, negotiate and carry out more or less integrated news coverage, sometimes an absence of effective management, and a lack of buy-in by all employees. A number of journalists at TBO told researchers that anticipated problems had either not materialized or vanished with seeing the quality or successes of the work of their colleagues, eventually gaining respect for journalists in other parts of the news organization as a result of convergence. If anything, these accounts show how changes and challenges in journalism are experienced, discarded or embraced on a distinctly individual level. A shift in doing newswork because of changing circumstances in the economy of the organization is, in other words, to a large extent dependent on the personal beliefs and behaviors of the journalist rather than the managerial skills or corporate ownership structure of the news.[39]

On the basis of content analyses of the news it is possible to argue that the concentration of media ownership and the convergence of news operations do not fundamentally challenge the fundamentals of basic news storytelling (such as a focus on institutional experts and elites as key sources, and a strict adherence to traditional news formats). However, as reporters and editors increasingly have to do their work in a context of individualized (and often contingent) contracts, cultural clashes, rapid transitions in required skill sets, and increased economic pressures, it is safe to say that newswork for its practitioners has become more risky, uncertain, stressful, and market-driven than one perhaps was aware of in the past. The key debate in the economic organization of news regarding difference or change is whether the drive towards synergy management and media convergence primarily benefits a corporate approach towards a more cost-effective standardizing and stream-lining of products across multiple properties, or if this process opens up new creative potential for better, more comprehensive, and inclusive reporting.[40]

The sociology of newswork

The sociological approach tracks the relationships between journalists and their more or less simultaneous existence in occupations, organizations, professional communities, and institutional settings.[41] This perspective typically tries to understand how journalists' efforts are constrained by organizational and occupational demands, focusing on the systematic, routinized or otherwise patterned actions, practices, and interactions by which journalists maintain themselves as journalists. In theories of newswork, this translates to an emphasis on the socialization that takes place once reporters enter a newsroom. Studies documenting the rather patterned and at times distinctly formulaic nature of work within news organizations, coupled with surveys among fulltime-employed reporters and editors, confirm such analyses.[42]

Beyond its non-permanent and contingent character, the kind of atypical employment as documented by the earlier mentioned IFJ report of 2006 remains largely invisible, as it effectively prevents journalists organizing collectively to make themselves or their concerns known. In this context all kinds of other informal organized networks have emerged, particularly on the internet. Early studies on such online networks of, for example, audio-visual media professionals suggest that beyond the expression and mobilization of interests, their effectivity to represent workers is limited.[43] On the other hand, informal networks of media workers have emerged online that contribute to a renewed sense of self among especially younger professionals in such industries. This new kind of self-identification among cultural laborers can be seen as a trans-local social movement of precarious workers, emerging beyond the traditional institutional contexts of governments, employers, as well as outside of unions or guilds.[44] Here, a shift of responsibility and accountability for employment and professional identity towards the individual coincides with a macro-level move away from institution-based to a post-national representation that is grounded in the impotence of people in their identities as citizens, consumers and workers "to shape their own social environment and [to] develop the capacity for action necessary for such interventions to succeed."[45] The late Pierre Bourdieu has been one of the fiercest critics of the increasing precariousness of work in the digital age, suggesting that living under precarious conditions prevents rational anticipation and, in particular, the basic belief and hope in the future that one needs in order to (individually or collectively) rebel against intolerable working or living conditions.[46]

The shift towards an individualization of labor counters the historical trend towards socialization and salarization, instead favoring more fluid and flexible notions of work – ushered in through rapid developments in technologies of communication, a decentralization of management practices and the fragmentation of markets. This does not mean that newcomers in journalism are not asked anymore to adapt themselves to existing ways of doing things, nor that reporters and editors are not expecting regular salaries for their work. It does suggest, however, that socialization today is quite different from the industrial master–apprentice model, where the aspiring practitioner would dutifully observe and copy an existing consensual creative process, and where newsroom socialization could be considered to be the best predictor for international news isomorphism and interinstitutional news coherence. This development runs parallel to processes of concentration and convergence in the news media. "Newsmagazines and newspapers preview their next editions on Websites that reporters and editors at other news institutions examine as soon as they are available. Newspapers advertise the next day's stories on cable news stations. The result is interinstitutional news coherence."[47]

Beyond the ongoing fragmentation of the workstyles of newsworkers lies a growing dependency of local and national news organizations on the services of two or three global multimedia information conglomerates that dominate world news: Reuters, the Associated Press (AP), and Agence France Press (AFP). Considering the dominance of these global agencies in the field of international reporting, they could be seen as "news instructors," influencing the standards of (Western) news values across the globe during the twentieth century.[48] Furthermore, Reuters, AP and AFP take advantage of the ongoing convergence within the news industries primarily through the formation of strategic alliances that increase their news gathering and distribution reach.

The individualization of labor on the one hand and the shift towards news dependency and organized networks on a global level on the other offer a different roadmap for the sociology of newswork. The relationship between employers and the employed is increasingly based on individualized, short-term, and contingent contracts rather than on companies assuming some kind of formal responsibility for the permanent employment and career development of the worker. This system has increased competition between individual workers for jobs instead of between companies for laborers, a process which keeps average wages down and increases an overall sense of insecurity among especially younger workers and junior employees. It further underscores the need for researchers who study the work of reporters and editors to recognize the limits of frameworks that document the presumed collective or group behaviors and attitudes in news organizations or professions. The news may become more the same, but the workstyles of journalists are increasingly different.

The culture of newswork

A long tradition of cultural approaches to news has documented the constraining force of broad cultural traditions and symbolic systems, and critically interrogated the historical or naturalized foundations of journalism.[49] Considering the mentioned concerns about the increasing coherence and isomorphism of news around the world, a cultural analysis of newswork tends to refer to the rather homogenous white, male and middle class makeup of the journalistic population in tandem with its overreliance on powerful business interests and ruling elites in traditional news coverage. However, current statistics on the identity of journalists are to an extent misleading as they tend to document exclusively fulltime employees and thus omit the growing legion of freelancers, temporary employees, and particularly contractual newcomers (among whom there is more diversity in terms of, for example, ethnicity and gender) in the industry. Second, the notion of "the elite" has become much more ambiguous than it was, for instance, 30 or 40 years ago. Considering that the most powerful institutions in terms of global governance today are (a wide variety of) multinational corporations and international non-governmental organizations rather than national governments or nation-based business interests, the claim of "elitist" or hegemonic reporting by journalists does not necessary indicate the perpetuation of a structural and coherent narrative.[50] What is a particular feature of newswork across media, nations and people engaged in any kind of journalism is its self-referentiality regarding a series of ideal-typical values and expectations: its news ideology.[51]

The twentieth-century history of (the professionalization of) journalism can be typified by the consolidation of a consensual occupational ideology among journalists in different parts of the world.[52] Although most scholarly work on journalism is reduced to studies of institutional and mainstream "hard" news journalism, research on other more feminine or so called "alternative" journalisms suggests journalists across genres and media types invoke more or less the same ideal-typical value system when discussing and reflecting on their work.[53] In the eyes of journalists, five ideal-typical values give legitimacy and add credibility to what reporters and editors do: public service, objectivity, autonomy, immediacy, and ethics. Journalists provide a public service as watchdogs or newshounds, active collectors and disseminators of information. They strive to be impartial, neutral, objective, fair and (thus) credible. They must be autonomous, free and independent to do their work effectively. They have a sense of immediacy, actuality and speed inherent in the concept of news. And they have a sense of ethics, validity and legitimacy. Newsworkers base their professional perceptions and practices on this ideology, but may interpret or apply it differently across media or news cultures.[54] Ideology does not presuppose that journalists (or those who claim to be journalists) think and act all the same – it does suggest, however, that in order to self-legitimize what they do they all implicitly or explicitly refer to one or more elements of the same set of ideal-typical values. This process can be observed by interviewing journalists or by analyzing news standards of different news outlets, locales, or even countries. "It is as if journalists were unconsciously multilingual, code-switching from neutral interpreters to guardians of social consensus and back again without missing a beat."[55] The value set of journalisms' ideology may not mean the same for everyone, nor is it necessarily internally consistent – but it does serve journalism to continuously reinvent itself.

What is important to note here is that none of these values can be considered exclusive to journalism as a profession. Some would argue that "as traditional distinctions between professional and popular communicators become less clear in this open, participatory, interconnected media environment, 'professional' journalists will not be distinguished by the products they produce nor the processes through which they do so. Rather, their norms will become increasingly definitive."[56] However, such norms and values take on meaning through the processes of gathering, selecting, editing, and disseminating any kind of public information as well as through the decision-making media logic of the medium, the news department, or individual practitioner (freelancer, stringer, correspondent) involved. The ideology of journalism cannot just be seen as enabling journalism as a profession or institution to self-police its borders – in the contemporary mediascape it is also a value system that in fact empowers each and every one to proclaim "Journalism!" when they see (or do) it. In terms of the work of journalists, its occupational ideology can be seen to act as a crucial qualifier in articulating the relationship between the self-similar packaging and formatting of news worldwide and the active role of the journalist in establishing a more or less distinct voice. Longitudinal surveys among journalists (in Western countries) show consistently how reporters and editors have come to consider explaining the news more important to their jobs than just reporting it. In content analyses, this preference particularly shows in the shrinking of time, space and visuals allotted to sources – whether experts, elites or others – while journalists themselves feature more and more prominently in (often their own) news reports.

As argued earlier, converging operations and multimedia newsrooms are transforming the practice and education of journalism worldwide. The disparity of approaches and models of teaching and researching multimedia reveal one thing at least: multimedia means different things to different people. The convergence process that characterizes multimedia poses challenges to departmentalized news organizations, and is generally considered to threaten a news culture that prefers individual expert systems and group-think over teamwork and knowledge sharing. Professional experience and the literature suggest that new media technologies challenge one of the most fundamental "truths" in journalism, namely: the professional journalists is the one who determines what publics see, hear and read about the world.[57] The combination of mastering newsgathering and storytelling techniques in all media formats, as well as the integration of digital network technologies coupled with a rethinking of the news producer–consumer relationship tends to be seen as one of the biggest challenges facing journalism in the twenty-first century.

In more or less converged news operations, the multimedia journalist has to make decisions about what kind of platforms to utilize when practicing his or her craft and in the case of multimedia productions has to oversee story packages rather than repurposing single stories in multiple formats. This relates to organizational features of convergent media and the competences of journalists working in such new media contexts. Applied research suggests how multimedia news operations prefer to organize people in teams and to arrange these working units in cross-departmentalized ways.[58] This advice is underscored by the experiences of multimedia newsrooms around the world. A survey by multimedia consulting firm *Innovation* – commissioned by the World Association of Newspapers – conducted in 2001 among media executives worldwide cited as the biggest obstacle to media convergence "the individualistic nature of journalists" (mentioned by 31 per cent of all respondents). If anything, these examples show how the cultural use of journalism's occupational ideology can be a tool for individual journalists to strategically resist, modify, or even counteract technology-driven innovation or imposed change in news operations.

Conclusion

What these contemporary articulations of dominant perspectives on newswork suggest, then, is a focus on the news-producing individual as the source of explanations for the content available in today's increasingly complex and at times overwhelming media system. In the strictest sense, this is not a novel argument. As an example one could consider how "the myopia of traditional definitions of news is proof enough that personal perspective colors news."[59] This may be true, but a long tradition of journalism studies regarding the role and actions of journalists within newsrooms and news organizations has also shown how much of their individual agency gets filtered out through socialization, editorial policies, ownership structures, and occupational ideology. Yet we find ourselves drawn into a discernibly different media ecology today which to some extent offers each and every individual the hardware, software, skill and post-materialist will to self-publish. Furthermore, scrutiny of each aspect of contemporary changes and challenges in the work and employment of journalists suggests that each trend, while amplified by new technologies, opens up creative affordances for individual journalists at the same time as it potentially restricts their editorial autonomy. Even though (global) news becomes more streamlined and standardized across media, the role and work of individual journalists is moving in an opposite direction. No doubt, this increases the opportunities for labor exploitation. Yet it also shows how an analysis of what is happening to journalism can move beyond discourses of imitation and change and facilitate the agency of journalists.

Notes

1 Martin Loeffelholz (ed.), *Theorien des Journalismus* (Opladen: Westdeutscher Verlag, 2000); Brian McNair, *Sociology of Journalism* (London: Routledge, 2003); Barbie Zelizer, *Taking Journalism Seriously* (Thousand Oaks: Sage, 2004).

2 M. Aldridge and J. Evetts, "Rethinking the Concept of Professionalism: the Case of Journalism," *The British Journal of Sociology* 54(4), 2003, 547–64; Eric Klinenberg, "Convergence: News Production in a Digital Age," *The Annals of the American Academy of Political and Social Sciences* 597, 2005, 48–64; Thomas Hanitzsch, "Establishing Equivalence in Comparative Journalism Research: Journalism, Editorial Organizations and Journalists as Objects of Inquiry," *Revista de Jornalismo* 8, 2006, 115–33.

3 Michael Schudson, "Four Approaches to the Sociology of News," in James Curran and Michael Gurevitch (eds.), *Mass Media and Society*, 4th edition (London: Hodder Arnold, 2005), 172–97.

4 I borrowed the term "workstyle" from several professional agencies in the field of management and human resources. See, for example, the site of a British professional coaching agency called The Results Agency (available at: www.theresultsagency.co.uk), Dutch agency Bureau Eveleens (available at: www.workstyle.nl), German work style management consultancy D@ccord 4u (available at: www.daccord4u.de), and Australian coaching agency MerryMentality (available at: http://www.merrymentality. com.au).

5 David Weaver (ed.), *The Global Journalist: News People Around the World* (Cresskill, NJ: Hampton Press, 1998).

6 International Federation of Journalists, "The Changing Nature of Work: A Global Survey and Case Study of Atypical Work in the Media Industry" (Switzerland: IFJ/ ILO, 2006). Available at: www.ifj.org

7 Mark Deuze, *Wat is Journalistiek* [What is journalism] (Amsterdam: Spinhuis, 2004).

8 Source: personal e-mail communication with South African journalism researcher Herman Wasserman August 4, 2007.

9 International Federation of Journalists, "Freelance Futures: World Survey of the Social and Economic Status of Freelance Journalists" (Brussels: International Federation of Journalists; 1999); G. Nies and R. Pedersini, "Freelance Journalists in the European Media Industry" (Brussels: International Federation of Journalists, 2003). Available at: www.ifj-europe.org

10 David Hesmondhalgh, *The Cultural Industries*, 2nd edition (London: Sage, 2007).

11 Henry Jenkins, *Convergence Culture: Where Old and New Media Collide* (New York: New York University Press; 2006); Mark Deuze, *Media Work* (Cambridge: Polity Press, 2007).

12 D.C. Feldman, "Toward a New Taxonomy for Understanding the Nature and Consequences of Contingent Employment," *Career Development International* 11(1), 2006, 28–47.

13 Barbie Zelizer, "The Culture of Journalism," in James Curran and Michael Gurevitch(eds.), *Mass Media and Society*, 4th edition (London: Hodder Arnold, 2005), 198–214.

14 L. McFall, "The Culturalization of Work in the New Economy: an Historical View," in T. Elgaard Jensen and A. Westenholz (eds.), *Identity in the Age of the New Economy: Life in Temporary and Scattered Work Practices* (Cheltenham: Edward Elgar, 2004), 9–33.

15 Mark Deuze, C. Neuberger and S. Paulussen, "Journalism Education and Online Journalists in Belgium, Germany, and The Netherlands," *Journalism Studies* 5(1), 2004, 19–29; Thorsten Quandt, Martin Löffelholz, David Weaver, Thomas Hanitzsch and K. Altmeppen, "American and German Online Journalists at the Beginning of the 21st Century," *Journalism Studies* 7(2), 2006, 171–86.

16 Mark Deuze, "The Web and its Journalisms: Considering the Consequences of Different Types of News Media Online," *New Media & Society* 5(2), 2003, 203–30; Pablo Boczkowski, *Digitizing the News: Innovation in Online Newspapers* (Boston: MIT Press, 2004).

17 Stephen Reese, "Understanding the Global Journalist: A Hierarchy-of-influences Approach," *Journalism Studies* 2(2), 2001, 173–87; A. Scholl and S. Weischenberg, *Journalismus in der Gesellschaft: Theorie, Methodologie und Empirie* (Opladen: Westdeutscher Verlag, 1998).

18 Richard Sennett, *The Culture of the New Capitalism* (New Haven: Yale University Press, 2006).

19 Paul Du Gay and Michael Pryke (eds.), *Cultural Economy: Cultural Analysis and Commercial Life* (London: Sage, 2002).

20 J. Storey, G. Salaman and K. Platman, "Living with Enterprise in an Enterprise Economy: Freelance and Contract Workers in the Media," *Human Relations* 58(8), 2005, 1033–54.

21 W. Lowrey and W. Anderson, "The Journalist Behind the Curtain: Participatory Functions on the Internet and their Impact on Perceptions of the Work of Journalism," *Journal of Computer-Mediated Communication* 10(3), 2005, available at: www.jcmc.indiana. edu; G. Gall, "New Technology, the Labour Process and Employment Relations in the Provincial Newspaper Industry," *New Technology, Work and Employment* 15(2), 2000, 94–107; T. Marjoribanks, "Strategising Technological Innovation," in Simon Cottle (ed.), *Media Organization and Production* (London: Sage, 2000), 59–75.

22 A. Kalleberg, "Nonstandard Employment Relations: Part-time, Temporary and Contract Work," *Annual Review of Sociology* 26, 2000, 341–65.

23 Shaping the Future of the Newspaper, "Outsourcing," Strategy Report 5.2 (World Association of Newspapers, April 2006), available at: www.wan-press.org

24 Available at: www.iht.com and www.onlinejournalismus.de

25 P. A. Reilly, "Balancing Flexibility-Meeting the Interests of Employer and Employee," *European Journal of Work and Organizational Psychology* 7(1), 1998, 7–22.

26 John Hartley, "Communicational Democracy in a Redactional Society: The Future of Journalism Studies," *Journalism: Theory, Practice, Criticism* 1(1), 2000, 39–47.

27 Ronald Inglehart, *Modernization and Postmodernization* (Princeton: Princeton University Press, 1997).

28 See Ronald Inglehart and C. Welzel, *Modernization, Cultural Change, and Democracy: the Human Development Sequence* (Cambridge: Cambridge University Press, 2005), 155; on weblogs, available at: www.blogherald.com

29 See especially the work of C. McKercher, *Newsworkers Unite: Labor, Convergence and North American Newspapers* (Lanham: Rowman & Littlefield, 2002).

30 D. H. Pink, *Free Agent Nation* (New York: Warner Business Books, 2001).

31 Schudson "Four Approaches."

32 Project for Excellence in Journalism, "Does Ownership Matter in Local Television News: A Five-Year Study of Ownership and Quality," (Washington, DC: PEJ, 2003). Available at: www.journalism.org

33 L. Kung-Shankleman, "Organisational Culture Inside the BBC and CNN," in Simon Cottle (ed.), *Media Organization and Production*, (London: Sage, 2003).

34 T. Marjoribanks, *News Corporation, Technology and the Workplace: Global Strategies, Local Change* (Cambridge: Cambridge University Press, 2000).

35 E. Louw, *The Media and Cultural Production* (London: Sage, 2001).

36 S. Quinn, *Convergence Journalism* (New York: Peter Lang, 2001).

37 Jane B. Singer, "Strange Bedfellows: the Diffusion of Convergence in Four News Organizations," *Journalism Studies* 5(1), 2004, 3–18; E. Huang, K. Davison, S. Shreve, T. Davis, E. Bettendorf, and A. Nair, "Facing the Challenges of Convergence: Media Professionals' Concerns of Working Across Media Platforms," *Convergence* 12 (1), 2006, 83–98; W. Silcock and S. Keith, "Translating the Tower of Babel Issues of Definition, Language, and Culture in Converged Newsrooms," *Journalism Studies* 7(4), 2006, 610–27; M. Dupagne and B. Garrison, "The Meaning and Influence of Convergence: A Qualitative Case Study of Newsroom Work at the Tampa News Center," *Journalism Studies* 7(2), 2006, 237–55.

38 Quote taken from trade magazine article: J. Stevens, "TBO.com: Then and Now," *Online Journalism Review* (April 3, 2002), available at: www.ojr.org

39 R. Beam, "Organizational Goals and Priorities and the Job Satisfaction of U.S. Journalists," *Journalism & Mass Communication Quarterly* 83(1), 2006, 169–85.

40 Mark Deuze, "What is Multimedia Journalism " *Journalism Studies* 5(2), 2004b, 139–52.

41 Zelizer, *Taking Journalism Seriously*, 47ff.

42 Mark Deuze, "National News Cultures: Towards a Profile of Journalists Using Cross-National Survey Findings," *Journalism & Mass Communication Quarterly* 79 (1), 2002, 134–49.

43 R. Saundry, M. Stuart and V. Antcliff, "Broadcasting Discontent—Freelancers, Trade Unions and the Internet," *New Technology, Work and Employment* 22(2), 2007, 178–91.

44 C. Bodnar, "Taking it to the Streets: French Cultural Worker Resistance and the Creation of a Precariat Movement," *Canadian Journal of Communication* [online] 31(3), 2006. Available at: www.cjc-online.ca.

45 Jurgen Habermas, *The Postnational Constellation*, tr. Max Pensky (Boston: MIT Press, 2001), 60.

46 Pierre Bourdieu, *Acts of Resistance: Against the New Myths of our Time* (Cambridge: Polity Press, 1998).

47 Michael Schudson, *The Sociology of News* (New York: W.W. Norton & Company, 2003).

48 Oliver Boyd-Barrett and Terhi Rantanen, "News Agency Foreign Correspondents," in Jeremy Tunstall (ed.), *Media Occupations and Professions* (Oxford: Oxford University Press, 2001), 127–43.

49 R. Renger, "Journalismus als kultureller Diskurs," in Martin Loeffelholz (ed.), *Theorien des Journalismus* (Opladen: Westdeutscher Verlag, 2001), 467–81; Barbie Zelizer, "When Facts, Truth and Reality are God-terms: On Journalism's Uneasy Place in Cultural Studies," *Communication and Critical/Cultural Studies* 1(1), 2001, 100–119.

50 D. Archibugi, D. Held and M. Köhler (eds.), *Re-imagining Political Community: Studies in Cosmopolitan Democracy* (Palo Alto: Stanford University Press, 1998).

51 J. Westerstahl and F. Johansson, "News Ideologies as Molders of Domestic News," *European Journal of Communication* 1, 1986, 133–49.

52 Mark Deuze, "What is Journalism Professional Identity and Ideology of Journalists Reconsidered," *Journalism Theory Practice & Criticism* 6(4), 2005, 443–65.

53 Lizbet van Zoonen, "A Professional, Unreliable, Heroic Marionette (M/F): Structure, Agency and Subjectivity in Contemporary Journalisms," *European Journal of Cultural Studies* 1(1), 1998, 123–43.

54 Pamela Shoemaker and Stephen Reese, *Mediating the Message: Theories of Influences on Mass Media Content* (New York: Longman, 1996).
55 Michael Schudson, "The Newsmedia as Political Institutions," *Annual Review of Political Science* 5, 2002, 263.
56 Jane B. Singer, "Contested Autonomy: Professional and Popular Claims on Journalistic Norms," *Journalism Studies* 8(1), 2007, 90.
57 Jane B. Singer, "Online Journalists: Foundation for Research into their Changing Roles," *Journal of Computer-Mediated Communication* [online] 4(1), 1998. Available at: www.jcmc.indiana.edu
58 K. Killebrew, *Managing Media Convergence: Pathways to Journalistic Cooperation* (Malden: Blackwell, 2004).
59 B. Kovach and T. Rosenstiel, *The Elements of Journalism* (New York: Crown Publishers, 2001), 109.

On Truthiness

Chapter 9

Rethinking Truth Through Truthiness

Keren Tenenboim-Weinblatt

The notion of truth – once essential to any understanding of journalism and democracy – appears to have fallen off the agenda of communication scholars. Depending on one's position in the field, truth as a theoretical concept has become obsolete, impertinent, banned, self-evident or too explosive to handle. When used, it is commonly put in quotation marks, to indicate irony or the author's recognition of its unattainability. This has resulted, among other things, in a widening chasm between scholars and journalists, who continue to hold truth and facts as "god-terms" despite the widespread currency of constructivist approaches.[1]

However, as the three essays in this section suggest, recent changes in the media and political environment may provide an impetus for rethinking the concept of truth and reincorporating it into academic discourse. To a large degree, these changes are embodied in the notion of truthiness, introduced by comedian Stephen Colbert in the inaugural episode of Comedy Central's fake punditry show *The Colbert Report*. Truthiness – selected as "word of the year" by the American Dialect Society (for 2005) and by Merriam-Webster's online community (for 2006) – refers to truth claims based on gut feeling or wishful thinking rather than facts or evidence. As Colbert satirically describes his own book (where he continues to play the part of a conservative pundit):

> It's not just some collection of reasoned arguments supported by facts. That's the coward's way out. This book is Truth – my Truth. I deliver my Truth hot and hard. Fast and furious. So either accept it without hesitation or get out of the way.[2]

Coming from a "fake journalist" and offering a critique aimed at both journalists and politicians, the notion of truthiness directs our attention to three interrelated dimensions of the changing regime of truth: 1) the practices of truth telling in contemporary political culture; 2) the standards and nature of truth in different sectors of the journalistic sphere; and 3) the ways in which journalistic "outliers" like Stephen Colbert and Jon Stewart challenge the authority of mainstream journalism, the definition of a journalist, and notions about what truth in journalism really is. Each author in this section focuses primarily on one of these three dimensions, and together they offer a provocative and multifaceted analysis of the meaning of truth in the new media and political environment, and of the complex interactions between politics, journalism and the academy in shaping the current regime of truth.

Michael Schudson explores the relationship between truth and politics, while focusing on the Bush administration and its truth-telling practices. Revisiting Hannah Arendt's discussions of truth and lying in politics and drawing upon a wide range of historical examples, Schudson argues that the Bush administration introduced a new form of relationship between truth and politics. Lying in politics is hardly a new phenomenon, observes Schudson, but the demotion of facts in the post-9/11 political culture adds a new dimension to the uneasy relationship of truth and politics, that is adequately (albeit not fully) captured by the notion of truthiness. According to Schudson, the disregard for facts in the political realm has prompted the need to resuscitate facts and truth within the academy, which along with journalism and other investigative agencies in and outside the government constitute a crucial arena for counteracting truthiness in the political realm.

James S. Ettema also foregrounds truthiness as a critical tool but directs our gaze to the journalistic world. He concurs with much of the criticism embedded in the notion of truthiness – particularly that aimed at Fox News-style programs – but suggests that some of the best and most truthful investigative stories are precisely those that "feel the news" at their readers and are based on a moral categorization of the facts. Ettema illustrates the intertwining of facts, values and narrative coherence in the pursuit of journalistic truth and, similarly to Schudson, sees the cultural moment of truthiness as "an opportunity to introduce a useful conception of truth" that will accommodate the contradictory forces shaping the daily work of journalists.

Jeffrey P. Jones turns our attention to the herald of truthiness – the satirist – and to the broader epistemological changes in the media and political culture that truthiness signifies. Truthiness, observes Jones, highlights a move from a journalism-centered regime of truth to a regime where citizens, politicians and various institutions and groups are involved in creative constructions of truth through widespread redactional practices. Jones considers the democratic potential of these practices but also warns against the dangerous repercussions of a political culture in which "truth in fact is less important than truth in essence." Satirists, he argues, play an important role in this new regime of truth, not by authoritatively asserting the truth (like "traditional" journalists) or by creating what Jones calls "believable fictions" (like certain partisan pundits), but by using redactional practices to fight truthiness on its own terms.

Significantly, each of the three authors introduces concepts and distinctions that transcend the dichotomy between relativism and absolutism and demonstrate the potential of employing diverse philosophical theories of truth to complicate and deepen our understanding of journalism and politics. One distinction, invoked by Ettema, is that between correspondence and coherence theories. Whereas correspondence theories suggest that truth consists in a relation to an objective reality – a proposition is true if it corresponds to the way the world is – coherence theories hold that truth consists in the proposition's relation to other propositions, that is, a certain assertion is true when and only when it belongs to a coherent system of judgments. Ettema cogently demonstrates how correspondence to the facts is necessary but neither sufficient nor always feasible in the journalistic pursuit of truth, and how central coherence considerations are to this complicated process.

The notion of "factual truth" is both defended and tweaked by Schudson, who acknowledges the vulnerability of facts and the impossibility of achieving a Habermasian consensus on what the facts are, but views factual knowledge as "the least bad system of knowing" and provides a contemporary interpretation of Arendt's and Lippmann's conceptualizations of truth and politics. His discussion of the role of academics, journalists and other experts in civil society and the government as professional (though imperfect) truth tellers sheds a new light on the debate over Lippmann's ideas on the relationship between expertise and democracy.

Finally, Jones's discussion of "truth in essence" – in contrast to factual truth – echoes the phenomenological conception of truth, originating with Husserl and Heidegger. The notion of "truth in essence" is usually invoked in the context of media products such as docudramas, biopics or historical movies, when complaints about truthfulness are met with the argument that techniques such as reconstruction, composite characters or time compression capture the essence of truth rather than simple factual accuracy. However, as Jones observes, "truth in essence" has come to be one of the defining qualities of a wide range of media products in the contemporary political culture, requiring scholars to critically reflect on the meaning and implications of this standard of truth.

Together, these three essays not only advance our understanding of the intricate relationship between truth, journalism and politics, but also elucidate the pathways for embarking upon the project of (re)taking truth seriously within communication studies. In exploring truth through the prism of truthiness, they remind us that such a journey can begin in the most unlikely venues.

Notes

1 Barbie Zelizer, "When Facts, Truth, and Reality are God-terms: On Journalism's Uneasy Place in Cultural Studies," *Communication and Critical/Cultural Studies*, 1, no. 1 (2004): 100–119.
2 Stephen Colbert, *I am America (and so can you!)* (New York: Grand Central Publishing, 2007), viii.

Chapter 10

Factual Knowledge in the Age of Truthiness[1]

Michael Schudson

In Charles Dickens' "Christmas Carol," Scrooge meets Marley's ghost but cannot believe it is really Marley's ghost. "Why," the ghost asks, "do you doubt your senses?" "Because," Scrooge replies, "a little thing affects them. A slight disorder of the stomach makes them cheats. You," he says, addressing the ghost, "may be an undigested bit of beef, a blot of mustard, a crumb of cheese, a fragment of an underdone potato. There's more of gravy than of grave about you, whatever you are!"

This is where we begin – with the fragility of human knowledge, the vulnerability of our perceptions, the uncertainty of our methods of validation. And yet, for all that, these days whole dissertations and books are being written based on a very surprising assumption: that there is a deep and widespread consensus on what the facts are.

I refer not to just any old facts. I refer to two specific facts: 1) facts established by the scientific community, particularly about global warming, and 2) reported facts, or their absence, particularly concerning whether there was a connection between Osama bin Laden and Saddam Hussein and whether Iraq in 2003 possessed weapons of mass destruction.

The revival of facts during the Bush administration

No prior US presidency raised so directly questions of ontology and epistemology. A cottage industry of articles, books and dissertations has been inspired by a self-righteous certainty about the factuality of climate change or the absence of factual evidence of weapons of mass destruction in Iraq. In 2004, Michael P. Lynch, a philosopher at the University of Connecticut and author of two prior volumes on the nature of truth, wrote *True to Life: Why Truth Matters*. It begins as follows: "In early 2003 President Bush claimed that Iraq was attempting to purchase the materials necessary to build nuclear weapons."[2] I came upon this quotation a week after sitting on a political science dissertation committee in which the candidate proposed a dissertation to help understand why something like half of the US voting population believed that we had in fact found weapons of mass destruction in Iraq and, furthermore, that Saddam Hussein had worked with Osama Bin Laden in planning the 9/11 terrorist attacks.

These misperceptions (how do I know these are misperceptions? How do you know? I will return to this matter later) have attracted great interest among both academics and political partisans. *New York Times* columnist Frank Rich subtitled his 2006 book on the Bush administration, "The Decline and Fall of Truth in Bush's America."[3] In liberal academic circles, possibly the most often repeated quotation (other than the "Mission Accomplished" banner behind President Bush on the aircraft carrier Lincoln) to come out of nearly eight years of the Bush administration comes from an unidentified White House source – whom knowledgeable people assume is Karl Rove – cited in a 2004 *New York Times Magazine* piece by journalist Ron Suskind. The White House aide remarked that Suskind and his fellow journalists were part of "what we call the reality-based community," a group defined as people who "believe that solutions emerge from (your) judicious study of discernible reality." But, the aide continued, "That's not the way the world really works anymore. We're an empire now, and when we act, we create our own reality. And while you're studying that reality – judiciously, as you will – we'll act again, creating other new realities, which you can study too, and that's how things will sort out. We're history's actors ... and you, all of you, will be left to just study what we do."[4]

This is a remarkably chilling statement – not because it is wrong but because it is both arrogant and true. Rove has taken the knowledge/power couplet very seriously indeed, and he takes it at its most cynical – not to suggest an inextricable link between knowledge and power but to assert an inevitable and abject subordination of knowledge to power.

Of course, the Bush administration follows in a long line of administrations that lie to the Congress and to the public and perhaps to themselves. Eisenhower lied about the U-2 flights (and then, when caught in the lie, apologized in considerable embarrassment). Kennedy dissembled over the Bay of Pigs, pleading successfully with the news media to withhold information journalists had picked up – but declaring the next year that it would have been better for the USA if the truth had come out. Johnson promoted the most flattering estimates of military success in Vietnam while ignoring more skeptical judgments. Nixon lied, hid, erased, and covered up. Reagan could not remember decision-making about Iran-contra. Clinton perjured himself over his sexual escapades. But if it would be a mistake to imagine that the Bush administration is unique in its contempt for truth, it would also be a mistake to assume that its falsehood is just more of the same. Earlier lies and evasions acknowledged the central value of truth. If hypocrisy is the homage vice pays to virtue, as La Rochefoucauld wrote, lying is the flattery that self-interest pays to truth. The Bush administration brazenly denies external standards of truth; truth is whatever we – the administration – make of the world, not what we find in it.

Grounded reality versus Bush administration "truthiness"

The term "reality" has itself become a proxy for antagonism to the Bush administration's policies. The *Washington Post* foreign correspondent Rajiv Chandrasekaran introduced his memoir of reporting in Iraq with a brief prologue concerning his encounter with John Agresto whose personal connection to Vice President Dick Cheney and his wife Lynn Cheney brought him to Iraq in 2003 to restore Iraq's 22 universities to operation. Agresto arrived with optimism and with his neo-conservative views intact. Nine months later, it was different. His visits to the universities around the country had become dangerous – and thus rare. He estimated that he would need a billion dollars to do the job the administration asked of him – and he received less than one per cent of that sum. He grew agitated as he spoke to Chandrasekaran. Gravely, he confessed, "I'm a neoconservative who's been mugged by reality."[5] Cut. End of scene. And then Chandrasekaran begins his book, taking readers inside the Green Zone in Baghdad whose bizarre unreality led American residents to refer to it as the "emerald city."

For a long time in the humanities and "softer" social sciences, including among some very rigorous and hard-nosed thinkers, the term "positivist" was thrown around as a damning epithet. Anyone who actually believed that conventional means of gathering data could get at something we might call truth or who believed that there really are facts about the world rather than competing ways of looking at the world was condemned as hopelessly naïve and probably dangerously reactionary.

Positivism was definitely out of fashion.

This has changed. One side of the change dates to October 17, 2005. On that evening, the opening episode of Stephen Colbert's "The Colbert Report" premiered on Comedy Central, and Colbert invented the word "truthiness." The word is defined by Wikipedia – who better? – as "a satirical term created by television comedian Stephen Colbert to describe things that a person claims to know intuitively or 'from the gut' without regard to evidence, logic, intellectual examination, or actual facts." Frank Rich adopts the term to refer to the story the Bush administration sold to the American public about the war in Iraq, a story "at variance with the facts that were known at the time" that nonetheless had "a slick patina of plausibility."[6]

Facts, in an old-fashioned positivist way, have been having something of a revival ever since. Even people who had once seemed to be ardent social constructionists – reality is a meaning we put together, not an unmalleable thing we find – were suddenly horrified to learn that many Americans believe Saddam Hussein helped plan the 9/11 terrorist attacks, and many Americans are confident that the American military discovered weapons of mass destruction stockpiled in Iraq. Others who have been critical of quantitative social science or public opinion polling or other constructions that claim to represent reality are outraged at the false reports the Bush administration concocted concerning the heroism of Jessica Lynch or the death of Pat Tillman. But what ground for horror or outrage about falsehood can there be if there is no access to a factual reality the propaganda betrays?

As Stephen Colbert said, "It used to be, everyone was entitled to their own opinion, but not their own facts. But that's not the case any more. Facts matter not at all. Perception is everything. It's certainty. People love the President because he's certain of his choices as a leader, even if the facts that back him up don't seem to exist." President Bush, Colbert said in his first use of the term "truthiness," backed Harriet Miers for the Supreme Court because, as Bush put it, "I know her heart," and as Colbert observed, "He *feels* the truth about Harriet Miers." And he adds, "And what about Iraq? If you think about it, maybe there are a few missing pieces to the rationale for war. But doesn't taking Saddam out *feel* like the right thing?"[7]

Hannah Arendt's defense of facts

"No one has ever doubted that truth and politics are on rather bad terms with each other," wrote Hannah Arendt, "and no one, as far as I know, has ever counted truthfulness among the political virtues. Lies have always been regarded as the necessary and justifiable tools not only of the politicians or the demagogue's but also of the statesman's trade."[8]

Arendt saw that power threatened truth, particularly "factual truth." Formal or rational truths like "two plus two equals four" are not as vulnerable as factual truth because "facts and events – the invariable outcome of men living and acting together – constitute the very text of the political realm." Factual truth is very vulnerable to politics – "it is always in danger of being maneuvered out of the world not only for a time but, potentially, forever. Facts and events are infinitely more fragile things than axioms, discoveries, theories – even the most wildly speculative ones – produced by the human mind; they occur in the field of the ever-changing affairs of men, in whose flux there is nothing more permanent than the admittedly relative permanence of the human mind's structure."[9]

But how, in our sophisticated age, could Arendt speak of "facts" at all? Even 40 years ago, when she wrote these words, she was of course well aware that the very concept of a fact was under indictment. She asked, "But do facts, independent of opinion and interpretation, exist at all? Have not generations of historians and philosophers of history demonstrated the impossibility of ascertaining facts without interpretation, since they must first be picked out of a chaos of sheer happenings (and the principles of choice are surely not factual data) and then be fitted into a story that can be told only in a certain perspective, which has nothing to do with the original occurrence?" Arendt conceded all this but then boldly asserted that these perplexities "are no argument against the existence of factual matter, nor can they serve as a justification for blurring the dividing lines between fact, opinion, and interpretation, or as an excuse for the historian to manipulate facts as he pleases."[10]

Arendt then offered an example of what she meant by this, an example that became a paradigm case for the rest of her essay. There is a story, she wrote, that Clemenceau, some time in the 1920s, was engaged in a discussion about the question of war guilt for World War I. He was asked what future historians would think about the question. He replied, "This I don't know. But I know for certain that they will not say Belgium invaded Germany." Arendt then added that this was not just up to the historians, that it would take "a power monopoly over the entire civilized world" to erase the fact that on August 4, 1914 German troops crossed into Belgium rather than Belgian troops crossing into Germany. And then – ever a realist – she noted that "such a power monopoly is far from being inconceivable, and it is not difficult to imagine what the fate of factual truth would be if power interests, national or social, had the last say in these matters."[11]

Is there any way out of this battle between politics and truth? Well, yes, there is, for Arendt, but it depends on how politics operates in a particular instance. Some polities tolerate or even encourage the establishment of institutions inside the polity that stand at arm's length from power. She cited the judiciary and the academy as two domains where "at least in constitutionally ruled countries, the political realm has recognized, even in the event of conflict, that it has a stake in the existence of men and institutions over which it has no power."[12] This is a point of fundamental importance. It is a messy point, to be sure. We know that the judiciary can be corrupted by power. We know that universities, although they may be in some corners a haven of critical and independent thought, are also eager to serve power. But we do not live in a perfect world nor will we. And the effort to invent and institutionalize the self-divided profession of truth telling or independent judgment may be as good as we get.

To the judiciary and the academy, I would add "experts" generally and independent journalism specifically.

Journalism and other resources for factuality

Journalism is not a perfect vessel of truth. Its coverage of politics is based on unspoken, often unconscious and sometimes unjustified assumptions about politics. In 1920 Walter Lippmann looked with distress upon the American journalism of which he was a part. He believed journalism was incapable of reforming itself, that it did not have the intellectual resources to present an accurate picture of the world. If it succeeded – and he still hoped it might – it would be because entities outside journalism – in government, in the universities, and in private organizations, all of which he called "political observatories" – would come to provide reliable research reports for reporters to relay to the public.[13] Lippmann did not believe that the public would do very much with these materials – people could not absorb it all even if they wanted to, and for the most part people just were not interested enough in the world beyond their doorstep. But either from the political observatories directly or through reports of them in the news, government would come to operate with a more realistic vision of the world.

Ninety years later, the problems of journalism today are of a different order. We see the deterioration of the economic structure that has sustained news gathering since the late nineteenth century. We see the erosion or demise of substantial local news organizations. The floundering of metropolitan daily newspapers is dire, but the picture is not all gloomy. First, the maturing of a more professional, detached, and analytical media over the past century and especially the past half century has been impressive. Nineteenth-century American journalism was a party-subsidized partisan press. It began to be a commercially driven but professionally produced press late in that century when, to the astonishment and outrage of European visitors, it seemed to develop a mania for reports rather than commentary and polemic. This transformation was rooted in economic, social and political changes that made a newspaper's political independence feasible, that made the press prosperous enough to support a large group of workers who began to take their collective reputation as reporters seriously, that made "science" a term of high praise, and that rejected the excessive enthusiasm of party politics. Still, US journalism up to the 1960s was frequently mediocre – less critical, less investigative, and more deferential to government office holders than it is today, and significantly more narrow in its outlook (notably concerning women, minorities, gays and lesbians, and most topics a few steps away from government, politics, and the economy). The news was less enterprising than today in exploring topics not already on the agenda of leading law-makers. In my judgment, historical studies of the press offer no grounds for nostalgia for the ghost of journalism past – nineteenth-century American newspapers were bitterly and wildly partisan in the cities while the country papers were generally bland.

Second, in the past decade, there has been a vast multiplication on the internet of the voices of civil society and exponents of media accountability. The rise of a global civil society, linked to the globalization of journalism itself, is powerful and transformative. There are many new journalistic voices (notably, bloggers) and new journalistic forms and forums (blogs, news aggregators, wikis, e-government sources). Meanwhile, conventional media that were once distributed locally have a new online presence that makes them nationally and globally available to hundreds of millions.

Third, many more organizations today are dedicated to informing citizens about public affairs in more systematic and ongoing ways than just the conventional news media. Some of the most important of these new "news organizations" are bureaus and departments in the government itself. Consider revelations about the use of national security letters. The FBI was authorized by various statutes that date to the 1970s to obtain private records without a court order or court review – telephone records, internet communication records, bank records, consumer credit records – but only if the FBI had specific reason to think that the entity whose records were being sought was a foreign power or agent of a foreign power. And only a very few senior FBI officials could issue a national security letter (NSL). The USA PATRIOT Act in 2001 broadened this greatly – many more FBI officials could issue the letters, the information sought no longer needed to relate to a foreign power, and the threshold for seeking the information was only that it be relevant to an investigation of international terrorism or espionage.

So, what happened thereafter? We know quite a lot about what happened thereafter: the FBI abused this power many times. How do we know? We know because of the Department of Justice Inspector General, Glenn Fine. Fine issued a report documenting the abuses, submitting his report to the Congress as well as to the FBI and the Justice Department, and because of course the press then reported it. That was in March, 2007. At that point, the Electronic Frontier Foundation filed a Freedom of Information Act lawsuit seeking further information on the FBI misuse of NSL authority. The FBI took its time. A federal judge ordered the FBI to release information responsive to that request. In July, 2007, the FBI disclosed a first batch of 1100 pages to the Electronic Frontier Foundation (EFF), all of which one can examine on the EFF website (www.eff.org). These disclosures show, among other things, that several cases of abuse of the NSL power that the FBI itself documented were forwarded to then Attorney General Alberto Gonzales, although Gonzales had denied knowledge of any civil liberties violations arising from the PATRIOT Act.

I do not deny that the PATRIOT Act increased government capacity to invade privacy and augmented the FBI's capacity to gather information secretly and without what might be judged to be appropriate judicial review. What I am pointing to, however, is that there is a culture that says this is wrong – or wrong unless absolutely necessary and ultimately reviewable. And I am also pointing out that in this case, and it is by no means a solitary case, knowledge of government wrongdoing came to light not through the efforts of the news media but primarily through the initiatives of investigative agencies internal to the government.

What is an Inspector General? There are over 60 Inspectors General with 12,000 staff members whose job is to investigate the agencies to which they are assigned and report to both the President and the Congress on their findings with recommendations for change or, more rarely, recommendations for prosecution. Usually the inspectors are looking for waste and fraud and other financial mismanagement, but sometimes their efforts are far more extensive. Inspector General Fine at the Department of Justice oversees a staff of 400 criminal investigators, auditors, and lawyers. And let me note one thing more: while a couple of agencies had Inspector Generals of a sort going back to the 1950s (although responsible to an agency head rather than to the President and the Congress), a law establishing the Inspector General as an institutionalized part of most major federal agencies was enacted only in 1978 as part of Congress's post-Watergate reforms.

These various developments – a more professional and critical press, a broader and globalized reach of civil society institutions linked and made public through new technologies, and the large growth of public information-generating research and investigation capacity in government itself and in non-governmental research (think tanks, opinion polling firms, university scientific and social scientific research, and advocacy research from public interest groups and foundations) have created a new information ecology. Think of the digital photographs soldiers took of their own acts of abusing detainees at Abu Ghraib prison. In 2004, these photos came to light because the US military itself initiated an inquiry, the technical ease of transmitting digital photography instantaneously across the globe made possible news media access to the photographs, old-fashioned investigative reporting and competition among US media outlets to break the story pushed the photographs into the public eye, and outrage in the Middle East forced President George W. Bush to respond and thus unintentionally validate the Abu Ghraib story as worthy of the front page.[14] The place of the press in this wider informational orbit must be re-described.

Despite the significant growth of this wider world of public information, it is still conventional journalism, for the most part, that translates a selected portion of this information into public currency. We still need journalists. We still need newspapers. Should newspapers pass from the scene (rather than passing from ink on paper to pixels on screens), democracy would be in grave danger. We still need journalists who get in the face of power – and are enabled to do so because their doggedness and their irreverence is protected by law, by a conducive political culture, and by a historical record of having served self-government well when they hunt down elusive or hidden facts. Democracy works better if we can guarantee journalists what Arendt called "the standpoint outside the political realm – outside the community to which we belong and the company of our peers." This standpoint, she wrote, is "one of the various modes of being alone," and she listed reporting among the outstanding "modes of truthtelling."[15]

Nothing I have said in defense of facts makes it easy to know facts or to trust in them. Facts are remarkably vulnerable. For one thing, they do not necessarily reach us and influence us even when the person who communicates the facts thinks that they obviously speak for themselves. A good example is the instance of Farnaz Fassihi, the *Wall Street Journal* reporter in Baghdad who sent a personal e-mail to friends that somehow got forwarded and forwarded and eventually wound up in the newspapers. In the email, she calmly talked about her everyday life in Baghdad and the dangers she faced. Somehow this impressed on people as none of her stories in the *Wall Street Journal* had that in the insurgency, life in Baghdad was dangerous! She was astonished.

There was nothing she said in her e-mail she had not written in other ways in her newspaper, but it had not broken through the indifference of the readers the way her personal story did. Not the facts, but the rhetoric in which they were communicated, seemed to make the difference.

Second, and perhaps related, the journalists in Baghdad waffled between wanting to communicate *only* facts, to keep their heads down and focused on what they could see right in front of them, and wanting to offer a larger framework that shows something of how those facts relate to or illuminate a larger context. Pressed by the Bush administration to "report the good news," they began to wonder if they were getting the story wrong by focusing on conflict, terrorism, mayhem, and death. Were they wrong to emphasize suicide bombings and fratricidal warfare when some schools were being re-painted and electricity in some neighborhoods being restored? Which facts are the right facts?

There are no final answers to such questions. Because there are no final answers, the reporters were rattled by the Bush administration' assault on them. They wondered, like Scrooge, whether they could or should believe their own senses, whether they might have been misled by that bit of beef or blot of mustard. The result, for correspondent Anthony Shadid of the *Washington Post*, was that he wrote a story that "reflected my own internal questioning more than it should have. And I think it reflected less than what I was actually seeing on the ground. And I regret that story, that's one of the stories that I count as a mistake." It came, he recalls, of "not sticking to what you're hearing, not sticking to what you're seeing."[16]

A statement can be judged true, in a Habermasian formulation, if all people would agree on it if they were to discuss all of human experience without any constraints for an indefinite length of time. But will we get everyone together? No. Will we ever command all of human experience even if we did? No. Will we deliberate indefinitely? No. There is no practical answer in this idealized situation.[17]

That does not mean that we cannot accept, provisionally, some things as facts when there is broad agreement among most of the most independent and most expert authorities among us acting with all appearance of integrity.

Toward a humble journalism

In journalism as in the university, a humility before the world, a humility before the facts, a humility before the contingent circumstance is appropriate and necessary, and a humility in relation to our own favored schemes and theories. "The acorn of good journalism is humility," writes Ken Auletta. It is the prerequisite for using the journalist's two "irreplaceable tools: The curiosity to ask questions and the ability to listen to the answers."[18] About the only thing we can be sure of regarding theories of the human condition is that they are wrong. *All* of them are wrong, except those too empty or tautological to actually stand as theories at all. The good theories – those that actually provide some sort of non-tautological framework for seeing the world   are routinely upended by events (the special pleasure of journalism) or by variations across time (the revenge of historians) or across cultures (the revenge of anthropology) or by variations among individuals (the revenge of what statisticians call the "normal distribution").

We cannot escape trying to make sense of our world. But we are forbidden from trying to do so without making a conscientious appeal to the facts. As imperfectly as we are able to know them. As mute as they sometimes are. It is the least bad system of knowing that we have.

Notes

1 This essay began as a much briefer presentation at the Annenberg Scholars Symposium in fall 2007, but it has undergone several transformations since. It became a full-length lecture at Texas A&M University's Glasscock Humanities Center series on "How Do We Keep Knowing?" in March, 2008. Parts of it appear also in "Facts and Democracy," the introduction to my book, *Why Democracies Need an Unlovable Press* (Cambridge, UK: Polity Press, 2008).
2 Michael P. Lynch, *True to Life* (Cambridge, MA: MIT Press, 2004), 1.
3 Frank Rich, *The Greatest Story Ever Sold: The Decline and Fall of Truth in Bush's America* (New York: Penguin Press, 2006).
4 Ron Suskind, "Without A Doubt," *New York Times Magazine*, 17 October 2004.
5 Rajiv Chandrasekaran, *Imperial Life in the Emerald City: Inside Iraq's Green Zone* (New York: Alfred A. Knopf, 2006), 5.
6 Rich, *The Greatest Story*, 2.
7 "Truthiness" in Wikipedia, retrieved 6/21/2007.
8 Hannah Arendt, "Truth and Politics" in Arendt, *Between Past and Future* (New York: Viking Press, 1968), p. 227.
9 Arendt, "Truth and Politics," 231.
10 Arendt, "Truth and Politics," 238.
11 Arendt, "Truth and Politics," 239.
12 Arendt, "Truth and Politics," 261.
13 Walter Lippmann, *Liberty and the News* (Princeton, NJ: Princeton University Press, 2007). Originally published in 1920.
14 For an excellent account of news coverage of US detainee abuse in Afghanistan and Iraq, see Eric Umansky, "Failures of Imagination," *Columbia Journalism Review* (September/October 2006).
15 Arendt, "Truth and Politics," 260.
16 Mike Hoyt and John Palatella and the editors of *Columbia Journalism Review*, *Reporting Iraq: An Oral History of the War by the Journalists Who Covered It* (Brooklyn, NY: Melville House, 2007), 135.
17 Raymond Geuss paraphrasing Habermas. Cited in Bernard Williams, *Truth and Truthfulness* (Princeton, NJ: Princeton University Press, 2002), 225.
18 Ken Auletta, *Backstory* (New York: Penguin Books, 2003), xvii.

Chapter 11

The Moment of Truthiness: The Right Time to Consider the Meaning of Truth*ful*ness

James S. Ettema

The notion of truthiness seems perfectly attuned to this moment of socio-political climate change when pre-millennial exuberance and post-9/11 earnestness have both cooled into the irony-rich atmosphere of the Later Iraq/Afghanistan Period. The notion seems uniquely suited to thrive in a mildly noxious climate that, despite enthusiasms released by a presidential campaign, retains elements of both a malaise about the conduct of politics and a moral panic about the direction of culture. A few years ago popular culture assured us that "the truth is out there." But not long ago in the form of pre-release advertising for the film "Michael Clayton," George Clooney's starring vehicle as a compromised lawyer, popular culture asserted that "the truth can be adjusted." In the same vein the second season of "Madmen," a melodramatic send-up of the advertising business in the 1960s, promised that the cable series would reveal "where the truth lies."

Yet a third manifestation of the moment is the rise to near-bestsellerdom of a brief meditation entitled *On Bullshit* by Princeton philosopher Harry Frankfurt.[1] With reference to the domains of commerce and politics Frankfurt defines bullshit as simply indifference to truth. Unlike liars who must engage truth in their attempt to deny it, bullshitters just plain ignore it in pursuit of their goals. "Your call is important to us" and "Your satisfaction is guaranteed" are annoyingly familiar examples from the domain of commerce. "Mission Accomplished" and "America is safer today" are more ominous examples from the domain of politics. And from yet another domain of human affairs: "Oh God, that was the best ever!" and "No, it's not you; it's me!" In all cases Frankfurt's concept adds a valuable third category of untruth. The Bush administration was a compelling testament to the analytical usefulness of the concept. Weapons of mass destruction in the hands of Saddam Hussein: mistake, lie or bullshit?

And yet I do not think Frankfurt's succinct definition of bullshit as disregard of the truth makes it synonymous with truthiness. Plausibility, for example, I take to be an essential element of truthiness but, as some of the previous examples indicate, not necessarily of bullshit. In so far as authorial intent can be accepted as offering insight into meaning we can turn to Stephen Colbert.

"Truthiness is, anyone can read the news to you. I promise to feel the news at you," said the current dean of America's fake news people when coining the term on his program. "As a journalist, it's not my place to editorialize. I'm here to objectively divide the facts into categories of good and evil. Then you make up your own minds."

The last line is, of course, a parodic skewering of the Fox News mantra, "We report. You decide." Resisting the temptation to reminisce about the best of Colbert's barbs, here is just one from his widely celebrated comments to the White House Correspondents' Association dinner in 2006. "The greatest thing about this man is he's steady," Colbert said, nodding toward President George W. Bush. "You know where he stands. He believes the same thing Wednesday that he believed on Monday, no matter what happened Tuesday." Thus did the satirist speak truth to a purveyor of truthiness.

Thinking about Colbert's introduction of truthiness on his program, however, wipes the grin from my face. As someone who has written a great deal about how some of the best news reporting does – and should – "feel the news at you" and "objectively divide the facts into categories of good and evil," I wonder who, in addition to hucksters and politicians, Colbert is teasing as purveyors of truthiness. Is it the news media or, even if unwittingly, is it us – academic critics of media? With this in mind I suggest that we, as critics sympathetic to good journalism, take this cultural moment   a moment marked in the phrase of *New York Times* columnist Frank Rich by the "decline and fall of truth in Bush's America"[2] – as an opportunity to introduce a useful conception of truth into our own theoretical program.

If that is truthiness, what's truth?

If we do not wish to subscribe to the notion that the truth is whatever can be imposed by a powerful regime, then to what notion should we subscribe? We have relentlessly analyzed the social construction of those pictures in our heads and thereby accomplished the deconstruction of journalistic objectivity. However, we have not put much effort into developing an understanding of truth that both journalists and their critics might be willing to embrace or, at least, that students and teachers could usefully debate in journalism school classrooms. Moreover, if we academic critics want to participate in, or even just appreciate, the calling-out of bullshitters with charges of truthiness, we do need to recognize some sort of truth that, presumably, has been subverted. I do not claim to solve the problem of truth here, but I think I have learned something relevant to that problem from my inquiries over the years into how journalists "feel the news at you" and "objectively divide the facts into categories of good and evil."

Most practitioners and many of their teachers would argue that journalists – *real* ones, that is – don't do those things or at least they shouldn't. To them, the fundamental nature of truth seems unproblematic as they brush quickly past questions of epistemology to those of ethics. "If journalists are ethical," admonished journalism educator John Merrill in *Journalism Ethics*, "they will use freedom to discover the truth."[3] In pursuit of this moral imperative Merrill, to his credit, clearly articulated a preferred conception of truth. "[T]here are facts, and true statements or claims describe those facts," Merrill wrote with S. Jack Odell in *Philosophy and Journalism*.[4] "This view that truth is a correspondence between what we say and the facts is referred to by philosophers as the *correspondence theory,* and it has had many champions."

For these educators the conception of truth as a no-nonsense correspondence between "statements" and "the facts" offers protection from the eternal night – both ethical and epistemological – of relativism. The light of truth seems threatened by flamboyant Continental (especially Gallic) theorizing, of course, but hardly less so by staid Anglo-American analytic philosophy. "We cut up the world into objects when we introduce one or another scheme of description," argued British philosopher Hilary Putnam.[5] "Since the objects *and* the signs are alike *internal* to the scheme of description, it is possible to say what matches what." That is to say, only because objects and signs cohere within a conceptual system describing the natural or social world can we determine a correspondence between objects and signs. Merrill and Odell, however, quickly dispatched coherence theories of truth. "In order to do justice to our notion of truth, we must at some point bring into the account reality or facts," they wrote, implying that a concern for coherence precludes such inputs to truth claims.[6]

From this perspective the satiric power of truthiness defends correspondence to the facts, shining in its simplicity, against the nihilism of coherence theories whatever their nation of origin. However, a great deal of journalism that cannot be accused (or at least convicted) of purveying truthiness indicates that correspondence to the facts is necessary but neither simple nor sufficient precisely because the story compellingly "feels the news at you" and "objectively divides the facts into categories of good and evil." My review of the *Chicago Tribune*'s extensive reporting on the need for death penalty reform provides an example. "With impunity, prosecutors across the country have violated their oaths and the law, committing the worst kinds of deception in the most serious of cases," began the first in a series of reports coauthored by Maurice Possley and Ken Armstrong. "They do it to win. They do it because they won't get punished."[7] Thus did these reporters feel the news at you.

With regard to the potent language Possley told me in an interview, "I think the comprehensive nature of the series allowed us to say things in a powerful straightforward way." He concluded, "You have a duty to present it in the most powerful way you can without overstepping your bounds." What made the report "comprehensive" for Possley – that is, what made the strong lead correspond to reality – is that he and Armstrong had examined all homicide convictions from across the USA overturned by higher courts due to prosecutorial misconduct since such misconduct was ruled unconstitutional in 1963.

They found that among the 381 cases, 67 defendants had been sentenced to death. And among the 67, 29 were convicted at retrial with four returning to death row while 24 were freed when they were acquitted, pardoned or charges were dropped. Thus did the reporters locate (objectively by any standard) facts that corresponded to their powerfully charged representation of reality – facts that fall, in this case, into the category evil. In the American system of justice, after all, every defendant, whether guilty or innocent, is entitled to a fair trial and to deny that right by prosecutorial misconduct is, *in fact*, wrong.

The analyses of overturned homicide cases established that prosecutorial misconduct was not readily quantifiable – the 381 cases, after all, were only those in which prosecutors were actually caught – but that it was not extremely rare. This count of 381 cases, however, was a far less crucial fact than simply that prosecutorial misconduct was practiced and tolerated *at all*. That 24 defendants sentenced to death were later freed when their convictions were overturned may, in fact, be a small number. But again, in fact, it is not small *enough*. *Tribune* readers, as I observed of this series, "were summoned to the moral logic that offers this unambiguous answer to the question of how many such injustices are too many: even one."[8]

In a subsequent series, reporters Ken Armstrong and Steve Mills continued to hold the Illinois criminal justice system accountable for its systemic injustices. "Illinois has claimed the dubious distinction of having exonerated as many Death Row inmates as it has executed," the series began. "But many of the circumstances that sent 12 innocent men to Death Row have been documented by the Tribune in numerous other capital cases." As is typical in investigative reporting, the series began by summarizing the facts: at least 33 defendants sent to death row were represented by attorneys who at some point had been suspended or disbarred; at least 20 defendants were sentenced to die based on flawed or obsolete forensics; at least 46 defendants were sentenced to die based on evidence that included a jailhouse informant, a form of evidence so unreliable that some states warn jurors to treat it with special skepticism. These systemic failures, according to the report, were among the most damaging of the "numerous fault lines running through the criminal justice system, subverting the notion that when the stakes are the highest, trials should be fail-safe."[9] By mapping these fault lines the series helped set the agenda for reform by estimating the type and frequency of systemic failures and indicating specific reforms that ought to be undertaken. In this way the passive correspondence of facts to statements were made to actively cohere within a meaningful and purposeful indictment of an institution that, in fact, exhibited an unacceptable level of moral disarray.

Correspondence and coherence, fact and story

Journalists and others who seek to tell the truth cannot always walk on the firm ground of unambiguous correspondence to obvious facts. Discussions with distinguished journalists indicate, however, that they know how to traverse that ground even though they were not given a conceptual map of it in the course of their education. To more closely examine their predicament I return to one of the most riveting interviews that Ted Glasser and I conducted for *Custodians of Conscience: Investigative Reporting and Public Virtue*.[10] Loretta Tofani, while a young *Washington Post* reporter, earned a Pulitzer Prize for her reporting on sexual assaults in a county jail against young men who were often charged with only minor crimes. Beginning her work Tofani expected both to hear differing stories from her sources and to construct her own story through a process of corroboration among those sources. She began by conducting detailed interviews with the victims:

> I collected a lot of stuff that was useless but what I put in [the story] were things that described or corroborated the crimes, *the story line in each of the cases*. Where the person was when it happened. How it happened: how the rapists approached him, where the guard was, whether he screamed, exactly what they did to him, exactly what they said to him. What the names were of the people who did it to him. How long it occurred. What he did afterwards – did he go the medical room? All the *essential questions* of what happened when he was raped and what happened afterwards. This was painful for the victims and so we ended up talking about a million different things during those interviews. Do you have a girl friend? What do you do in real life?[11]

The interviews provided a great deal of information with the potential to become the facts of the case; but the reporter understood that the "essential questions," those most relevant to "the storyline in each of the cases," concerned not only the occurrence of rape but also the problems in the jail (e.g. poor design, inadequate staffing) that allowed the abuse of people who were not hardened criminals but had jobs and girl friends in real life. The facts of the attack itself (e.g. screams of the victim) along with its circumstances (e.g. location of the guards) and consequences for the victim were all what we called in the book, following Durkheim, "moral facts" that endowed events in this jail with their moral as well as socio-political meaning. Again a reporter objectively divides the facts into categories of good and evil.

Through these interviews fact and story emerged together into the light of public scrutiny. The facts that became the reality of what was happening in the jail were summoned from among all those available because the essential questions to be asked had been identified by the essential storyline of investigative reporting: people who do not deserve what befalls them nonetheless are victimized by an unjust system. To verify fact and story the reporter could not, of course, compare the victims' accounts to "what really happened." She could only compare their accounts to other accounts that she could elicit. She explained:

> The first thing was getting the jail medical workers to talk to me which was not an easy task. Only a couple of them did. I went to their homes at night and asked them. They were very disturbed about all the rapes they were seeing. Over time, as trust developed, they gave me the medical records of these rape victims. From those medical records, I could see that, in fact, these men had been raped ... There was clear evidence like semen in rectums and there were physical injuries like bruises and broken bones. And then, I talked to the rapists themselves about what they had done. Their stories corroborated the victims' stories. It was only coming to the end of that line – really fleshing out each individual story – that I became certain that it was true.[12]

The reporter's awareness that only by "fleshing out each individual story" could she know the facts is a testament to the mutual constitution of fact and story and the centrality of coherence to the practical production of truth claims. To flesh out the stories Tofani always tried to triangulate three sources – the victim, the medical record, the attacker – or at least compare two sources. And yet, in one case that she used in her series she had only the word of the victim:

> I talked to another, more experienced reporter about it; and I said, "Look, there's no real corroboration." He asked me a lot about this guy – what he was like. I had spent a lot of time talking to this guy and I said that he really did seem disturbed about it and he was able to describe it in very complete detail. Even when I would talk to him about it weeks later, the details would not change and he seemed to have it very clear in his mind that this had happened. The other reporter felt it was solid enough. I wasn't sure, but I trusted his judgment and went with it.[13]

The journalist could also allow herself to be convinced of this victim's story not only by its consistency but by its fit within the larger pattern of stories from other victims caught in this hellish place. The essential facts were corroborated by both their correspondence to, and coherence within, a very particular and terrible sort of situation – jail rape – that had become readily, if painfully, recognizable to the reporter.

The reporter's task may seem to be what Steven Pepper called multiplicative corroboration, in which separate stories provide the same fact as when multiple scientific experiments yield identical results.[14] Here several sources – victim, medical record, attacker – all provided an identical fact: rape. However, corroboration for the reality of rape was not provided merely by the use of the word "rape" which might never have been uttered by the sources. Rather, corroboration emerged from a painstaking piecing together of the facts that the reporter had elicited from sources. Thus, the medical record corroborated the victim's account not because both sources repeated exactly the same information but because the accounts of each provided a series of distinct but related items that matched up in a coherent way and that, in turn, could justify the use of a particular description: rape. This, Pepper called, structural corroboration.

The series that emerged from these reportorial labors reconstructed harrowing encounters between victims and attackers all caught in a system that allowed it to happen. Here Tofani writes of the motives of the attackers as shaped by the system:

> Francis Harper, a convicted armed robber, decided to teach a lesson to the inmate who switched the television channel in the county jail. Harper decided to rape him ... "The basic thing was to keep fear in the air to keep that respect," Harper said. "I was aggressive because I was afraid."[15]

And here she writes of a young man as victimized by the system:

> Kevin Parrish, a 20-year-old student from Upper Marlboro, was arrested on a drunk driving charge at 3 a.m., Feb. 20 and taken to the Prince George's County Detention Center. He was to wait there a few hours, until his mother could arrive with $50 to bail him out. But his mother came too late.[16]

Again a skillful reporter "feels the story at you."

Fact, story and value in daily reporting

The previous example comes from the journalistic genre of investigative reporting which explicitly seeks to reveal and interpret morally meaningful facts. But daily assignment reporting also yields examples of the inter-connectedness of fact, story and value in establishing the kind of truth about which journalism – and the rest of society – should deeply care. Here is an example from my examination of the coverage given to the 1992 death in the USA of a Japanese exchange student. The student was shot by a homeowner when he and his American host, both in costume, approached the wrong house in search of a Halloween party. The incident came to be called the "Freeze Case" because the homeowner had shouted "Freeze" at the boys which the exchange student had probably understood as "Please." The US press framed the story as an international incident that brought shame to America. "All of Japan's national TV networks here took time during their national news programs tonight to offer a lesson in English," wrote the *Washington Post*'s T.R. Reid from Tokyo. "In tones of amazement and terror, the news anchors explained how the word 'freeze' can be used to mean, 'Don't move or I'll shoot!'"[17]

When a jury found the homeowner not guilty of manslaughter Reid again tuned in to the Japanese media. "Virtually all media reports here took the verdict as confirmation of their worst stereotypes about the United States: a sick country that has lost its greatness amid nagging social problems and constant fear," he wrote. "[A] recurrent theme in today's Japanese reports was that [the homeowner] won acquittal because most Americans consider it normal to shoot and kill an unknown visitor at the door." The next day, Reid reported that the student's family would file a civil suit against the home-owner: "an American-style remedy for their American loss." The story went on to reiterate the Japanese diagnosis of an American sickness. "All the national Japanese newspapers ran editorials today on the so-called 'freeze case'," Reid reported. "Nearly all referred to the United States as 'The Gun Society,' and the consensus view was expressed by the *Yomiuri Shimbun*, Japan's biggest newspaper: 'The pathology of life in The Gun Society is horrifying.'"

In an interview Reid explained why all this Japanese talk became facts worth reporting. "It's very, very expensive for the *Washington Post* to keep me and my wife and three children in this country. So damn it, I better teach Americans something to justify this." Reid claimed the role of social observer, but hardly a disinterested one. "When I first came here, rich Japan and how they got rich and how they became a world super power, that was my story," he said. "Now I feel that my story is how they became a world *social* power, how they became such a peaceful, free society. We Americans have got to learn this somewhere." The effect of Reid's reporting, as I observed of these stories, "was to fix America in the humiliating gaze of the people who, at that moment, could most readily evoke self-doubt, anxiety and guilt. America, even if stereotyped and misunderstood, stood exposed and ashamed – at least in these carefully crafted news texts."[18] This crafting of America's shame in the sight of the Japanese is another powerful example of the objective reporting of moral fact.

Finally, consider an example of how the objective reporting of moral facts not merely avoided the truthiness peddled by officials but actually critiqued it and this from the news organization with the deepest of commitments to just-the-facts journalism. As an Associated Press reporter Byrna Brennan covered civil wars in Nicaragua and El Salvador from 1986 to 1989. This was a time in which journalists were actively questioning the Cold War meta-frame that, for more than four decades, had provided both reporters and officials with a standardized geo-political worldview. But while journalists had grown skeptical, Washington continued to promote the interpretation of world events in terms of East–West politics. In an unpublished memoir of her years covering warfare in Central America, the reporter wrote:

> It's a very sad situation, but you must explain it and explain it a different way than Washington explains it which is in terms of politics. I don't agree that everything is politics. A lot of it is years of inequity. A lot of it is a very unfair system – situations that people in the United States don't

quite understand without the proper background. Unfortunately, out of Washington, its gets lumped into East–West and good–bad. It's just not that way.[19]

One dispatch out of El Salvador that clearly reflected this view began by noting that the USA had provided $2.7 billion for a war that had killed 65,000 people. Still the fighting continued. The story went on to report:

> Other matters have become more threatening at the moment and a mood is growing in some quarter that El Salvador's agonies can only be resolved by correcting the wrongs that caused them in the first place.
>   The economy is shattered and the political and social sectors are in upheaval ...
>   In the countryside, where most of the war has been fought, peasants eke out only a subsistence living.
>   Few, if any, hold out hope for a battlefield victory or an end to the bloodshed by means of the new regional peace initiative.[20]

The reporter spoke of "propaganda out of Washington" in an interview with me but she declined to characterize this or any other stories as an attempt to counter that propaganda. She maintained that her reporting was merely her best effort to cover what was happening on her beat – just the facts. "You're painting these small pictures of a time in history," she said. And appearing frequently among these small pictures were images of apolitical civilians caught up in the conflict. Here is one of many examples:

> LAS TROJES, Honduras – Natividad Jesus Figueroa, pausing occasionally to listen to the thunder of distant shelling, wonders why his family and neighbors have been pulled into a war that has poured over the Nicaraguan border and into his back yard.
>   "The [Honduran] army came and said to clear the area," Figueroa said in a recent interview. "So suddenly we are part of the war."[21]

Figueroa's home had become a free fire zone when Nicaraguan government forces attacked Contra rebel bases inside Honduras. "We left under a blanket of fire," he says of the urgent evacuation. "We were allowed to leave with only our shoes. We lost everything." The story continues:

> "This is a problem we didn't create," said the president of the [Honduran] national congress, Carlos Montoya. "It's the Contras, on the borders. It's a no-man's land there."
>   The US government, which will be giving $100 million in military and nonlethal aid to the Contras this year, said it "is studying the problem."

"We have to identify the problem," said an official for the U.S. Agency for International Development, who spoke on condition that he not be further identified.

Of this story I have previously observed, "The U.S. official's comment was, of course, reported with scrupulous adherence to the forms of objective reporting but in juxtaposition with Figueroa's story, it is difficult to read the comment that the U.S. government was 'studying the problem' with any attitude other than irony."[22] While the official promised that a program would begin the next year, the reporter countered with own authorial voice in the story: "But that doesn't seem soon enough for the people streaming into Las Trojes and the townspeople." Then the reporter gave voice to one of the townspeople: "This year of the $100 million from President Reagan is $100 million of death," Martinez said. "It will be a cemetery here."

So yet again a skillful reporter "feels the story at you." My reading of the essential moral facts in this story is informed by the American philosopher Richard Rorty who thought that stories – both nonfiction and fiction – were more valuable to mankind than philosophical treatises. Journalism among other story forms can facilitate, in Rorty's terms, "imaginative identification with the details of others' lives" and thereby promote "a loathing for cruelty," "a sense of the contingency of selfhood and of history," and beyond that "a sense of human solidarity."[23] Of this goal he wrote:

> The view I am offering says that there is such a thing as moral progress, and that this progress is indeed in the direction of greater human solidarity. But that solidarity is not thought of as recognition of a core self, the human essence, in all human beings. Rather, it is thought of as the ability to see more and more traditional differences (of tribe, religion, race, customs, and the like) as unimportant when compared with similarities with respect to pain and humiliation – the ability to think of people wildly different from ourselves as included in the range of "us."[24]

Just as journalists must make choices with moral (and simultaneously epistemological) implications when they report and write so, I would argue, citizens must make choices when they read. As a member of this interpretive community I chose to read the story of Natividad Jesus Figueroa and the others forced to flee with only their shoes as a very small picture of a time in history that nonetheless addressed the sort of moral progress that Rorty envisioned – an expanded range of "us."

Survival of the reality-based interpretive community

The intertwining of correspondence and coherence along with other indivisible conceptual pairings encountered in these reporters' work – fact and story, truth and value – may seem to threaten journalism with schizophrenia. But journalists simply must learn to live with such threats. I take the metaphor of schizophrenia from Michael Schudson's argument that "the news media should be self-consciously schizophrenic in their efforts to perform a democratic function."[25] That is, following the requirements of classical democratic theory, the news should help citizens think through their political preferences. And yet, recognizing that most citizens are just not paying attention, the news must in, Schudson's terms "serve as a stand-in for the public, holding the governors accountable – not to the public (which is not terribly interested), but to the ideals and rules of the democratic polity itself."[26]

Schudson's provocative endorsement of schizophrenia is relevant here because it identifies the journalistic goals – an informed public and accountable officials – that purveyors of truthiness aim to subvert. At this point, however, I might be accused of being in league with those culprits by seeming to argue that news is essentially and inevitably truthy. I plead not guilty – and *not* by reason of schizophrenia. That is to say, I think that there is truth to be known and told and to be distinguishable from truthiness. And I think Stephen Colbert nailed that distinction when he nailed George Bush as someone who "believes the same thing Wednesday that he believed on Monday, no matter what happened Tuesday." Similarly, Scott McClellan, the presidential press secretary from 2003 to 2006, observed in his memoir *What Happened*, "To this day, the president seems unbothered by the disconnect between the chief rationale for war and the driving motivation behind it, and unconcerned about how the case was packaged."[27]

To put Colbert's and McCellan's arguments into more philosophical language we can look again to Hilary Putnam, the coherence theorist who nonetheless maintains that "there are experiential *inputs* to knowledge; knowledge is not a story with no constraints except *internal* coherence."[28] Reality may be subject to no single correct "scheme of description" but not all such schemes are equally adequate or defensible. These schemes "depend upon our biology and our culture; they are by no means 'value free'," as Putnam maintained. "But they *are* our conceptions, and they are conceptions of something real."[29]

Indifference, if not imperviousness, to "experiential *inputs* to knowledge" mark the particular truthiness of the Bush administration in contrast to the painstaking process of eliciting and piecing together experiential inputs demonstrated by Loretta Tofani. Thus as academic critics who are skeptically post-modern but nonetheless sympathetic to the goals of journalism, we ought to muster some intellectual umbrage, rather than just ironic bemusement, at the comments of a Bush aide (widely thought to be Karl Rove) who mocked the "reality-based community" of journalists and warned them that "judicious study of discernable reality" is "not the way the world really works anymore." Speaking just before the 2004 election to a *New York Times Magazine* writer, the aide explained:

> We're an empire now, and when we act, we create our own reality. And while you're studying that reality – judiciously, as you will – we'll act

again, creating other new realities, which you can study too, and that is how things will sort out.[30]

These comments provided Frank Rich, a self-professed member of the reality-based community, with the point of departure for his book, *The Greatest Story Ever Sold*. Tracing the mistakes and lies but mostly the bullshit attributable to the Bush administration concerning Iraq, he maintained that those "new realities" asserted by the presidential aide came undone "when actual reality, whether in Iraq or at home, became just too blatant to be ignored."[31] That is to say, in the language of philosophy, not all schemes of description are equally adequate for capturing the realities of Iraq, home or anywhere else. And the schemes of description that prove superior to others are those that consider correspondence *and* coherence, fact *and* story, truth *and* value. These considerations – all of them – remain essential to the survival of the beleaguered reality-based community.

Thus, while truthiness may be the politically or economically motivated indifference to experiential inputs, truth*ful*ness is far more than merely a regard for such inputs. That is to say, it is more than a regard for correspondence between facts and statements. Truthfulness is the result of a judicious regard for the entire range of considerations noted above. And as I have tried to show, such regard, although usually unarticulated, has been essential to journalism all along, no matter what teachers and practitioners may sometimes assert. The cultural climate in which truthiness emerged may change again. Be that as it may, truthfulness is unlikely to flourish in any climate if we do not tend to its careful articulation for the benefit of our students and anyone else who may care.

Postscript

Noting the sudden death in mid-2008 of Tim Russert, the NBC Washington bureau chief, David Remnick wrote in *The New Yorker*, "Beyond his family, Russert's passion was politics, and he cared enough about the game to try to keep it and its players, honest."[32] Given, especially, the tenuous interest of the public in politics this is as good a mission statement for journalism as any. This mission and Remnick's praise for its accomplishment is most fully meaningful, however, only if journalists, critics and any of the public who may care understand that truthfulness, along with its cognates such as honesty, begins but does not end with facts.

Notes

1 Harry Frankfurt, *On Bullshit* (Princeton, NJ: Princeton University Press, 2005).
2 Frank Rich, *The Greatest Story Ever Sold: The Decline and Fall of Truth in Bush's America* (New York: Penguin Books, 2006).

3 John C. Merrill, *Journalism Ethics: Philosophical Foundations for News Media* (New York: St. Martin's Press, 1997), 116.

4 John C. Merrill and S. Jack Odell, *Philosophy and Journalism* (New York: Longman, 1983), 70.

5 Hilary Putnam, *Reason, Truth, and History* (Cambridge: Cambridge University Press, 1981), 52.

6 Merrill and Odell, *Philosophy and Journalism*, 73.

7 James S. Ettema, "Journalism as Reason-Giving: Deliberative Democracy, Institutional Accountability and the News Media's Mission," *Political Communication* 24, no. 2 (2007): 148.

8 Etterna, "Journalism and Reason-Giving," 149.

9 Etterna, "Journalism and Reason-Giving," 150.

10 James S. Ettema and Theodore L. Glasser, *Custodians of Conscience: Investigative Journalism and Pubic Virtue* (New York: Columbia University Press, 1998).

11 Cited in Ettema and Glasser, *Custodians of Conscience*, 138 (emphasis added).

12 Etterna and Glasser, *Custodians of Conscience*, 139.

13 Etterna and Glasser, *Custodians of Conscience*, 140.

14 Stephen C. Pepper, *World Hypotheses: A Study in Evidence* (Berkeley, CA: University of California Press, 1942).

15 Ettema and Glasser, *Custodians of Conscience*, 121.

16 Etterna and Glasser, *Custodians of Conscience*, 116.

17 Cited in James S. Ettema, "Crafting Cultural Resonance: Imaginative Power in Everyday Journalism," *Journalism* 62, no. 2 (2005): 140.

18 Etterna, "Crafting Cultural Resonance," 142.

19 Cited in James S. Ettema, "Discourse that is Closer to Silence than to Talk: The Politics and Possibilities of Reporting on Victims of War," *Critical Studies in Mass Communication* 11, no. 1 (1994): 9.

20 Etterna, " Disclosure that is Closer to Silence," 9–10.

21 Etterna, " Disclosure that is Closer to Silence,", 14–15.

22 Etterna, " Disclosure that is Closer to Silence," 14.

23 Richard Rorty, *Contingency, Irony, and Solidarity* (New York: Cambridge University Press, 1998), 190.

24 Rorty, *Contingency, Irony and Solidarity*, 192.

25 Michael Schudson, *The Power of News* (Cambridge, MA: Harvard University Press, 1995), 211–12.

26 Schudson, *The Power of News*, 217.

27 Scott McClellan, *What Happened: Inside the Bush White House and Washington's Culture of Deception* (New York: PublicAffairs, 2008), 202.

28 Putnam, *Reason, Truth, and History*, 54.

29 Putnam, *Reasom, Truth and History*, 55.

30 Cited in Rich, *The Greatest Story Ever Sold*, 3–4.

31 Rich, *The Greatest Story Ever Sold*, 4.

32 David Remnick, "Postscript: Tim Russert," *The New Yorker*, 23 June 2008, 27.

Chapter 12

Believable Fictions: Redactional Culture and the Will to Truthiness

Jeffrey P. Jones

The fatal premise of news is this: that it simply imitates reality or nature; it is transparent, representational and unconstructed. Therefore, so long as it avoids bias, remains impartial and sticks to plain facts in plain language, it is true, and can enforce its truth throughout the world.

John Hartley

The scary part is that our desire to seek the truth is a lot weaker than our desire to tell ourselves what we want to hear, to perpetuate our own beliefs. The truth is not like that, it's not something that comes to us at our convenience.

Errol Morris[1]

When comedian Stephen Colbert performed for President George W. Bush and the Washington press corps at the White House Correspondents Dinner in 2006, the video recording of the event became one of the most widely circulated and talked about political events of the year on the internet. One observation rarely mentioned was that Colbert's performance wasn't entirely new material. Colbert had delivered many of the best comedic bits in the debut episode of his faux pundit talk show on Comedy Central, *The Colbert Report*, when he unveiled the concept of "Truthiness." The playful term refers to the tendency for bloviated television pundits (such as Fox News's Bill O'Reilly, of whom Colbert's character is a direct parody) and right-wing politicians alike to gleefully trumpet their illogical, gut-centered way of thinking, irrespective of evidence or facts. By essentially repeating this routine in his speech, Colbert used the occasion for a wide-ranging assault on the president, the Washington press corps, and the broader political culture of Washington. In such a culture, the president has shown he can willfully ignore realities and define truth as he wishes, while a dutiful press corps – through its norms, routines, and practices – not only plays along but helps to construct and justify the mirage. Repeatedly Colbert points to the ways in which inconvenient truths can simply be brushed aside in such an environment. "Guys like us," he says (including the president in the statement), "we don't pay attention to the polls. We know that polls are just a collection of statistics that reflect what people are thinking in 'reality,' and reality has a well known liberal bias."

Through the concept of truthiness, Colbert extends the parodic critique of a television personality (who the citizenry can ultimately ignore) to the most powerful person in the world (with whom we don't have that luxury). In turn, Colbert highlights the deleterious effects that can result from a political culture where "truth" is increasingly up for grabs. Truthiness encompasses the believable fictions proffered by the Bush administration – that Saddam Hussein is essentially the same as Osama Bin Laden; that the insurgents are essentially terrorists; and that waging war in Iraq is essentially the same as waging war against those responsible for the terrorist attacks of 9/11. In short, truthiness points to a political culture where truth *in fact* is less important than truth *in essence* (or what Manjoo calls "true enough").[2] Moreover, believable fictions are not just lies, but fictions that the news media are implicated in creating.

Every society, Michel Foucault argues, has a "regime of truth" that is comprised of "the types of discourse it harbours and causes to function as true; the mechanisms and instances which enable one to distinguish true from false statements, the way in which each is sanctioned; the techniques and procedures which are valorized for obtaining truth; the status of those who are charged with saying what counts as true."[3] For much of the twentieth century, the news industry served as a primary institution in America's regime of truth. The discourse it produced was called "news," based on its supposedly "objective" reporting techniques, was what society "cause[d] to function as true," and was central to the status granted to the news industry as arbiters of that truth in public life. Journalists and reporters were granted special access (into our homes and into the halls of power) and authority in both establishing and sanctioning discourses of truth, and often reified that monopoly position by reminding us of the vital role they played in mediating reality (captured best in their rhetoric of holding a "mirror to the world"). But what happens if that special access and authority are denied? What if citizens demote news from its privileged place in their homes or challenge its monopoly status as a mediating institution by turning to other discourses and means of arriving at truth? And what if government officials also challenge that monopoly by elevating other sources (from talk show hosts to fake reporters) and including other means (i.e. more proactive information management across media outlets and platforms) for establishing and disseminating truth?

As John Hartley points out, the fatal premise of the news industry is the belief that its product mimetically represents "truth," and therefore is either synonymous to truth or is a trustworthy means for achieving it.[4] What makes such a premise "fatal" (as opposed to simply flawed) is that once society challenges the premise or stops believing it is accurate, the press increasingly finds its legitimacy as arbiter of truth in public life crumbling. In his discussion of the rhetoric of documentary form (including news), Bill Nichols notes how this house of cards can fall. "Beliefs stem from shared values and ... shared values take on the form of conventions," he argues. "These include conventional ways of representing the world in documentary (sober-minded commentators, visual evidence, observational camera styles, location shooting, and so on) as well as conventional ways of seeing and thinking about the world itself. Subvert the conventions and you subvert the values that compel belief."[5] Through the conventions of news, journalists rhetorically assert that audiences should believe that what they produce is "the truth," and that truth is based on agreed upon "facts." The public, as this chapter argues, may no longer be buying this rhetoric.

Truthiness, thus, is an apt term for highlighting the ways in which American political culture is moving away from its previous journalism-centered regime of truth and is increasingly being subverted (if not replaced) by a broadly discursive, media-centered epistemology where various actors (politicians, institutions, movements, bloggers, talk show hosts, and so on) are involved in a dispersed and widespread creative construction of truth. To be sure, journalism and news will continue to provide important conventions and foundational ingredients to these constructions. Nevertheless, news's place at the center of the regime of truth in public life is under siege in a digital world. A variety of tools and avenues now exist for such constructions and subversions, all of which derive from a renewed sense of agency that numerous public actors are displaying in constructing alternative truths about politics than that traditionally offered by journalism. Changes in technology are such that citizens have assumed greater control over how they engage and interact with information, thanks in part to the ways in which content flows across and through convergent media. In this context, we witness how "newly emerging technologies 'free' information from any particular actor, function, or context. Communication, in this new environment, is the work of appropriating information from disparate sources into a coherent whole. Communication is literally and genuinely constitutive."[6]

It is this changed landscape with which journalism – as a practice, profession, and set of normative conventions and routines for the establishment of social reality (and truth) – must contend. The challenges to journalism in the digital era are not just economic (that is, how the press must reconfigure business, production, or distribution models to address shifts in consumer behavior and advertising dollars). Rather, those challenges are also manifest in how the usage and availability of digitally networked technologies have helped transform public *expectations* of who in society has legitimate discursive authority and who gets to participate in the formulation of reality and truth. In short, citizen-consumers have recognized their own power to be participants in defining the world (and often in opposition to the world created by mainstream news and media outlets), a realization that increasingly calls into question the institutionalized legitimacy of traditional journalistic practice.

But to suggest that this challenge to journalism's regime of truth is solely the product of technology or the emancipatory feelings brought on by technological change would be a case of technological determinism at its worst. Rather, this chapter begins by briefly examining some of the cultural forces in

American society (some quite old, some more recent) that have contributed to such challenges, and that have helped create the conditions for the rise of truthiness. The chapter then examines Hartley's theoretical model for under-standing this changed relationship between citizens, information, and truth through what he calls a redactional society, and how such practices are manifest in both television and digital technologies.

Although one could investigate numerous redactional practices that present challenges to journalism's regime of truth (such as blogging,[7] citizen journal-ism,[8] video sharing sites, and so on), the analysis here centers on two different forms of political and cultural expression. The first I call "believable fictions," those rhetorical appeals created by political partisans across a variety of media that seem to encapsulate the behaviors Colbert has identified with the term "truthiness." Here, factual truth is elided because the evidence marshaled by fictional truth is sufficient to merit belief. Under such conditions, truth in fact is unnecessary because truth in essence is good enough. Hence, I analyze sev-eral examples from the political right and left to show how that is so. The chapter then examines a second set of practices in popular media that are fre-quently derided as cynical entertainment or scorned as dangerous substitutes for news and information (and at times seen as a threat to the regime of truth established by "legitimate" news institutions). That is, I turn the tables on fake news satirists such as Colbert and Jon Stewart, examining their own redac-tional practices and what some critics might argue is their own brand of tru-thiness. I argue that in contradistinction to the believable fictions of political partisans, satire and parody have become important forms of social discourse in contemporary political culture, and in turn, have reinvigorated the search for political and social truth via these redactional practices in the wake of journalism's moment of crisis.

But before moving forward, it is necessary to consider first some of the social and political forces that have not only challenged journalism's regime of truth but continue to shape the redactional practices that constitute truthiness. I briefly sketch several key factors that have made "truth" a contested target in broader ideological struggles of late.

Anti-intellectualism, anti-elitism, and the onset of truthiness

Both Foucault and Hartley note that truth is a social process and the product of contestation. "There is a battle 'for truth,' or at least 'around truth'," Foucault contends, with truth being understood as "the ensemble of rules according to which true and false are separated and specific effects of power attached to the true."[9] Tracing the word's etymology, Hartley points out that "truth is a product of war, and is itself adversarial. There is not, and never has been, an original truth." Instead, truth is "a relational or orientational term, expressing the social relations of often warring parties."[10] Both theorists therefore remind us that societies engage in struggles *over* truth, as opposed to the modern Enlightenment myth of struggles *for* (locating) truth. The point is helpful in highlighting the battles over truth that have been waged on numerous fronts in American society in recent years – in particular, in the realm of culture with specific iterations in the realm of politics.

Written in the wake of the McCarthy years, Richard Hofstadter's classic book, *Anti-Intellectualism in American Life*, provides an insightful historical analysis of American culture and the relationship between fundamentalist religion and broader cultural suspicion of learning and educated elites, and how those two have been conjoined repeatedly in political life. He demonstrates the recurrent tendency of religious fundamentalism in American society and its ever vigilant "revolt against modernity" that becomes manifest in political fundamentalism. Hofstadter argues that "the secularized fundamentalist mind begins with a definition of that which is absolutely right, and looks upon politics as an arena in which that right must be realized."[11]

Yet in the years after Hofstadter's analysis, the left too engaged in its own questioning of truth, in particular through the postmodern and postcolonial thinking advanced in American universities. Academics attacked the Enlightenment belief that fact and truth were somehow neutral things to be discovered or revealed through objective processes. Instead, scholars argued that both are used as weapons of the powerful, thereby maintaining that truth is often relative and history is subjective. Postmodernism and post-colonialism both questioned the notion of "Truth" and its natural existence in any form except in relation to systems of power. As the ramifications of this thinking played itself out through revisionist history, a focus on race/class/gender, and critiques of Western imperialism in all its manifestations and imbrications, conservatives began to proclaim universities as a dangerous bastion of godless, America-hating, liberal elites. Conservatives would use such charges to mount another political and cultural offensive in the 1980s through a revival of religious fundamentalism yoked to the Reagan Revolution and a culture war. The political right had learned to exploit conservative beliefs that the absolute truth of God and the greatness of America were somehow linked and somehow under attack by liberals, and to mobilize those beliefs and feelings for success at the ballot box.

What also occurred around that time was an active labeling of news media as "liberal," perhaps beginning in the Nixon era, but gaining serious social and political traction as an effective rhetoric in the early 1990s during the presidency of George H. W. Bush (despite the cheerleading from the same news media during the Persian Gulf War). Bush's electoral loss was followed by a wave of conservative populism, as Republicans regained control of both houses of congress by employing rhetoric that painted Washington elites as out of touch with common people. Newt Gingrich, as newly elected Speaker of the House, routinely attacked the media as purveyors of a liberal agenda, out-of-step with mainstream America, and an institutional force out to destroy the new Republican majority. As one journalist noted of Gingrich at the time:

"However (his) strategy might be described, it is clear that he is not playing by the traditional journalistic conventions in Washington. ... His attacks are far more consistent, far more calculated, than typical complaints from politicians. Ultimately he appears intent on destroying the mainstream media's credibility—its most precious asset."[12]

But it was right-wing media itself that became perhaps the most effective in propagating the myth of a "liberal media" that can't be trusted to supply the truth. Beginning with Rush Limbaugh in the early-1990s, talk show radio hosts flooded the airwaves with rhetoric that the "mainstream media" were really a cabal of liberals destined to destroy middle-class America and its supposed conservative values.[13] Limbaugh built a media empire around this myth, with himself and his media products as the necessary antidote. Roger Ailes, who produced Limbaugh's failed syndicated television show in the early 1990s, was hired in 1996 to spearhead the launch of Fox News, and subsequently introduced the network's marketing brand, "Fair and Balanced." Although labeled a news network, Fox News's prime-time hours were quickly filled with right-wing talk show hosts such as Bill O'Reilly and Sean Hannity. In the process of furthering the myth of a liberal media, the network used opinionated talk (not reporting) to help propel the network to the top of the cable news ratings.

With George W. Bush's re-election in 2004 and Republican control of all three branches of the federal government, a perfect storm of postmodern anti-intellectualism merged with political power and pushed through the echo chamber of right-wing media. Recognizing a fearful press that repeatedly displayed a refusal to challenge them directly (including such journalist stalwarts as Tim Russert, Bob Woodward, and Judith Miller), the Bush administration mastered the art of information management (as has been thoroughly detailed by political communication scholar Lance Bennett).[14] As a senior advisor to President Bush impatiently explained in 2004, the days of the "reality-based community" were over. "That's not the way the world really works anymore," this person stated. "We're an empire now, and when we act, we create our own reality."[15] From stem cell research to evolution and global warming, political power was put to use to disavow any and all facts or claims to scientific truth that might contradict the desired reality that right-wingers wished to create.[16] It is in this environment that Colbert's notion of "truthiness" was born.

Susan Jacoby, in her book *The Age of American Unreason*, has taken up where Hofstadter left off. Unlike the repeated eras of fundamentalism that Hofstadter describes, Jacoby contends that we live in a time of politicized anti-rationalism, where "facts are whatever folks choose to believe."[17] This anti-rationalism is the product of a resurgent religious fundamentalism, she argues, but abetted by infotainment-driven mass media, a culture of distraction, and an education system that has produced citizens incapable of dealing with what she calls "junk thought." While Jacoby offers a more scholarly corollary to Colbert's parodic treatment of the same phenomenon, there is nevertheless an

Arnoldian quality to her critique of the Philistines here, one that is eerily similar to the screeds against television and popular culture that are repeatedly trotted out for many of society's ills.[18]

What seems to be a fundamental point that Jacoby overlooks is not so much the continued ignorance of people in spite of increased levels of access to education or the supposed absence of skills and abilities that Jacoby contends are missing from people today (skills that might assist people in deciphering truth from lies, or science from junk thought). Instead, it is the willingness of elites – be they corporate, religious, or political – to openly and actively play people for fools by lying to and misleading them, all the while sowing seeds of doubt, cynicism, indifference, and confusion that affect the citizenry's relationship to public life and social thought. The result has been an increasing tendency for people to distrust elites (political, educational, corporate, media), yet having little recourse except to turn to competing elites in response. This is what Farhad Manjoo, in his book *True Enough: Learning to Live in a Post-Fact Society*, describes as a move from generalized trust – a belief in the authority of strangers, such as experts – to particularized trust, that is, trusting in people who are only like us.[19] What has resulted is a blurring of the line between truth and untruths, as well as the ascendancy of the postmodern idea that truth is relative and constantly up for grabs. Mass media – including journalism – have simply become an amorphous mass of rhetoric for many citizens, with little in the way to help delineate the value of different discourses. NBC News is no different than Fox News, CNN no different from *Oprah*. Truth has no specific location on the channels. What exist are only different appeals *as truth*. And facts are simply what different interpreters make of them. It is in this regard that at least one aspect of the practice of redaction can be understood.

Truth in a redactional society

Amidst massive changes in information and communication technologies and the public's relationship to them, John Hartley has advanced the idea of a "redactional society," where citizens increasingly produce "new material by a process of editing existing content," he argues.[20] "Redaction is a form of production not reduction of text," and a means through which citizens attempt to "sort out order from [the] chaos" of information abundance.[21] Such processes become perhaps the central means of political and social engagement. "It is redaction," he contends, "not original writing (authorship) as such, that determines what is taken to be true, and what policies and beliefs should follow from that."[22] Hence, Hartley provides a useful model through which to understand how citizens are making sense of public life through active textual engagement with it, thereby "learning how to share, deploy, trust, evaluate, contest and act upon collective knowledge" in politically meaningful ways that operate outside the traditional confines of elite issue/news framing and agenda setting.[23] In assessing the broader social implications of such engagements, Hartley asks, "are we in a period where it is not information, knowledge and culture as such that determine the age but how they are handled? If so, then a redactional society is one where such processes are primary, where matter is reduced, revised, prepared, published, edited, adapted, shortened, abridged to produce, in turn, the new(s)."[24]

This redactional society is partly the product of profound public discontentment with journalism's regime of truth.[25] For instance, in his study of the alternative media practice known as "culture jamming" (an often humorous form of anti-corporate redaction made popular in the 1980s and 1990s in the USA), Michael Strangelove points to those frustrating features of mainstream media that often inspire culture jammers to appropriate and alter media content. "Commercial media," he notes, "inhibits audiences' ability to see interconnections, cumulate information, organize it into patterns, and draw conclusions about actions and consequences within the social system."[26] With convergence culture, citizens have the tools and means by which to redact mainstream media messages, leading either to new truths or the contestation of truths offered by traditional sources.[27]

Lest one think this is solely the product of digital technologies (popularly manifest in web activities), Hartley is making his case through television, a medium widely criticized for its structured lack of interactivity. Redaction need not be limited to the action of users, however, for it can be a central process within television texts themselves. For instance, elsewhere I have examined the ways in which *The Daily Show with Jon Stewart* is built on the redactional practices of interconnection, accumulation, reordering, and conclusion drawing – constructions that, in comparison with cable news outlets such as CNN, might actually do a better job of informing voters of the greater truths at stake in a presidential election.[28] Likewise, in his arguments for how *The Daily Show* supports a monitorial citizenship that redactional culture allows, Jenkins notes the powerful potential for a more active citizenry: "In such spaces, news is something to be discovered through active hashing through of competing accounts rather than something to be digested from authoritative sources."[29]

Redactional culture is perhaps easiest to identify through the practice of blogging, where bloggers author their own ideas, but also typically allow for numerous contributions that are not original material (such as video clips, links to news articles, material from other websites, and so on). While the redactional nature of these sites often results in charges that blogs are little more than rumor mills (at best) and hysterical digital mobs (at worst), Jane Singer contends that bloggers, like journalists, are also "committed to truth— but they have quite different ideas of how best to attain it and what to do with it."[30] Bloggers, she argues, "see truth as emerging from shared, collective knowledge. ... The blogger's truth is created collectively rather than hierarchically. Information is not vetted before its dissemination but instead through the process of disseminating multiple views: truth, in this view, is the result of discourse rather than a prerequisite to it."[31]

And it is here where the ethos of public participation in the construction of knowledge and the power of networks in helping society achieve this meets with the ideals that John Dewey and James Carey have articulated.[32] "Public opinion is not formed when individuals possess correct representations of the environment," Carey contends (summarizing Dewey's argument with Walter Lippmann), "even if correct representations were possible. It is formed only in discussion, when it is made active in community life."[33] The problem with news media is that they fail this important societal function. "The purpose of news," Carey continues,

> is not to represent and inform but to signal, tell a story, and activate inquiry. Inquiry, in turn is not something other than conversation and discussion but a more systematic version of it. What we lack is the vital means through which this conversation can be carried on: institutions of public life through which a public can be formed and can form an opinion.[34]

As with other social conversations, it is less important that what is said in a redactional culture is necessarily new or original – only that members of society feel personally engaged in conversation and know that they can contribute and be participants to it. New technologies, then, have enabled an assortment of redactional practices. But as the next section demonstrates, redaction is not limited to digital technologies. Rather, as with the historical context offered above, the will to craft and create alternative truths to that offered by journalistic elites runs across and through all forms of media. The question for society is in what ways are these creations positive or negative.

Believable fictions

> When he talks about New York, people see it ... and they feel it, and if a number isn't quite right, or is off by a small amount, nobody will care, because it rings true to them.
>
> Republican strategist defending presidential hopeful Rudolph Guiliani's repeated use of facts and statistics that weren't accurate.[35]

While the democratic potential of such changes are evident, we should also consider the negative ramifications of redactional practices in the formulation of "truth" when used by partisans. Both the political right and political left have demonstrated tendencies to engage in the construction of "believable fictions," constructions of reality where truth *in fact* is less important than truth *in essence*. Indeed, the word "truthiness" is designed to highlight this sleight of hand in the contested terrain of *politically* motivated constructions of truth.

The 2004 presidential campaign offered several examples of the dueling "truth-in-essence" narratives offered by both the political right and left.

One notable example occurred through the actions of Swift Boat Veterans for Truth, a group composed of Vietnam veterans with a long history of antipathy toward John Kerry. They produced television ads asking, "Can America trust a man who betrayed his country?" a question built on false representations such as soldiers who served "with" John Kerry (as opposed to "under") and soldiers who "are his entire chain of command" (missing numerous people, including deceased presidents Johnson and Nixon).[36] Although the ads themselves were factually inaccurate, they would prove rhetorically successful as a truth-in-essence narrative because they were built upon the fact (or truth) that Kerry had returned to the USA after the war to become a leader in the anti-war movement. With the "traitor" label already planted in public consciousness through documentary evidence, the new accusations could circulate freely as believable fictions. While the mainstream press would eventually debunk the ads as inaccurate representations of the truth of Kerry's service record in Vietnam, a considerable amount of time passed (and a significant amount of political damage accrued to Kerry) while these believable fictions were played out as if true in the press, on television, and across the internet.

Also from the political right, perhaps the most outrageous example of citizen-derived truthiness in a redactional culture is Conservapedia. This on-line encyclopedia was inaugurated as a "much-needed alternative to Wikipedia, which [the site claims] is increasingly anti-Christian and anti-American."[37] It seeks to offer conservative definitions of contested words and terms, from evolution and global warming to dinosaurs and kangaroos. While such an endeavor is, on its face, patently absurd, the notion behind the site is quite powerful. These are the *real* truths, the site proclaims, and the ability now exists for conservatives and Christians to create their own public space where they need not endure the falsities propagated by the anti-Christian and liberal establishment that have dominated public thought through their ability to define the world. Such a site is the culmination of years of effort to challenge the supposed hegemony of liberal media, government, and academics, and it does so by the establishment and control of language upon which reality is built. Although there is no way of telling whether such a site will be used by enough people for Conservapedia to actually affect public thinking (as, for instance, Fox News has been successful in challenging central tenets of journalistic practice and the audience's relationship to news). Nevertheless, simply by its mere existence, the site actively challenges the belief that other such locations for the establishment of definitional truth (from Wikipedia to Encyclopedia Britannica and Webster's) are legitimate. It challenges its users to question *all* such informational resources for their ideological biases first before using them. Thus, the truthiness of Conservapedia is not in its ideas or "definitions," as much as its epistemology.

From the other side of the ideological spectrum, Michael Moore offered enough visual evidence in his film *Fahrenheit 9/11* to argue that George W. Bush is, in essence, moronic, lazy, a tool of the oil industry, and the wrong man for the job. Whether Bush is, in fact, any of those things is debatable.[38] Truth-in-essence narratives dominate the film: Bush's family relationship to the House of Saud is a central reason for the war in Iraq; that war is fought by the working class; Eric Clapton's "Cocaine" signifies rumors of Bush's drug use in the past. All of these claims might be true in fact, but the film does not depend on factual evidence to sway the audience. Which leads to perhaps the most interesting aspect of the film – its enormous popularity. *Fahrenheit 9/11* appeared during the 2004 presidential campaign season and became the largest grossing documentary of all time. Although we can only speculate why millions of audience members went to see the film, the one thing that is abundantly clear is that Moore's jeremiad seemed to fill a void within public discourse. The film provided an avenue for audience outrage, contempt, laughter and scorn toward a man and an administration many frustrated citizens had come to revile. As has been well documented, a compliant and timid press had done a terrible job in challenging the Bush administration's myriad lies and distortions in the lead-up to and execution of the Iraq War and the US's resulting occupation of that nation.[39] Moore's truthiness therefore became an antidote to Bush's own truthiness in the absence of hard hitting journalism dedicated to the pursuit of truth.

These examples attest to how believable fictions can be offered through both old media (film and television) and new (websites). While one might be tempted to claim that several of these are little more than traditional dirty campaign tactics deployed in the digital age, I suggest they speak more broadly to the disputed nature of truth and how it is derived in contemporary society. Citizens are now more involved in the construction and circulation of public truth than simply its reception. Anyone can create a fake photo montage of John Kerry and Jane Fonda at an anti-war rally, for example, and forward it to his or her friends (as was done in the 2004 campaign). Such believable fictions can be anonymous, with little hope of being traced to a particular source (therefore possibly making them *more* believable, especially in an era when news media are trusted so little). Also, viral e-mail letters are related to what new media scholars refer to as the power of reputation or "reputation management."[40] In the old regime, it was *institutional* trust and reputation that mattered in the circulation of information and truth. With viral e-mails, an altered version of the "two-step flow" of political influence is in effect. Influence now may come from those with the time, willingness, and wherewithal to connect and be connected to the creation and/or dissemination of such believable fictions through personal networks. Finally, the hierarchy of public truth creation and dissemination between elites and publics (in this instance) has been reversed. The "logic of convergence politics," Jenkins points out, is that citizens can adroitly "use grassroots media to mobilize and mainstream media to publicize."[41] In short, redactional culture allows for a more widely dispersed and creative construction of truth than that offered by the old regime, for better or worse.

Truthiness meets satire

In his book *Journalism and Truth*, Tom Goldstein relates a discussion between Jon Stewart, host of Comedy Central's faux news program *The Daily Show*, and Ted Koppel, anchor of ABC's *Nightline*, over how the Swift Boat incident in 2004 highlights problems between journalism and the production of "truth." Stewart critiques the news media for abdicating their duty to portray reality accurately and help society arrive at truth because they have shown themselves as conduits for lies, misstatements, and other forms of proactive information management (such as those that have been the hallmark of the Bush administration). Koppel defends the press, arguing that journalists are offering the facts in the case (that these vets "were in Vietnam," that they "were on swift boats," and that "they are saying these things" now), even though he admits that "the truth may not catch up for another week or two or six."[42]

While Koppel admits that the difference between truth and fact "is the great problem with journalism," he nevertheless contends that the truth will eventually be discovered. Stewart, on the other hand, sees a news media more committed to process (dutifully repeating what authorities say, however ridiculous or untruthful) than to producing or revealing truth, even when that truth is readily available "in the public record."[43] If facts, truth, and reality are the "god-terms" of journalism, as Barbie Zelizer contends, then according to Stewart, the press needs to recognize that the first of these terms alone does not have a necessary relationship to the other two.[44] Furthermore, slavish devotion to certain factual reporting (for instance, that it is vitally important to report that A said B about C) can create conditions where truth and reality become lost in the process. Journalistic production of facts – a traditional defining feature of journalism – is simply no longer good enough in the contemporary context.

Jon Stewart is a satirist of politics, but he is also a satirist of news media. Both he and Stephen Colbert have been celebrated – even by journalists – for pointing out important truths that journalists are not providing and that seem sorely missing from public debate.[45] Their comedic efforts remind us of the role that satire and parody can play in uncovering and announcing truths in an era of political spin and information management. One of the central redactional techniques used to do so is the faux anchor employing edited video footage to make his critique through humorous quips. Yet one might argue that Stewart and Colbert are engaged in redactive truthiness – extracting statements by politicians and reporters from news footage, mashing them together in creative ways, generally removing such discourse from the specific context of enunciation or broadcast and adding a new spin as to what these people, statements or events mean. Although there is not space here to offer a detailed analysis of these and other techniques, several scholarly treatments of these shows do just that,[46] including a few that also focus on the nature of these shows in relation to traditional journalistic practice.[47] If such redaction occurs here as well, what then, if anything, makes them different from the believable fictions of partisan media described above?

Satire is a fundamentally different enterprise primarily because of its intent to interrogate taken-for-granted facts and truths as an act of deconstruction. Satire is a discursive means of scrutinizing through playful means. It ideally should lead the audience to move beyond taking news and information from authoritative sources at face value, and instead engage with the material in ways that lead to an examination and questioning of it. By comically playing with the political, Bakhtin suggests, one can gain a greater sense of ownership over it, and in turn, feel empowered to engage with it. Satire and parody not only strip politics bare, but they also invert political pretentions, standing falsities on their head. It is this vertigo that is both humorous and enlightening. As G. K. Chesterton writes, "The essence of satire is that it perceives some absurdity inherent in the logic of some position, and ... draws the absurdity out and isolates it, so that all can see it."[48]

Truthiness too is about inversions – not the head, but the gut; not the brain, but the heart; not reality "as is," but reality as "must be." Satire and parody, then, become important means through which truthiness can be countered *on its own terms*. Through their redactional techniques, Stewart and Colbert's faux journalism and punditry play by the same rules, and consequently, have the power to counter truthiness with their own pastiche of truthfulness. Satirists use redaction to expose lies, while partisans use redaction to create them. The old journalistic regime of truth was, in part, built on the Miltonian self-righting principle enunciated in *Areopagitica*, "Let [Truth] and Falsehood grapple; whoever knew Truth put to the worse, in a free and open encounter?" But these satirists and parodists recognize that simply asserting the older conventions of truth against the newer constructions of truthiness is not the most effective option in this day and age of information management. They understand that today, truth is as much about how it is sold as any inherent or self-evident quality truth itself possesses. Put simply, redactional techniques are also a means by which truthiness must be challenged.

These techniques are similar to those employed by documentary filmmaker Errol Morris and what some consider his postmodern approach to truth. In his dramatic reenactments of the varying "eyewitness" accounts of the murder of a Dallas County police officer in the film *The Thin Blue Line*, Morris never presents the viewer with the *one true version* of the murder among these competing accounts of the truth. That doesn't mean that he believes there is no truth. Nor does it mean he isn't advancing what he believes is the truth in this case. Instead, he simply chooses to do so through means other than the traditional authoritative voice of documentary film (another truth-establishing convention). Morris lets those who seek to establish an authoritative, yet ultimately self-serving and manipulative truth indict themselves through their questionable versions of truth. He therefore allows the viewer to question not only those versions, but also the "authority" of those who seek to make such authoritative claims in the first place.

Similarly, Stewart allows those in power to speak, including the news media. But through his techniques of redaction, he is less involved in fabricating new truths (as with partisan redactionists) as he is in leading viewers to question the truths they are being offered and the authority of those making the assertions. The satirical awareness of truthiness, therefore, is this: it doesn't offer up truth against lies as much as "show how lies function as partial truths" or, as I have termed them, believable fictions.[49] Satire and parody have attacked lies before, but here they are attacking truthiness – *a particular mediated way of creating believable fictions*. In that regard, satire and parody participate in a postmodern episteme, a questioning of truth more than an authoritative assertion of it. As Stewart has argued, "Our audience can watch without feeling like we're grabbing them by the lapels and shouting, 'This is the truth!' in their faces. Our show is about not knowing what the truth is."[50]

To make these assertions is not to prescribe satire and parody as substitutes for professional journalism. Rather, it is to say that in the absence of hard-hitting journalism, in the presence of masterful information management, in the era of postmodern understandings of truth, and amidst technological changes that allow for new avenues of persuasion, evidence, proof and belief, rhetorical forms such as satire and parody have become important means for locating and grounding truth amidst such slippery terrain. That is, they have become an effective (if not also necessary) means for addressing truthiness and a viable and proven way to challenge believable fictions.

Conclusions

While I have attempted to highlight how truthiness is more than simply a sleight of hand by conservatives, there is little doubt that Colbert's critique is squarely aimed at right-wing media and politicians. But we must also recognize that politicians and media are, first and foremost, concerned with audiences. Therefore, we must include not just pundits, journalists and politicians in this discussion, but also the willfully believing audiences as well. For as Hartley notes, truth is "the end product (hopefully) of a mixture of fact, fiction, fabrication and faking whose chief characteristic is that the audience – with much encouragement – continues to believe in it despite the odds."[51] Furthermore, he notes, "this is what makes the politics of reading so important, since a truth is not produced by the mere act of utterance, by whatever authority, in whatever medium. A truth is produced in the act of reading."[52] To fully appreciate the moment we are in, therefore, we must note that such a state of affairs is more than the product of a rogue administration or the heads of media corporations. Instead, truthiness is the product of a political culture in which citizens are full participants in such a will to believe. Sarah Palin can conjure the fiction that she opposed the "Bridge to Nowhere," despite all evidence to the contrary, because some voters willfully believe it to be true. And so too with enumerable other fictions of the McCain–Palin campaign in 2008: for some voters, facts and reality are ultimately less important than a belief that the things they are being told are true enough.

With fear that I may be drawing the lines too starkly, I nevertheless propose that there are two stories of redactional culture being offered here. One is the world illuminated by Hofstadter, Jacoby, Manjoo and Colbert, where elites and citizens alike have demonstrated a will to truthiness in their redactional practices. It is a world driven by a fearful belief that things aren't what elites say they are, but instead are what our hearts tell us are true. The other is a story of satirists, bloggers and others who cling to the possibilities that redaction provides for the horizontal establishment of truth (or the questioning thereof). It is based on hope and a trust in people and a reassertion of beliefs that the known world can be derived or formulated by different communicative relationships. Technology in the first instance allows for negation; in the second, it emblematizes reformulation. Both, though, are based on a distrust of elite-established truth. Both also question journalism's regime of truth, turning it on its head with truths created from the bottom up. Thus, redactional culture signals a move toward a dispersed and widespread creative construction of truth, further signaling a world in which journalism will have to reassess and perhaps redefine a role it has assigned itself (and taken for granted) for far too long.

Notes

1 Errol Morris, "Truth Not Guaranteed: An Interview with Errol Morris." Interview by Peter Bates. *Cineaste* 17, no. 1 (1989): 16–17.
2 Farhad Manjoo, *True Enough: Learning to Live in a Post-Fact Society* (Hoboken, NJ: Wiley, 2008).
3 Meaghan Morris and Paul Patton, eds., *Michel Foucault: Power, Truth, Strategy* (Sydney: Feral Publications, 1979), 46.
4 John Hartley, *Tele-ology: Studies in Television* (London: Routledge, 1992), 52–53.
5 Bill Nichols, *Introduction to Documentary* (Bloomington, IN: Indiana University Press, 2001), 55–56.
6 Michele H. Jackson, "Fluidity, Promiscuity, and Mash-ups: New Concepts for the Study of Mobility and Communication," *Communication Monographs* 74, no. 3 (2007): 409.
7 Jane B. Singer, "The Marketplace of Ideas—With a Vengeance," *Media Ethics* 16, no. 2 (2005): 1, 14–16; Jane B. Singer, "Contested Autonomy: Professional and Popular Claims on Journalistic Norms," *Journalism Studies* 8, no. 1 (2007): 79–95.
8 See "Who is a Journalist?" *Journalism Studies* 9, no. 1 (2008): 117–31.
9 Morris and Patton, eds., *Michel Foucault*, 46.
10 Hartley, *Tele-ology*, 48.

11 Richard Hofstadter, *Anti-Intellectualism in American Life* (New York: Vintage, 1962), 135.
12 J. McCartney, "Used and Abused," *American Journalism Review* 17 (April 1995): 39.
13 Eric Alterman, *What Liberal Media? The Truth about Bias and the News* (Chicago, IL: Basic Books, 2004).
14 Lance Bennett, *News: The Politics of Illusion*, 7th ed. (New York: Longman, 2007).
15 Frank Rich, *The Greatest Story Ever Sold: The Decline and Fall of Truth from 9/11 to Katrina* (New York: Penguin Press, 2006), 3.
16 Chris Mooney, *The Republican War on Science* (New York: Basic Books, 2005); Wendy Wagner and Rena Steinzor, eds., *Rescuing Science from Politics: Regulation and the Distortion of Scientific Research* (New York: Cambridge University Press, 2006).
17 Susan Jacoby, *The Age of American Unreason* (New York: Pantheon Books, 2008), 29.
18 Neil Postman, *Amusing Ourselves to Death* (New York: Penguin Books, 1985); Neil Gabler, *Life, the Movie: How Entertainment Conquered Reality* (New York: Knopf, 1998).
19 Manjoo, *True Enough*, 225–30.
20 John Hartley, "Communicative Democracy in a Redactional Society: The Future of Journalism Studies," *Journalism* 1, no. 1 (2000): 39–47; John Hartley, "From Republic of Letters to Television Republic? Citizen Readers in the Era of Broadcast Television," in *Television After TV: Essays on a Medium in Transition*, ed., Lynn Spigel and J. Olsson (Durham, NC: Duke University Press, 2004), 386–417.
21 Hartley, "From Republic of Letters to Television Republic?" 402.
22 Ibid.
23 Henry Jenkins, *Convergence Culture: Where Old and New Media Collide* (New York: New York University Press, 2006), 226.
24 Hartley, "Communicative Democracy in a Redactional Society," 44.
25 See, for instance, "Views of Press Values and Performance: 1985–2007; Internet News Audience Highly Critical of News Organizations," *The Pew Research Center for the People and the Press*, August 9 2007. Retrieved from: www.people-press.org
26 Michael Strangelove, *The Empire of Mind: Digital Piracy and the Anti-Capitalist Movement* (Toronto: University of Toronto Press, 2005), 113.
27 Jenkins, *Convergence Culture*.
28 Jeffrey P. Jones, "'Fake' News versus 'Real' News as Sources of Political Information: *The Daily Show* and Postmodern Political Reality," in *Politicotainment: Television's Take on the Real*, ed. Kristina Riegert (New York: Peter Lang, 2007), 129–49.
29 Jenkins, *Convergence Culture*, 227
30 Singer, "Contested Autonomy," 85.
31 Ibid.
32 Don Tapscott and Anthony D. Williams, *Wikinomics: How Mass Collaboration is Changing Everything* (New York: Portfolio, 2006); Yochai Benkler, *The Wealth of Networks* (New Haven, CT: Yale University Press, 2006); John Dewey, *The Public and its Problems* (New York: Henry Holt, 1927); James W. Carey, *Communication as Culture* (New York: Allen & Unwin, 1989).
33 Carey, *Communication as Culture*, 81.
34 Carey, *Communication as Culture*, 82.
35 See Michael Cooper, "Citing Statistics, Giuliani Misses Time and Again," *New York Times*, November 30 2007.
36 www.swiftvets.com
37 John Cotey, "Conservatives Create Own Wiki Site," *Contra Costa (CA) Times*, March 24 2007: F4.

38 See numerous documentary film responses, including *Fahrenhype 9/11* and *Celsius 41.11*, as well as "Michael Moore: Cinematic Historian or Propagandist?" *Film & History* 35, no. 2 (2005): 7–16.

39 Rich, *The Greatest Story Ever Sold*; Bill Moyers, "Buying the War," *Bill Moyers Journal*, PBS, Original airdate, April 25 2007.

40 Jodi Dean, Jon W. Anderson, and Geert Lovink, eds., *Reformatting Politics: Information Technology and Global Civil Society* (New York: Routledge, 2006), xxvii.

41 Jenkins, *Convergence Culture*, 220

42 Tom Goldstein, *Journalism and Truth: Strange Bedfellows* (Evanston, IL: Northwestern University Press, 2007), 23.

43 Goldstein, *Journalism and Truth*, 22.

44 Barbie Zelizer, "When Facts, Truth, and Reality are God-Terms: On Journalism's Uneasy Place in Cultural Studies," *Communication and Critical/Cultural Studies* 1, no. 1 (2004): 100–119.

45 Rachel Smolkin, "What the Mainstream Media Can Learn from Jon Stewart," *American Journalism Review* (June/July 2007). Retrieved from: www.ajr.org

46 Geoffrey Baym, "Representation and the Politics of Play: Stephen Colbert's *Better Know a District*," *Political Communication* 24, no. 4 (2007): 359–76; Amber Day, "And Now ... the News? Mimesis and the Real in *The Daily Show*," in *Satire TV: Politics and Comedy in the Post-Network Era*, ed. Jonathan Gray, Jeffrey P. Jones, and Ethan Thompson (New York: NYU Press, 2009); Jeffrey P. Jones, *Entertaining Politics: New Political Television and Civic Culture* (Lanham, MD: Rowman & Littlefield, 2005).

47 Geoffrey Baym, "*The Daily Show*: Discursive Integration and the Reinvention of Political Journalism," *Political Communication* 22, no. 3 (2005): 259–76; Jones, "'Fake' News versus 'Real' News."

48 Quoted in George A. Test, *Satire: Spirit and Art* (Tampa, FL: University of South Florida Press, 1991), 28.

49 Linda Williams, "Mirrors Without Memories: Truth, History, and the Thin Blue Line," in *Documenting the Documentary*, ed. Barry Keith Grant and Janet Sloniowski (Detroit, MI: Wayne State University Press, 1998), 389.

50 Jones, *Entertaining Politics*, 115.

51 Hartley, *Tele-ology*, 47.

52 Hartley, *Tele-ology*, 52.

Afterword

The Troubling Evolution of Journalism[1]

Peter Dahlgren

Journalism appears to have reached some historical juncture, and we are justified in being troubled by these developments. Since our horizons have the benefit of only limited historical hindsight, we are still very much in the middle of things, and it is thus at times difficult to get a clear perspective – while it is of course all too easy to draw conclusions about an uncertain future based on the past. The preceding contributions in this volume offer us many helpful insights from a variety of specific angles, and shed light on a number of key themes concerning contemporary journalism. While the overarching picture may still elude us, we have here a number of important puzzle pieces that help move our understanding forward.

The wonderfully alliterative themes that structure this collection will also serve to organize my reflections here. I'll begin with some remarks on the larger societal forces that are impacting on the traditional model of journalism and its audiences. From there I'll explore some implications of the newer technologies, and then address tabloidization and truthiness and their challenges to traditional journalism, ending with a discussion about transitions and possible new traditions. I find myself nodding in agreement with most of what the previous contributions offer; I'll be addressing a few specific points, but my remarks here largely try to extend and deepen some of the basic strands of thought. At bottom, I emphasize what I see as being journalism's fundamental raison d'être, namely democracy. Democracy, however, is not just an abstract or formal system, but must also be a way of life, whose impact guides thought and action in everyday contexts. From that perspective, the role of journalism extends[1] beyond the basic elements of providing correct and relevant information: it must also touch us, inspire us, and nourish our daily democratic horizons. This is of course a tall order, but nothing less will do.

Tradition: the fading of classical journalism?

As an institutionalized set of practices located within the media, journalism evolves with the transformation of society, culture, and media institutions. Its traditions are not just predicated on professional practices, but also on the institutional and material circumstances that frame them. Already a decade and a half ago authors were asserting that the "high modern" or "classical" paradigm of journalism was waning.[2] This historical mode took shape early in the previous century and based itself on traditional liberal ideals about democracy and citizenship. In this framework, mass media journalism is seen as providing reports and analyses of real events and processes, and contributing to defining the public agenda. Through its narratives, classical journalism lays claim to accurate and impartial renderings of a reality that exists independently of its telling, and which is external to the institutions of journalism. It is aimed at a heterogeneous citizenry that basically shares the same public culture, and citizens use journalism as a resource for participation in the politics and culture of society. Journalism in this mode serves as an integrative force and as a common forum for debate. Even if journalism in the real world has never fully operated in this way, this paradigmatic normative model of how it should be has guided our understanding and expectations of it.

The media industries are following the general patterns found in the global economy. Massive media empires have emerged on a global scale, concentrating ownership in the hands of a decreasing number of mega-corporations. As the commercial imperatives of the media have hardened over the past few decades, the balance between public responsibility and private profit has been steadily tipping in favor of the latter. Within journalism and its media environment we are familiar with the harsh market imperatives that increasingly bulldoze over journalistic values, and what this means in terms of allocation of resources, staffing, news values, and so forth. Also, pressures from political power centers can raise issues of bias, too close relationships with elites, or lack of political nerve in defining the topics of discussion.

Further, the rise of an array of new genres in the media that in various ways compete with journalism also contributes to putting mainstream journalism in a defensive position, hemmed in by threatening forces. For example, the very definition of what should be deemed journalism (as well as who is and is not a journalist) becomes cloudy, as journalism's boundaries become challenged on several fronts by public relations, popular culture, advocacy political communication, non-news information, ad hoc or citizen journalism, user-generated content, and other phenomena.

Journalism has always had its (necessary) critics, but in these changing circumstances, it appears increasingly demoralized and powerless, as expressed by journalists themselves.[3] Academic critics further chart these problems.[4] If we look more broadly towards information in the digital era, the processes cementing the dynamics of privatization in telecommunication and the cultural industries continue, not least in the transition from mass media to the new information and communications technology (ICT) landscape.[5] The intensification of the drive to maximize profits impacts all the more on the social relations between technical innovators, corporate owners, government, and citizens in ways that are detrimental to democratic ideals. News and the functions of information distribution end up in the hands of businesspeople and managers who have little exposure to or engagement with the traditions and ethics of journalism.

The critical watchdog function and the protection of freedom of expression are not part of the cultural traditions of these actors. This media concentration not only reduces diversity, it contracts the potential domain of critical journalism. Journalists employed by a large mega-conglomerate will generally avoid topics that might damage its wide-ranging interests. When they don't, the consequences can be devastating for their careers.[6] C. Edwin Baker[7] argues that relying on market forces in the media industries is turning into a disaster for journalism and democracy. Moreover, such policies do not even "give the people what they want": people's tastes are not primordial, and can be gradually habituated to what is being offered.

Protean audiences

The changes within journalism have to do with what is happening both within its own institutions as well as in the larger socio-cultural landscape of late modernity. Thus, today, other factors add to the dilemmas. For example, journalism's position within people's ensemble of information sources has been downsized. What the public knows about the world is to a declining degree a result of traditional journalism; its role in democracy is thus being altered, reduced. It is not just a question of a reduced audience, but also one that is evolving in its social and cultural profiles. Media audiences today parallel the major tendencies at work within the overall changes of late modern society, where concepts such as heterogeneity, fragmentation, niche building and individualization have become emblematic.

The notion of the "audience" has been evolving along with the media and with researchers' shifting theoretical and empirical orientations;[8] in the age of interactive media it becomes especially challenged.[9] Also, the relationship that people have with the media – both the traditional mass media and the newer digital media – are becoming more multidimensional, as media encounters become contextualized in new ways within people's lives. Not least, the new technologies give people much more control over what kind of information they receive, and when and how they receive it.

Among media audiences we can also note declines – to various extents – in the "reading publics" of most Western democracies, especially among the young, as image-based media take on stronger positions within news and current affairs. Also, while citizens are becoming increasingly socially fragmented amongst themselves (i.e. seen horizontally), specific market niches emerge from continuing societal segmentation, thus making a hierarchical (i.e. vertical) differentiation more pronounced. Overall, the strong concept of "the public" as the voice of the inclusive citizenry moves more toward a weak version of media spectatorship, complemented by a plethora of smaller, more exclusive and often interactive, online publics.

Audiences become more "nomadic" and mobile, make more individual choices, and have more technological capacities at their disposal to avoid being the traditional "sitting ducks" of mass-mediated communication. As the media in their various forms saturate daily life, it becomes increasingly difficult to identify the specific attention a specific group of people accord a specific media output. The situation becomes fluid, and difficulties measuring audiences multiply: the 2007 report by Project of Excellence in Journalism on *The State of the News Media* formulates it this way: "With audiences splintering across ever more platforms, nearly every metric for measuring audience is now under challenge as either flawed or obsolete ... "[10]

However, if inadequate journalism can be seen as a failure for democracy, a form of disempowering, it is also the case that at some level democratic theory also requires citizens to take some responsibility for the well-being of democracy. Translating this normative postulate into some fruitful policy remains elusive, however. While it can be argued that contemporary journalism has been contributing to the lowering of audiences expectations as it drifts further from the traditional ideals of the profession, it is not the case at this point in history that simply reverting to "quality journalism" in the traditional sense will automatically attract larger audiences. This is a real economic dilemma, even for those who espouse high journalistic ideals.

Professional response

In this crisis, many journalists and editors feel a profound professional frustration, and there have been a variety of responses in recent decades. In the USA, the Committee of Concerned Journalists formed in 1997 and published a major study asserting the importance of normative professional frameworks.[11] Another ambitious call to reconstruct journalism is found in Meyer,[12] who looks at the current media situation from the standpoint of the interplay between the profession and the new economic parameters. No doubt the robust public (also called civic) journalism movement constituted the most visible effort in recent years to redirect journalism's contemporary trajectory.[13]

Another extensive response to the crisis of journalism is found in the above-mentioned annual reports on *The State of the News Media*, by the Project of Excellence in Journalism, affiliated with the Columbia University Graduate School of Journalism, and funded by the Pew Charitable Trusts. They offer a detailed annual online report; the current one, for 2008, is its fifth. The seriousness of the situation is reflected on the first page of the first report: "Journalism finds itself in the middle of an epochal transformation, as momentous as the invention of the telegraph or television."[14] While these reports offer detailed accounts and statistics of the decline in traditional journalism and the difficult transitions to a new media alignment, they are not simply an exercise in alarmist rhetoric: the reports constitute a sustained, probing analysis, looking at the different media, audiences, economics, technologies, while identifying trends and offering measures in both the long- and short-term perspective to facilitate the transitions in ways that will be as fruitful as possible.

Attentive – but disconnected citizens

However, at some point, audiences must feel that they can actually use journalism in some way. One of the mainstays of traditional journalism has been that it offers news and information precisely so that citizens can participate in a meaningful manner. Yet this is predicated on the assumption that the political mechanisms for such civic input are functioning. Thus, we have to take into account not just media performance alone, but also how it is actually functioning in terms of democracy's dynamics, and how citizens experience it in relation to the political process. A recent study in the UK took as its point of departure the concept of "mediated public connection," that is, that citizens share an orientation to the public world beyond their private concerns, and that this orientation is maintained chiefly by a convergence in the media that they consume.[15] The major problem identified is that the majority of the respondents who still maintained this public connection, do not feel there is a clear link between such attention and any opportunities for any civic action; journalism makes no difference in their roles as citizens. The authors found "little evidence of UK citizens having had access to 'communities of practice ... through which they could act together in the public world; the result must be to make it more difficult to build ... 'plausible narratives of the self' that link citizenship to the rest of everyday life."[16]

Here we hit a sort of bottom line: the fundamental role of journalism in democracy is to link citizens to political life. If citizens are at least attentive to the media – if they are thus "connected" – this is an important pre-condition for engagement. Yet, if they see little possibility to actually participate, if they have little chance to see themselves as engaged citizens, then the problems for journalism – and democracy – run very deep. In a sense, the future of traditional journalism is ultimately tied to the development of democracy – which in turn remains an ongoing and very problematic challenge.

Technology: ambivalent signals and adapting to the cyber-environment

The internet and other related/integrated forms of ICT have, as in so many sectors, revolutionized the way journalism gets done, altering the processes of newsgathering, production, storage, editing, and distribution.[17] Not least the multimedia character of news production is altering the basic patterns of production and dissemination. Newspapers and other traditional news organizations are going through a tumultuous time of difficult restructuring. While traditional news organizations have developed their online presence, the host of newer, "non-press" actors such Yahoo and Google, also compete for audience attention.

Further, we also find specialized providers catering to target "communities" for particular news, ads, and lifestyle information (about, for example, financial matters, hobbies, health) as part of this new mix. From another horizon we see alternative news organizations, such as Indymedia,[18] various kinds of do-it-yourself citizen-journalism such as Wikinews,[19] and sites that engage in critical analyses of mainstream news and information, for example MediaChannel.[20] For example, Corporate Watch[21] monitors the actions of major corporations and financial institutions, while One World[22] emphasizes news about environmental issues and democracy and PR Watch.

Turning our attention to mainstream online journalism, the chapters by Pablo J. Boczkowski and Mark Deuze in this collection, deriving from their respective field studies of how newswork is carried out in the new environment of multimedia newsroom, illuminate in a helpful way what is going on. From Boczkowski we understand that the extensive infrastructure of mediation, with journalists and editors all the more monitoring one another, obstructs diversity. In an almost paradoxical manner, the increase in both the transparency and the number channels of journalism tends to intensify mimicry, with more voices saying the same things. Also, the basic temporal patterns of work, with their established periodicities, become ruptured. I also take it to be a key point here that technology per se is not deterministic; however it does play a key role in shaping the editorial dynamics that decide what kinds of stories get told, who gets to tell them, how they are told, and which publics are to be addressed. One may well lament this missed opportunity for traditional mainstream journalism to diversify, though given the economic logic our level of surprise should be moderate.

Mark Deuze, in his work, underscores a political economic perspective on the conditions of online journalistic production. As in the mainstream media, the increasing "casual employment" among journalists serves to weaken their professional standing. Generally, the culture of the new capitalist era that drives the restructuring of journalistic work signals a deterioration of working conditions: functional flexibility, outsourcing, and offshoring all contribute to sapping professional solidity. And with so much information circulating in cyberspace, journalistic work encompasses all the more editing and packaging, and less original writing. A flip side to this is found in the development of various forms of non-professional online journalism; and here especially I feel we have to be cautious about making categorical evaluations as to their contributions to journalism and democracy (see below).

In another similar study of a news organization, Klinenberg[23] found that the extensive restructuring brought on by the interplay of economic pressures and technological possibilities of multimedia convergence resulted in more work pressures on the staff, with them having less time than before the reorganizations for preparing and writing stories. The goals of productivity, efficiency and profitability pushed traditional journalistic values even further to the margins. Clearly, in the massive transitions underway, it would be foolish to conclude that such will always be the case, but it does underscore that "better" technology does not always automatically lead to "better" journalism. We cannot accurately analyze the impact of technology on traditional online journalism and journalists while being blind to political economy. Thus, while digital technologies are changing journalistic production practices, within traditional news outfits these developments do not necessarily promote journalistic values or quality, but rather are aimed at enhancing short-term profits.[24]

Enter the amateurs – with professional tools

Increasingly, however, it is not just professional journalists who are engaged in journalism online. Today many assert that we are in the age of Web 2.0, with the large array of new and relatively inexpensive multimedia platforms and applications available to the general public. Chadwick[25] underscores several trends relevant to our concerns here: as broadband becomes increasingly available, the issue of bandwidth scarcity recedes, thereby making the multimedia character of the net more accessible as a user-friendly utility in everyday life, for a vast array of communication activities, including what we might call grassroots journalism. Citizens are more and more able to circumvent the traditional packaging of journalism and retrieve – and produce – information for themselves, thus "eliminating the middleman." The historical story-telling role of journalism is being complemented by large flows of socially relevant electronic information between people and organizations outside of mainstream journalism.

Organized groups with sophisticated information skills are not only providing their members with useful materials, but are in some cases functioning as sources for journalists. For example, environmental groups or consumer activists who target the sweatshops of transnational corporations often also serve up the information for the mainstream media. Who is and who is not a journalist in this context becomes increasingly fuzzy as a variety of information functions arise to sort, sift and funnel data electronically in differing organizational and societal contexts. The boundaries between journalism and non-journalism in cyberspace are becoming even blurrier than in the mass media. In short, there is massive civic information sharing going on in cyberspace that increasingly tends to bypass the classical modes of journalism production and dissemination. The traditional top-down mass communication model of traditional journalism is being challenged in this new media environment, with the increase in horizontal, civic communication, including journalistic modes.

New tools of journalism offer new practices, new possibilities; from the early "computer-assisted reporting" in the 1980s to today's multimedia production, the digital revolution has offered new modes of doing journalism, not just ways of doing old things better. More people are doing things online that can be classified as journalistic. These developments evoke questions about the extent to which journalism can reinvent itself and still be seen as "traditional journalism." While we should be concerned about what is happening to traditional journalism, not least from the standpoint of the political economic and organizational pressures that whittle away at its professional strengths – we can at least take some comfort in the situation engendered by the new technology. From the standpoint of democracy and civic participation, with the proliferation of material available from so many different organizations – journalistic and otherwise – and the easy and continual updating, accessible and extensive archives that can be searched, and downloaded, this new era offers enhanced possibilities for engaged citizens to gain political knowledge and access a broader range of ideas and debates. Moreover, this cyber public sphere offers sites and spaces for political participation, as well as the opportunity for more citizens to do journalism in one form or another. Of course, the advent of large numbers of non-professionals into the realm of journalism also introduces new sets of problems; I'll return to those shortly.

In general, the emergence of the internet and related ICTs as mass phenomena over the past two decades has made a profound impact on all areas of modern life. From a perspective of cognitive neuroscience and media ecology as well as from the inspiration of Marshall McLuhan and Niklas Luhman, Julianne H. Newton's chapter explores the consequences of the new media landscape for journalism as well as how we live our lives more generally. I agree completely with her overall view that journalism needs to develop new forms of expression, attempt new genres, establish new kinds of relationships with its audiences; one senses that we have just begun to explore the multimedia possibilities of the new technologies. Audiences need to be engaged not just cognitively, but also intuitively, via non-conscious dimensions. This raises issues, in the online context, of not only what is and is not journalism, but also the status and role of emotionality (see below); these topics will unavoidably remain with us. While her focus on the journalist's mind can certainly be very useful, I would also underscore that we must not lose sight of the fact that journalism is not generated just by individual journalists, but by large organizations, conditioned by an array of internal and external constraints.

Tabloidization: the wrong target?

One could argue that the media industries' economic response to journalism's difficulties has to a considerable extent taken the form of increased tabloidization. The term has several connotations, and in the introduction to a milestone anthology on this topic,[26] Sparks delineates several basic aspects. A dominant one is the pattern in which news values lead to a focus on scandals, entertainment, celebrities, sports, etc., to the neglect of traditionally important areas such as society, politics, and economics. Thus, less attention is given to serious news in the context of the overall media mix. Also, tabloidization can have to do with issues of taste, where critics castigate what they see as inappropriate and even vulgar displays.

In her contribution on the tabloidization discussion to this volume, Elizabeth Bird observes that there are indeed a variety of characteristics that are attributed to this journalistic tendency, but that we still have not arrived at a final definition of what it actually is. (She also reminds us that such is also the case with traditional journalism and its standards of truth and objectivity ... .) She rightly chides the debates in this regard: if we can't agree on what it is about tabloidization that we are so worried about, how dangerous can it ultimately be? This is a good rhetorical point, yet she does also acknowledge that what the critics refer to can still be justifiably viewed as problematic, not least that the circulation of such journalism can be seen as taking place at the expense of other possibilities for journalistic contribution. For even if much of journalism consists of sensationalism, scandal, personalization, excessive dramatization, and the derailing of civic-oriented news values, democracy can still be nourished if the mix continues to contain relevant information that is useful for citizens, regardless of what forms it may take. But as even this core element continues to evaporate, however, the warning signals should rightly go off.

The element of storyness is often mobilized as lamentable features of tabloidization, but as Bird reminds us, narrative is an inexorable element of journalism. Specific story structures tend to recur in journalism, serving as recognizable frames. While it is true that certain such frames tilt towards emotionality and personalization, I find that Bird is right on target in arguing that it is not storyness per se that is the problem. Rather, it is the basic ideological elements that comprise a specific frame – the way of seeing the world or particular issues that the frame invites (and by implications, deflects). Stories not only fill a basic human need, but they also, I would argue, following Bruner,[27] have an epistemological status: narrative constitutes a way of knowing the world. Stories serve as a device for conveying meaning, by structuring sequences, attributing motives, highlighting circumstances, and so forth. This does not compete with, say, the scientific epistemological mode of knowledge, but rather serves to complement it.

This theme that we really need not be so concerned about tabloidization as sensational and emotional stories, but rather focus instead on the ideological implications that the story frames offer – the moral of the story, as it were – is nicely highlighted in Carolyn Kitch's chapter on how the reporting of death and its emotional consequences can be framed. The examples she mobilizes underscore that the real issues are not about emotionality or personalization per se, but rather about specific ideological implications, in the context of prevailing political issues or atmospheres. And in highlighting several times the journalistic choices made in arriving at narrative closure, she reminds us that journalism consists of ongoing decision making: what topics to address, and how to present them. The options chosen could always, at least theoretically, have been otherwise.

Positive popularization

The media have always wanted to reach large audiences, and it can be argued that tabloidization is but an extreme form of popularization, that is, simply strategies to gain larger audiences. This is intrinsically neither good nor bad – popularization in practice need not be negative per se,[28] even if the distinctions between acceptable popularization and deplorable tabloidization will remain contentious. Popularization can mean making the public sphere available to larger numbers of people via more accessible formats and styles of presentation, helping people to feel incorporated into society as citizens. It can involve taking up topics and experiences from the realm of private experience and introduces them as important and contestable topics within the public sphere.[29] In a diverse media landscape, popular forms of journalism can address those segments of the population who may feel excluded by more highbrow formats and discursive registers; such forms can engage, evoke, and provoke, serving as catalysts for discussion and debate.[30]

There are, in other words, versions of popularization. Thus, while popularization can lead directly to the obvious pitfalls and becomes, simply, tabloidization in the negative sense, especially if the bedrock of relevant civic information vanishes, it is not always certain that merely clinging to traditional journalistic formats per se is the best way to defend democracy in a time of dramatic socio-cultural change. Hence, I am in full agreement with what Herbert J. Gans expresses in his chapter, namely that we should shift our attention from tabloidization as a negative trajectory and instead look to how popularization can be fruitfully used to enhance civic involvement.

It is certainly true that media output must be "opportunistic" in regard to audiences – be tuned into their tastes, expectations, and so forth. Yet it is also the case that the media themselves bear a responsibility in structuring the horizons of expectation: offering more fun and placing less demands on the audiences leads to expectations of, well ... more fun and less demands. Such developments are at the heart of much of the controversy within journalism today, and they will continue to evoke debate. The big challenge, it would seem, is to develop new popular forms that will both resonate with large audiences and also communicate in meaningful ways about important matters.

Truthiness – and plural realities

A cornerstone of traditional journalism has always been its commitment to truth. Yet one need not be a professional philosopher to understand that the notion of "truth" can be slippery. Once we move beyond correspondence theory and basic, incontestable factual reality things can get complicated. Yet complication does not justify capitulation – which is the implication in the satiric notion of truthiness. James S. Ettema's chapter illuminates some of the issues journalists confront in pursuing the truth, as well as some of the more sophisticated investigative strategies they can use in getting closer to it. In a time when relativism appears to be gaining some legitimate ground, both journalists and readers need helpful tools for orientation. Notions like "structural corroboration" the Ettama discusses, as well as others, can serve as practical, critical criteria for assessing the veracity of texts (a theme I will return to below).

In journalism, a commitment to the truth must remain a part of the bedrock, even if this commitment has to be tempered by insights into the difficulties in attaining the truth as well as in defining it in complex situations. In that vein, I also align myself with the commitment to factual truth that Michael Schudson expresses in his chapter. I would probably lean more towards the philosophical achool of critical realism than the positivism that he invokes; it is my sense that critical realism as a platform is more conducive to epistemological self-reflections. However, any further such hair-splitting is beyond our discussion here.

Prismatic truth

The Bush administration's indifference to truth, its refusal to be constrained by factual reality, and instead bank on the intensity of feelings, was of course deeply troubling in itself, but it was also dangerous in that it could easily set precedents for the future – in politics and the media. Coupled with the economic logics that constrain journalism, one could imagine that such a downward ethical slide could easily continue if not actively opposed – and the uphill struggle would always be more difficult. In responding to such tendencies today, there have naturally been many critical comments from journalists and academics. We should also note the importance of political humor in this context, and in the political arena generally. I certainly support what Jeffrey P. Jones writes in his chapter about satire and parody as an intervention to expose the "believable fictions" – the deceptions, disinformation, and spin – of the political class, as well as the inadequacies of journalism. This is all the more central in the era of truthiness. Jones makes the point that such comic intervention should not replace journalism (the *Daily Show with Jon Stewart* cannot be faulted if many viewers perceive it as journalism), yet we should by all means treat political humor as an integral and necessary dimension of the public sphere. Laughter is healthy – as a critical intervention for democracy, as well as for our spirits.

Such humor has as its point of departure the idea that there is a truth, and it is in principle accessible to us. The classic problems of knowledge and truth, however, will always remain with us, and not just in journalism. Relativism is not a nasty, unnecessary disease, but arises out of the Enlightenment's understanding of our epistemological limitations; since Kant we have become quite aware of the conditions that shape our knowledge of the world. To occasionally engage in self-reflection on what we know – and how we know it – is not just useful but should also be essential to the craft and profession of journalism (as well as just about any other human context). To acknowledge that our knowing is situated and contingent does not mean that we cannot know things, that truth – in the sense of accurate knowledge and understanding about human affairs – is always beyond us. Rather, such self-deliberation encourages us not least to check our facts. More profoundly it can also help us maintain a degree of humility about our knowing and a curiosity about that which lies beyond it. Truthiness, on the other hand, tells us not to worry about all that silly stuff, and just go with the flavor of the feelings.

For journalism, as for all of us in our everyday lives, much of the world consists of non-negotiable factual truths, in the sense that they are solid, they cannot legitimately be negotiated or bent. In this realm, journalism simply has to get the information right. Other domains of human activity are more open to interpretation, their meanings can be negotiated, contested. For example the significance of the statement "The prime minister is having big political problems," would most likely be contingent on a point of view. Yet, even with solid facts there can be different ways to frame them, using different premises, and so on. The tensions around truth thus include not just disputes over facts, but also over the significance that should be attributed to the facts, which in turn often has to do with perceptional frameworks and normative pre-dispositions. In the face of some degree of inexorable relativism, a defense via adherence to a stilted notion of formal objectivity only takes us so far. The truth may in fact be multidimensional, and even if not all versions have equal validity in our own eyes, others may see it differently, depending on ideological premises: for example does deregulation to increase market forces enhance or restrict freedom in society? Thus, journalism's commitment to the truth, its focus on the facts, remains crucial, yet will not alleviate it from having to deal with the plural nature of social reality.

This has in a sense always been the case, but I would suggest that we could expect that this epistemological challenge to journalism will continue to grow, as more and more social actors are using a growing number of outlets on the sprawling internet. As I mentioned above, we can anticipate that public knowledge will continue to derive increasingly from non-professional or non-traditional journalistic sources, with more new genres and hybrid forms emerging. This is being fed by the growing diffusion of, access to, and skills in using new media technologies, especially among the young. Within journalism, high standards must of course be maintained in regard to the accuracy of facts, source veracity, document authenticity, and so on. At the same, a tension arises: the prismatic character of social reality confronts monolithic versions of the world. This becomes especially salient in the context of globalization of communication between individuals, groups, institutions, publics, and political cultures, as well as within national societies divided by political horizons, ethnicity, and culture. There are in principle many possible stories to tell about the same phenomenon. Journalism, in all its heterogeneous forms, is today accentuating this all the more. Yet it must somehow maintain its commitment to the truth.

Cyber citizen journalism: towards a "multi-epistemic order"?

This dilemma becomes clearly exemplified when we look at alternative and activist media. They have a long history; their relevance today continues to grow, as the new technologies help facilitate such forms of engaged journalism and amplify their visibility.[31] On the internet there is a vast array of such journalistic sites and activity, and they diverge in significant ways from the mainstream mass media.[32] At the same time, as is often pointed out, the dichotomization of "mainstream" and "alternative" journalism is not always as obvious as one may suspect at first glance. There is evidence for varieties of "crossovers" in terms of actual practices, suggesting that treating the distinctions as characterized by a continuum rather than a rupture makes good sense, especially given the emergence of a small but growing cadre of "hybrid" journalists, with one foot in each sector.[33]

Yet, certainly it would be foolish to minimize the contrasts between mainstream news media, and those who explicitly challenge its worldviews, such as Alternet, Zmag, and Fair.[34] The network established by the Independent Media Centers, Indymedia, mentioned above, is the most extensive and well-known of the online alternative news services and is a good case in point. Viktor Pickard[35] suggests that the basic model behind Indymedia is fundamentally different from and incompatible with profit-based corporate news organizations. Journalistically, Indymedia sees itself as an oppositional force, offering a decisively alternative world view to that found in the mainstream commercial media. As Hyde[36] frames it, Indymedia can be understood in part as a response to the profit-driven journalism of the corporate media, and at the same as a manifestation of the tradition of the alternative press in the USA which has now gone online. To this we can add other versions of cyber citizen journalism, with individuals and groups from many political and epistemological directions feeding the media with raw empirical materials, edited reports, commentaries, discussions, debates, political manifestos using an array of technological platforms.

A prismatic notion of truth is anchored in what we might call an emerging "multi-epistemic order," where it becomes generally understood and accepted that all storytelling is situated, all perspectives on society are contingent – not in least in a world where political communication is dispersed within a complex media matrix of global character. However, at the same time we will continue to need workable criteria for distinguishing better stories from less good ones, accurate accounts from distortions, truths from falsehoods. How will traditional journalism position itself within this new epistemic regime, and what will in fact constitute "journalism" under these new media conditions? Will traditional journalism remain the prime institution – with which various modes of alternative cyber citizen journalism locks horns? Or will traditional journalism's position continue to erode?

I suspect that the traditional referent of "objectivity" will recede as a compelling professional and ideological strategy for legitimacy, while the notion of "truth" will remain operative, despite all its difficulties. As the traditional, mono-epistemic model continues to decline, and the multi-epistemic one continues to gain prominence, how do we maintain – normatively and in practice – what we might call baseline criteria for standards of journalistic quality? How do we pursue the truth – and avoid truthiness? If "objectivity" has traditionally been known as the front-line legitimating concept for good journalism, but is now harder to assert in a convincing manner in the new media environment, we may fall back on some of the other notions closely associated with objectivity – and still find them viable – and promote them to front-rank attributes. Thus, we have:

Accuracy: adherence to that which is factually indisputable
Fairness: representing a pluralism of voices
Transparency: via self-reflection and self-revelation, making visible the production process, as well as the limits to one's own knowing
Accountability: checks and consequences for malpractice, such as lies, errors, and truthiness.

These are solid criteria for journalistic quality, and would yet, it seems, allow for a sense of the plural nature of reality.

Thus, theoretically it seems to be possible to hold onto the ideal of truth and mobilize criteria for good journalism even in a multi-epistemic order. In practice, however, what is troubling is the degree of non-communication we already see between disparate actors in the public sphere as well as in certain forms of competing journalism. The classic danger of the fragmented public sphere comprised of disparate political actors with little or no common communicative ground risks being compounded by the development of a multi-epistemic order within journalism itself. Maintaining a minimal shared public culture so that political adversaries – in the street, home, parliament, online – can talk to each other in a meaningful way is essential. However, if the multi-epistemic environment means a cognitive segregation among groups, where respective worldviews are reinforced by journalisms that do not connect with each other, democracy's dilemmas will be deep indeed.

Journalism within late modern democracy, whether of the traditional or the alternative mode, will remain a terrain of institutional difficulty, professional uncertainty, and political contention. We will have to hope that it will also remain a terrain of imagination and creativity.

Notes

1 Some short sections of this text appear, in different form, in my book *Media and Political Engagement: Citizens, Communication, and Democracy* (New York: Cambridge University Press, 2009).

2 See for example, David Altheide and Robert Snow, *Media Worlds in the Post-Journalism Era* (New York: Aldine de Gruyter, 1991); Daniel Hallin, "The Passing of the 'High Modernism' of American Journalism," *Journal of Communication*, 42, no. 3 (1992): 14–25.

3 Among this literature are James Fallows, *Breaking the News* (New York: Vintage Books, 1997); Leonard Downie, Jr. and Robert G. Kaiser, *The News About the News* (New York: Vintage, 2003); Tom Fenton, *Bad News: the Decline of Reporting, the Business of News, and the Danger to Us All* (New York: HarperCollins, 2005); Neil Henry, *American Carnival: Journalism Under Siege in an Age of New Media* (Berkeley: University of California Press, 2007).

4 The following books exemplify this trend: David Croiteau and William Hoynes, *The Business of Media: Corporate Media and the Public Interest* (Thousand Oaks, CA: Pine Forge Press, 2001); William A. Hatchen, *The Troubles of Journalism*, 3rd ed. (Mahwah, NJ: Lawrence Erlbaum, 2005); Herbert J. Gans, *Democracy and the News* (New York: Oxford University Press, 2003); Ben Bagdikian, *The New Media Monopoly* (Boston, MA: Beacon Press, 2005); Robert McChesney, *Communication Revolution: Critical Junctures and the Future of the Media* (New York: The New Press, 2007).

5 Dan Schiller, *How to Think About Information* (Urbana: University of Illinois Press, 2007).

6 See the collection of accounts of the dire personal experiences among journalists in Kristina Borjesson, ed., *Into the Buzzsaw: Leading Journalists Expose the Myth of a Free Press* (Amhurst, NY: Prometheus Books, 2002).

7 C. Edwin Baker, *Media, Markets and Democracy* (New York: Cambridge University Press, 2002) and C. Edwin Baker, *Media Concentration and Democracy: Why Ownership Matters* (New York: Cambridge University Press, 2006).

8 See for example, Denis McQuail, *Audience Analysis* (London: Sage, 1997); Pertti Alasuutari, ed., *Rethinking the Media Audience* (London: Sage, 1999); Karen Ross and Virginia Nightingale, *Media and Audiences: New Perspectives* (Maidenhead, UK: Open University Press, 2003).

9 Sonia Livingstone, "On the Relation Between Audiences and Publics," in *Audiences and Publics: When Cultural Engagement Matters for the Public Sphere* ed. Sonia Livingstone (Bristol: Intellect, 2005), 17–41.

10 The Excellence in Journalism Project 2007, *The State of the News Media* (www.stateofthemedia.org).

11 Bill Kovach and Tom Rosentiel, *The Elements of Journalism: What Newspeople Should Know and the Public Should Expect* (New York: Three Rivers Press/Random House, 2001).

12 Phillip Meyer, *The Vanishing Newspaper: Saving Journalism in the Information Age* (Columbia, MO: University of Missouri Press, 2004).

13 Useful overviews can be found in Paul S. Voakes, "A Brief History of Public Journalism," *National Civic Review* 93, no. 3 (2004): 25–35; Tanni Haas and Linda Steiner, "Public journalism: a reply to critics," *Journalism* 7, no. 2 (2006): 238–54.

14 State of the News Media, 2003, Overview:1 (www.stateofthemedia.org).

15 Nick Couldry, Sonia Livingstone and Tim Markham, *Media Consumption and Public Engagement : Beyond the Presumption of Attention* (Basingstoke: Intellect, 2007).

16 Couldry *et al.*, *Media Consumption*, 188.

17 See for example Stuart Allan, *Online Journalism* (Maidenhead: Open University Press, 2006), for an overview; see also Donald Matheson, "Weblogs and the epistemology of the news: Some trends in online journalism," *New Media and Society* 6, no. 4 (2004): 443–68; Lynne Cooke, "A visual convergence of print, television and the Internet: charting 40 years of design change in news presentation," *New Media and Society* 7, no. 1 (2005): 22–46.
18 Indymedia (www.indymedia.org).
19 Wikinews (www.wikinews.org).
20 Media Channels (www.mediachannel.org).
21 Corporate Watch (www.corpwatch.org/).
22 One World (www.oneworld.org/).
23 Eric Klinenberg, "Convergence: News Production in a Digital Age," *The Annals of the American Academy of Political and Social Science*, 597 (2005): 48–64.
24 Jim Hall, *Online Journalism: A Critical Primer* (London: Pluto Press, 2001).
25 Andrew Chadwick, *Internet Politics: States, Citizens and New Communication Technologies* (New York: Oxford University Press, 2006).
26 Colin Sparks and John Tulloch, eds, *Tabloid Tales: Global Debates Over Media Standards* (Lanham, MD: Rowman and Littlefield, 2000).
27 Jerome Bruner, *Actual Minds, Possible Worlds* (Cambridge, MA: Harvard University Press, 1986).
28 See for example, Peter Dahlgren and Colin Sparks, eds, *Journalism and Popular Culture* (London: Sage, 1992).
29 For instance Sonia Livingstone and Peter Lunt, *Talk on Television* (London: Routledge, 1994); Irene Costera Meijer, "The Public Quality of Popular Journalism: Developing a Normative Framework," *Journalism Studies* 2, no. 2 (2001): 189–205, and Irene Costera Meijer, "The Paradox of Popularity: How Young People Experience the News," *Journalism Studies* 8, no. 2 (2007): 96–116.
30 See Mick Temple, "Dumbing Down is Good for You," *British Politics* 1, no. 2 (2006): 257–73.
31 For overviews and historical perspectives see John Downing, *Radical Media: Rebellious Communication and Social Movements* (London: Sage, 2000); Chris Atton, *Alternative Media* (London: Sage, 2002); Bob Ostertag, *People's Movements, People's Press: The Journalism of Social Justice Movements* (Boston: Beacon Press, 2007); Mitzi Waltz, *Alternative and Activist Media* (Edinburgh: University of Edinburgh Press, 2005); Ostertag, *People's Movements*.
32 See Olga Baily, Bart Cammaerts, and Nico Carpentier, *Understanding Alternative Media* (Maidenhead, UK: Open University Press, 2007); for an enthusiastic rendering of current developments, see Dan Gillmor, *We the Media: Grassroots Journalism by the People, for the People* (Sebastopol, CA: O'Reilly Media, 2004).
33 This point is explored in Tony Harcup, "'I'm Doing This to Change the World': Journalism in Alternative and Mainstream Media," *Journalism Studies* 6, no. 3 (2005): 361–74.
34 www.alternet.org, www.zmag.org, www.fair.org
35 Viktor W. Pickard, "United yet autonomous Indymedia and the struggle to sustain a radical democratic network," *Media, Culture and Society* 28, no. 3 (2006): 315–26.
36 Gene Hyde, "Independent Media Centers: Cyber/Subversion and the Alternative Press". *First Monday: Peer-Reviewed Journal on the Internet* 7, no. 4 (2003). www.fitstmonday.org

Index

Related titles in the *Shaping Inquiry in Culture, Communication and Media Studies* series:

Explorations in Communication and History
Edited by Barbie Zelizer

When and how do communication and history impact each other? How do disciplinary perspectives affect what we know?

Explorations in Communication and History addresses the link between what we know and how we know it by tracking the intersection of communication and history. Asking how each discipline has enhanced and hindered our understanding of the other, the book considers what happens to what we know when disciplines engage.

Through a critical collection of essays written by top scholars in the field, the book addresses the engagement of communication and history as it applies to the study of technology, audiences and journalism. Driven by fundamental questions about disciplinary knowledge and boundary marking, such as how communication and history change what the other notices about the world, how particular platforms encourage scholars to look beyond their disciplinary boundaries, and which cues encourage them to reject old paradigms and embrace new ones, the book both navigates the terrain connecting communication and history and raises meta-questions about its shaping. In so doing, it elaborates our understanding of what communication and history have to give each other, how they build off of each other's strengths and often subvert each other's weaknesses, and what we can expect from the future of disciplinary engagement.

Contributors: Elizabeth S. Bird, Richard Butsch, James Curran, Susan J. Douglas, Anna McCarthy, Robert McChesney, John Nerone, David Paul Nord, John Durham Peters, Michael Schudson, Peter Stallybrass, Paul Starr.

A comprehensive introduction by Barbie Zelizer contextualises these debates and makes a case for the importance of disciplinary engagement for teaching as well as research in media and cultural studies and each section has a brief introduction to contextualise the essays and highlight the issues they raise, making this an invaluable collection for students and scholars alike.

ISBN 13: 978-0-415-77733-9 (hbk)
ISBN 13: 978-0-415-77734-6 (pbk)
ISBN 13: 978-0-203-88860-5 (ebk)

Available at all good bookshops
For ordering and further information please visit:
www.routledge.com

Related titles from Routledge:

Reporting War
Journalism in Wartime
Stuart Allan and Barbie Zelizer

Reporting War explores the social responsibilities of the journalist during times of military conflict. News media treatments of international crises, especially the one underway in Iraq, are increasingly becoming the subject of public controversy, and discussion is urgently needed.

Each of this book's contributors challenges familiar assumptions about war reporting from a distinctive perspective. An array of pressing issues associated with conflicts over recent years are identified and critiqued, always with an eye to what they can tell us about improving journalism today.

Special attention is devoted to recent changes in journalistic forms and practices, and the ways in which they are shaping the visual culture of war, and issues discussed, amongst many, include:

- the influence of censorship and propaganda
- 'us' and 'them' news narratives
- access to sources
- '24/7 rolling news' and the 'CNN effect'
- military jargon (such as 'friendly fire' and 'collateral damage')
- 'embedded' and 'unilateral' reporters
- tensions between objectivity and patriotism.

The book raises important questions about the very future of journalism during wartime, questions which demand public dialogue and debate, and is essential reading for students taking courses in news and news journalism, as well as for researchers, teachers and practitioners in the field.

ISBN 13: 978-0-415-33997-1 (hbk)
ISBN 13: 978-0-415-33998-8 (pbk)
ISBN 13: 978-0-203-49756-2 (ebk)

Available at all good bookshops
For ordering and further information please visit:
www.routledge.com

Handbook of Journalism Studies

Karin Wahl-Jorgensen and Thomas Hanitzsch

This handbook charts the growing area of journalism studies, exploring the current state of theory and setting an agenda for future research in an international context. The volume is structured around theoretical and empirical approaches, and covers scholarship on news production and organizations; news content; journalism and society; and journalism in a global context. Emphasizing comparative and global perspectives, each chapter explores:

- Key elements, thinkers and texts
- Historical context
- Current state of the art
- Methodological issues
- Merits and advantages of the approach/area of studies
- Limitations and critical issues of the approach/area of studies
- Directions for future research.

Offering broad international coverage from top-tier contributors, this volume ranks among the first publications to serve as a comprehensive resource addressing theory and scholarship in journalism studies. As such, the *Handbook of Journalism Studies* is a must-have resource for scholars and graduate students working in journalism, media studies and communication around the globe.

ISBN 13: 978-0-8058-6342-0 (hbk)
ISBN 13: 978-0-8058-6343-7 (pbk)
ISBN 13: 978-0-203-87768-5 (ebk)

Related titles from Routledge

Journalism After September 11

Barbie Zelizer and Stuart Allan

'The best critique yet of how the media responded to September 11, 2001.'
Jon Snow, *Channel 4 News*

'This is not a book just for journalists but for everyone concerned about democracy, freedom of speech and our future.'
Phillip Knightley, *author of* The First Casualty

The events of September 11 continue to resonate in powerful, yet sometimes unexpected ways. For many journalists, the crisis has decisively recast their sense of the world around them. Familiar notions of what it means to be a journalist, how best to practice journalism, and what the public can reasonably expect of journalists in the name of democracy, have been shaken to their foundations.

Journalism After September 11 examines how the traumatic attacks of that day continue to transform the nature of journalism, particularly in the United States and Britain. It brings together an internationally respected group of scholars and media commentators to explore journalism's present and future, by engaging with such pressing issues as trauma, free speech, censorship, patriotism, impartiality and celebrity.

The book raises vitally important questions regarding what journalism can and should look like today. In providing answers it addresses topics such as: journalism and public life at a time of crisis; broadsheet and tabloid newspaper coverage of the attacks; the role of sources in shaping the news; reporting by global news media such as CNN; Western representations of Islam; current affairs broadcasting; news photography and trauma; the emotional well-being of reporters; online journalism; as well as a host of pertinent issues around news, democracy and citizenship.

Communication and Society
Series Editor: James Curran

ISBN 13: 978-0-415-28799-9 (hbk)
ISBN 13: 978-0-415-28800-2 (pbk)

Available at all good bookshops
For ordering and further information please visit:
www.routledge.com

Printed in the USA/Agawam, MA
November 19, 2010

555222.069